The Paradox of Loyalty

THE PARADOX OF LOYALTY
AN AFRICAN AMERICAN RESPONSE TO THE
WAR ON TERRORISM

edited by
JULIANNE MALVEAUX
REGINNA A. GREEN

With a Foreword by Cornel West

Third World Press, Chicago

Third World Press
Publishers since 1967

First Edition
Printed by R. R.Donnelley

10 09 08 07 06 05 04 03 02   10 9 8 7 6 5 4 3 2 1
Cover Artwork by Paul Collins

Library of Congress Cataloging-in-Publication Data
The paradox of loyalty: an African American response to the war on terrorism /
edited by Julianne Malveaux and Reginna A. Green.
    p.cm.
    Includes bibliographical references.
    ISBN 0-88378-243-X (alk. paper)
1. September 11 Terrorist Attacks, 2001-Public opinion. 2. War on Terrorism, 2001-Public opinion. 3. African Americans-Attitudes. 4. Racism-United States-Public opinion. 5. Patriotism-United States-Public opinion. 6. Equality-Public opinion. 7. United States-Foreign relations-2001-Public opinion. 8. Public opinion-United States. I. Malveaux, Julianne. II. Green, Reginna A.

HV6432.7 P37 2002
973.931-dc21

                                                    2002073285

Permissions to Reprint
Brian Gilmore, "Stand by the Man, originally published in *The Progressive*, January 2002.
Haki R. Madhubuti, "Hard Truths: September 11, 2001 and Respecting the Idea of America," originally published in *Tough Notes: A Healing Call for Creating Exceptional Black Men*, Third World Press, 2002.
Aaron McGruder, "The Boondocks." Distributed by Universal Press Syndicate.
John Edgar Wideman, "Whose War?: The Color of Terror," originally published in Harper's, March 2002.

To the victims of terrorism throughout history and all over the world
Especially those Africans whose lives were disrupted by European terrorism
Those Native Americans whose lives were shattered by American terrorism
Those Tulsans whose lives and livelihoods were incinerated by the terrorism
of economic envy

Those Blacks and Jews who were lynched in the South and elsewhere

Victims of the Holocaust

Palestinian and Israeli victims of terrorism in the Middle East

Victims of domestic police brutality, yet another form of terrorism,

And the individuals in New York, Pennsylvania, and Virginia,

Especially the children who lost their lives
on September 11, 2001

Contents

Foreword   XI
Cornel West

Preface   XIII

One   Only the Strong Survive   1
       Necessary Changes
          Gail E. Mitchell with Andrea Benton Rushing   3

Two   Dateline: September 11, 2001   13
       Toppling Towers, Tested Power
          Julianne Malveaux   15
       Using Your Spiritual Resources
          Rev. Willie F. Wilson with Andrea Benton Rushing   18

Three I Pledge Allegiance?   27
       Patriotism Comes in Black
          Cheryl Poinsette Brown   29
       Stand by the Man
          Brian Gilmore   38
       Hard Truths: September 11, 2001 and Respecting the Idea of America
          Haki R.Madhubuti   46
       Terrorism, Muslim Profiling and the "Enemy"
          Askia Muhammad   51

Four   **Lift Every Voice**   61
            Young Black America's Response to September 11th:
            Black Youth Continue to Define Their Political Ideology
                Melanie L. Campbell   65
            Speech Before the U.S. House of Representatives - September 16, 2001
                Congresswoman Barbara Lee   76
            Whitewash
                Roland Martin   78
            Do You See What They See? Do You Hear What They Hear?:
            Two Black Women Share Their Candid Thoughts on September 11th
            and the War on Terrorism
                Tamara A. Masters Wilds   84
            The War Within: African American Public Opinion on the
            War Against Terrorism
                Karin L. Stanford   95

Five   **What is Terrorism?**   117
            Whose War: The Color of Terror
                John Edgar Wideman   120
            Fighting Men, Silent Women?
                Marcia Ann Gillespie   129
            Enemies, Both Foreign and Domestic: Tulsa, 1921
            and September 11, 2001
                Kimberly C. Ellis   134
            Where Were You When the Revolution Was Televised?
                Reginna A. Green   159

Six   This Land Was Made For You and Me   167
          The Death Penalty in this Great Nation of Ours
              Danny Glover   171
          White Man's Pass: The Heightened Danger of Racial Profiling
          in the Post 9/11 World
              Laura W. Murphy   175
          Shared Status: A Global Imperative
              Julianne Malveaux   185

Seven An Island of Tranquility in a Sea of Discontent:
          U.S. Foreign Policy and the War on Terrorism   199
          Globalization, Racism and the Terrorist Threat:
          Incorporating an Afro-Caribbean Response
              Orville W. Taylor   201
          The U.S. War on Terrorism and Foreign Policy Justice
              Ron Walters   223

About the Contributors   235
About the Editors   239
Acknowledgements   240

FOREWORD

Julianne Malveaux is the leading multimedia progressive journalist of her generation. For over a quarter of a century, she has upheld a bold vision of justice and equality on television and radio as well as in her columns and books. Her sheer brilliance, courage and wit have gained her a large following of informed citizens and persons of all colors here and abroad. During the Ice Age of Reagan and Bush Sr. she was one of the few critics to highlight the vast concentrations of corporate power and its concomitant wealth inequality. In the flashy times of Clinton, she was nearly alone in keeping close track on the escalating incarceration rates and expanding prison industrial complex. Now in these arrogant moments of Bush Jr., she has examined the so-called "election" and its aftermath with insight.

Reginna Green, a young, brilliant journalist in her own right, builds on the rich legacy of Julianne Malveaux. She has already made major strides in bringing her tremendous talent, discipline and energy together in order to tell painful truths about our present plight and predicament.

In this timely text Malveaux and Green take on the major matter of the early twenty-first century: Bush Jr.'s "war on terrorism." There is no doubt that September 11, 2001 will forever live in the American memory as a day of infamy. Nearly 3,000 precious lives flushed out by mass murderers in the name of rage and revenge against American foreign policies in the Middle East. All of us found ourselves wrestling with the question: What are we to make of this ugly situation? My first response to the attacks on the World Trade Center was visceral. I was in a Times Square hotel when the first plane flew into the tower. I had come to New York City to campaign for my brother Fernando Ferrer for mayor. September 11th was election day. I saw the second plane hit the second tower. My first thought was Times Square would be hit next. I looked down below and saw people running across the street and huddling around the news strip to witness the replay and report of the attacks. Although I live under the threat of death everyday from potential racist, domestic terrorists, I thought that I may not get out of the hotel alive owing to subsequent attacks on Times Square.

I was deeply upset about the precious lives in the World Trade Center and the possible even probable attack on the hotel. Yet I was not afraid. I felt I had been in this situation before — many times. Then I thought how many times I had undergone the experience of being unsafe, unprotected, subject to arbitrary violence and hated. Despite my job at Harvard and home in downtown Boston, I was still a "nigger" in America. To be an American "nigger" is to be unsafe, unprotected, subject to arbitrary violence and hated. I concluded that 9/11 had initiated a painful process of the "niggerization" of America—we all are now unsafe, unprotected, subject to arbitrary violence and hated. The country known for its upbeat optimism–now has the blues. Maybe it can learn something from the blues people in its midst who have known the night side of the American past and present.

Julianne Malveaux and Reginna Green are bone of the bone and flesh of the flesh of a people who have been terrorized by the very government that now declares a war against terrorism around the world. In their calls for justice not revenge; democratic defense of rights and liberties not authoritarian efforts of false security; and robust dialogue not overt or tacit censorship they voice the best of the black intellectual tradition as well as the core of progressive politics.

As you read through this volume you understand why Julianne Malveaux, along with her precious vision and legacy, is a national treasure. She and Reginna Green have brought together the most significant voices in this country to examine the various dimensions of the United States' declared "war on terrorism." We ignore their voices at our own peril.

—Dr. Cornel West

PREFACE

We spent September 11, 2001 together. We didn't plan it that way. We both planned to be at our respective desks across town from each other, working. But the day ended up being one of those that screamed out for connection; because we are sisterfriends, we ended up together, crying, watching television, talking, reaching out to our respective friends, and fielding calls from folks who sought us out. Parents, friends, blasts from the past, and even casual acquaintances were on the phone.

Everyone in America thought about themselves and we thought about our lives on that day. Few of us thought about race first, but eventually it came up. It came up for us when we watched television and saw no black commentators. Not until *Nightline*, late at night, did melanin hit the screen accompanied by the incandescent voices of Maya Angelou and Bebe Moore Campbell who spoke of spirit, unity, resilience, and connection.

We were troubled and we talked about our trouble. It was an interesting conversation we had since our generational divide is such that the elder of us thinks race first or second, while the younger of us thinks race third or fourth. Still, we both agreed that race mattered in the "war on terrorism," although we could not agree how. We heard black folks mumbling and grumbling about the ways we were ignored in media, about the ambivalence that many felt about our country and its foreign policy, about our history and legacy of fighting for the right to fight.

Mary Frances Berry coined the term "the paradox of loyalty" in *Long Memory: The Black Experience in America*, the book she wrote with John Blassingame in 1986. We have long been intrigued by the phrase, thinking it the perfect distillation of the mixed feelings that many African Americans feel about our country. African Americans are the perfect Americans; caught between hope and despair, believing in the American dream despite evidence to the contrary because our disbelief would make us nihilistic and disengaged. African Americans who vote, engage, and criticize America are, in our opinion, the ultimate Americans, offering their criticism as a form of service, pushing our nation to embrace the words, "one nation, indivisible" that are recited when the flag is pledged.

Race matters. That sentiment was the impetus for compiling this anthology. We had an idea, Haki Madhubuti at Third World Press was interested, and it was on. Along the way we discovered similar voices and discordant ones. We also discovered issues about the way voices are heard. The publisher of the *Richmond Times-Dispatch* told Julianne that after he printed her immediate reaction piece (see Toppling Towers) with the headline "Provoked?" on the front page of the paper, some of the machines that carried the article were vandalized. The attack on the World Trade Center seemed to suggest that all of us Americans should be in the same boat. But, as Julianne puts it, some of us have been riding and some rowing; some have been hit hard by the economic response to the war on terrorism; others have been coasting along, profiting, and even flaunting the profits.

This book aims to reflect the range of responses within the African American community to the events of September 11, 2001 and the subsequent "war on terrorism." The essays which comprise this book—from the visceral words of Gail Mitchell, a survivor of both the World Trade Center bombing of 1993 and the 9/11 terrorist attacks, to the academic essays by Dr. Kimberly Ellis and Dr. Karin Stanford—paint a picture of a response to a "war" that is not only colored by race and experience but also by patriotism, loyalty and safety. The words of Haki Madhubuti and Askia Muhammad are as penetrating as they are true. Melanie Campbell and Tamara Wilds with essays which bridge the reactions to 9/11 and the "war on terrorism" between Black youth and Black seniors. Dr. Orville Taylor's contribution adds an Afro-Caribbean response. Danny Glover makes the connection between domestic social policy and foreign policy as succinctly as could possibly be made in his November 2001 speech at Princeton University that is reprinted here. Laura Murphy of the American Civil Liberties Union tackles the metamorphosis of "driving while black" into "flying while brown." Congresswoman Barbara Lee lends her dissenting voice to these pages. John Edgar Wideman and Brian Gilmore provide this volume with thoughtful, critical essays based on raw emotion. Rev. Willie Wilson of Union Temple

Baptist Church in Washington, D.C. brings a spiritual response in this publication of his sermon given on September 16, 2001. Cheryl Poinsette Brown reminds us that patriotism is not the intellectual property of only white Americans. Marcia Gillespie analyzes what 9/11 and the "war on terrorism" means for women worldwide. Aaron McGruder graces these pages with the always pointed and thought-provoking humor strip "Boondocks." Contributions to this volume are further explored in section introductions, written by Julianne, and other comments by Reginna and by Andrea Rushing, who graciously agreed to edit two of the essays included in this volume.

We believe in this book. We believe in it because it is African Americans who share some of the most sought-after freedoms in the world, but who also exist in a society that is racist and ethnocentric, characteristics shared by our country's foreign policy and the current "war on terrorism." And like the Japanese who were perceived to be national security threats and rounded up and sent to internment camps during World War II, African Americans know that while we may live here, it does not always feel as if we are of here. This relationship colors our experiences and informs our perceptions of what took place September 11, 2001 and the weeks and months thereafter. There is no doubt that Americans of color—from those who were enslaved to those who were interned—see the perils of the "war on terrorism" much more clearly and vividly than those who are members of the privileged class who wage it.

We are excited to have brought together a group of thoughtful and talented writers to explore the African American response to the "war on terrorism." We are especially delighted to join the established voices of John Edgar Wideman and Marcia Ann Gillespie with emerging voices like those of Tamara Wilds and Kimberly Ellis. We are excited that our conversation is cross generational and policy oriented. The choir we have pulled together doesn't always sing from the same sheet music. But our difference sings America, a nation that has often (but not always) encouraged free speech and embraced difference.

CHAPTER ONE

Only the Strong Survive

Only the Strong Survive

Gail Mitchell is long, tall, tough, a talk much stuff and take none black woman I have known for nearly 30 years. I remember, when I pledged Iota chapter of Delta Sigma Theta in 1973, she put us Pyramids through our paces. I remember working to get a smile out of her and watching her retreat behind the angles and planes of her classical face. She is the last person I would think of as a victim, the last one I'd think of as living in the middle of a meltdown. But when members of the Social Action Commission of Delta talked about September 11th, one of her good friends shared that Gail was a double survivor, having been in the World Trade Center when it was bombed in 1993. Gail's perspective, it was said, had been altered by the tragedy of September 11th. We talked. She wrote. We talked. I was too gripped by the raw edges in her voice to edit her work, so I enlisted a sisterfriend and colleague, Dr. Andrea Rushing, to take Gail's raw emotion and turn them into an essay.

We begin this book with Gail's testimony because her truth is the basic truth, the foundation upon which we must build any discussion about an African American perspective on the war on terrorism. We, Black folks, are so integrally woven into the fabric that we call America that an attack on any building or institution (except, perhaps, the United States Senate) will affect us. At the same time, we are so invisible to white America that an attack that includes us becomes so "color blind" that it excludes us. How many know that Lisa Jefferson, the GTE operator who talked and prayed with Todd Beamer, one of the heroes of UAL Flight 93 was an African American woman? How many know that Captain LeRoy Hunter, one of the pilots who died, was African American? Should it matter? While Gail Mitchell does not dwell on race in her description of surviving September 11th, she suggests in her concluding remarks that African American survivors and heroes got much less attention than their white counterparts. For Mitchell, then, race matters.

The main thing she shares, though, is not a racial perspective, but a human, riveting account of being in the eye of the storm, walking through it, coming home, and reflecting. Jerry Butler, one of our culture's richest lyricists, says, "Only the strong survive." Gail Mitchell is a survivor who has transcended her survival to speak about the necessary changes we must make to transform our society, to collectively survive.

–J.M.

2

NECESSARY CHANGES
Gail E. Mitchell with Andrea Benton Rushing

Looking back a year later, with much more critical and questioning minds than we had in the immediate and extended 24-hour coverage of the events and the aftermath of September 11, 2001 we realize that Black women's voices were silenced: No reporters, television anchors, analysts or pundits. Although many of us did not see the significance of enforced silence then, we now realize why institutional racism and sexism created it.

My original introduction to Gail Mitchell came from the thoughts she put on paper. Those words did not prepare me for a woman who graciously talked to me for hours. You are about to read her account of a day she compares to Armageddon and her later reflections on the still-stunning event. Rather than trying to bury those awful hours or turn away from her tears and fears, she relates to them. Gail Mitchell is more than a survivor of two World Trade Center attacks; she is a compassionate, intelligent and outraged "overcomer." Although she would modestly deny it, she belongs in the circle of bodacious, testifying women like Sojourner Truth, Rosa Parks and Anita Hill.

You will be chilled and astonished by her story. Her words are ones we have been unknowingly waiting for.

"Can I get a witness?" We are unbelievably fortunate to have found just the right one.

–Andrea Benton Rushing

SEPTEMBER 11, 2001

It's hard for me to believe that I'm here with you today. You see, I've survived an earthquake, the February 26, 1993 bombing of the World Trade Center, and the September 11 attack on the World Trade Center, too. Raised as a Catholic, I know I'm blessed to be alive and, though going through emotional suffering in the aftermath, in my right mind today. I know the Creator still has work for me to do. Part of that work is to tell you my story because so few Black voices have been heard.

Nothing about September 11, 2001 prepared me for what lay ahead, though, looking back, I remember that I had been a little restless the night before. I got up at my usual 5:30 a.m. time so I could get to work between 8:00 a.m. and 8:30 a.m. The day was beautiful: the sun was shining brightly and the sky was a glorious blue. It was one of the clearest days of the year. When I looked out my bedroom window and saw the Twin Towers, I thought about how beautiful they were and how fortunate I was to have spent so much time there, working for the Port Authority of New York and New Jersey. I remember thanking the Creator because I'd just celebrated my fiftieth birthday with my mother and sister on a trip to Hawaii, Australia, New Zealand and Fiji. Getting dressed I listened to radio as I always did in the morning. There were the usual delays on the train to work. As the train doors opened at Cortlandt Street stop, a man in a suit behind the bars where you exit the station was saying, "A bomb, a bomb, get out, get out!" I've lived in New York City so long that I'm accustomed to the unusual, so I just thought the man was a little crazy and I stayed very calm. I had no idea that an unparalleled disaster had already started to happen and that I would see its second stage with my own astonished eyes.

My usual exit was inaccessible, so, still calm, I walked the entire platform and left by another staircase. In the lobby of the building I heard a security guard screaming, "Hurry up, hurry up, get out, get out." When I ran into the street, I was in a storm of noise, paper, and indefinable debris. My mind took in the details, but couldn't fit them into a pattern. When I saw the North Tower on fire with smoke billowing out of the windows, my first thought was, "Is that the 88th floor where I work?" Even though I had lived through the 1993 World Trade Center bombing, even though I'd kept in my mind the idea that since that event hadn't destroyed the Towers and the people responsible for it would come back, I couldn't imagine what had happened. At first I thought it was an explosion from one of the mechanical rooms. I began counting the floors to try to figure out if my floor was on fire. I began to think about my colleagues—seventy-five of them died that day—and wondered if they were all right. My body began to shake, on the inside and the outside, like jelly. Kirby, a co-worker who's an engineer, grabbed my shaking body and hugged me very tightly. I asked him if it was my floor on fire. He insisted that it was above my floor and told me not to worry. When we began to count the floors together, we realized that the smoke was coming from the floors around the nineties. I asked Kirby if his wife Kelly was at work. She was and she worked on the 73rd floor. Now it was my turn to comfort him. Knowing his wife as I did, I told him not to worry, because she had already left the burning building and was probably on her way home. I was right as I found out several days later.

It's amazing how the details stick in my mind; my adrenaline must have really been racing. While I was standing in the middle of Vessey Street in front of the post office, I saw people hanging out of the building, waving handkerchiefs, screaming for help. Then, suddenly, in the middle of all the confusion I saw a huge jumbo jet and wondered why it was flying so low. Before I could think clearly, there was an enormous roar and an explosion. The plane had flown into the South Tower. A huge fireball that looked like the mushroom cloud over Hiroshima in 1945. It covered everything in its path. It was chaos; all anybody could hear were violent screams of people running to get out of its way, and you could see pieces of the plane, paper, and body parts. Within a few minutes there were Air Force fighter planes circling overhead, but at first that also terrified me because I thought it was another attacking plane. It took me time to realize they were U.S. planes.

As I ran to the next block, I turned around and saw people jumping from the windows of the World Trade Center. It wasn't like it appeared on television. I was there watching people choosing to die this way rather than burn to death, and I wondered what choice I would have made if I were in that inferno. They continued to jump. Some, pitifully, all by themselves. Others, mostly men and women, holding hands, jumping together. If I live a thousand years, I will never forget the thumping noises their bodies made when they hit the pavement. My co-worker Kirby and I passed a young woman, crying hysterically, and saying over and over, "My mother is in there." He tried to comfort her the same way he did me, as if he had no worries of his own. Kirby kept telling her, "She will be all right." The three of us walked down another block. I told them I had to find a telephone, so I could call home. Some people's cell phones could get incoming calls, but couldn't call out. Mine wasn't working at all. There aren't a lot of pay phones in the area, and every one had at least 15 to 25 people on line waiting to use it. After some time, I finally reached my mother to let her know that I was all right.

While I was waiting for the telephone, I heard someone saying that a plane had flown into the Pentagon and that the government was looking for eight planes altogether. Since three planes had already struck, there were five more to come. "Oh my God what next? Armageddon?" So many things went through my mind and I, accustomed to being in charge of my important and complicated job, felt so very helpless. Waiting gave me time to realize that there were about 50,000 people in the World Trade Center complex at that time of day and most of them worked in the Twin Towers. Still waiting, I began to see people whom I knew coming from the building, and I asked them what floor they came from to see if I could receive any reassurance about colleagues from the 88th floor. People with head, arm, and leg injuries passed me. Since the World Trade Center was a few blocks from Beekman hospital, many people walked there on their own while sirens from police and fire department vehicles shrieked in the background.

Then I heard a rumbling noise like a large, heavy freight train was passing. The earth shook. People screamed. A loud explosion. I watched in disbelief as the South Tower began to collapse like a stack of Sunday pancakes. The top of the building fell to the side and floors toppled onto each other. I don't have the words to describe the noise. I'd survived an earthquake before and the ground on which I was standing felt like I was in another one. As the building fell, an immense cloud of gray smoke, as huge as a tidal wave, seemed to cover everything. It rose very quickly and moved just as quickly enveloping everything in its path. The small diameter of Lower Manhattan was enveloped by smoke within minutes. I stood there helpless while the buildings were pulverized. My job, leasing space at the World Trade Center and responding to tenants' concerns about that space, made me fairly knowledgeable about construction. That's probably why I noticed that marble, glass, gypsum, concrete, metal, fabrics, papers, computer equipment, furniture, cafeteria equipment, automobiles were destroyed quickly and completely.

I began to run, trying not to breathe in the awful air, worried that if I did, I would suffocate. In a survival mode and powered by adrenalin, my intuition ordered me, "Run north, run north!" I live in Queens; the easiest way to get there from Manhattan was across the 59th Street and the Queensborough Bridge. I walk a lot, but I rarely run. Afraid that I was going to die, I ran so fast that I got to Canal Street before the North Tower fell. I had managed to

6

make a phone call home before I started to run. Now I wanted to call again because I realized that my family probably did not know whether or not I was caught in the debris and smoke. It wasn't any easier to find a working telephone the second time. I began walking once again and met my friend Diane. She saw the look on my face and asked me where I was coming from. All I could do was point in the direction of the disaster. After a big hug, she made me sit down. I had suffered so many shocks that I was weary and numb. Although I had not eaten or drank anything all morning, I was neither hungry nor thirsty.

There was a church near where Diane worked and its phones were working. I talked to another friend's mother because my own mother's line was busy. Exhilarated to be alive in the face of so much destruction and death, I told her I was fine. I thought I was, but what I should have said was "I was blessed to survive" because I wasn't fine then, and, I later learned that, like other people who came through the catastrophe, I will never again be "fine." The Gail Mitchell who left home that gorgeous Tuesday morning is, no matter how she looks on the outside, forever changed on the inside.

Many nearby places of business were setting up tables with water and other cold beverages so that passers-by could have something to drink. A dazed man passed me with a bloodied head and gray matter all over him. A medical technician asked him sit down in order to take his blood pressure. He gave him a wet cloth to wipe his face. At first the man wouldn't stop, as if he didn't understand what the technician was saying. Finally he sat down, drank something and had his pressure taken. Then he got up and continued his walk, continuing to stare without seeming to see, and he never uttered a word.

As I sat in my friend's office, radios reported that all modes of transportation had stopped running. The only way to get from Manhattan back to my home in Queens was to cross a bridge. I didn't even think about spending the night in Manhattan. What if gas pipes and water mains started bursting? My friend Diane also lived in Queens, so we gathered our belongings, and, not knowing how we were going to make it, decided to walk across the 59th Street bridge. I realized that, even if the subway was working, I did not want to be underground. "If we are attacked again, let me die above ground." Six of us left and began walking north. My memory comes in bits and pieces and I can't remember what street we were on, but I know we passed some housing projects where people were sitting around listening to music and children were in the playground. I could not believe that they didn't know what was going on. I wondered whether they cared.

We finally saw a bus stop and got on a bus that took us to 14th Street. We walked to Madison Avenue and boarded a bus that took us to 59th Street. We walked from Madison Avenue to the 59th Street bridge and, then, like hundreds of other people, we walked across the East River. Looking to the right and there was a huge cloud, but the World Trade Center was no longer there. Although I couldn't believe the emptiness I saw and wondered if I was dreaming, a hole opened in my heart. I was so afraid a bomb would fall before I could get across the bridge. The Air Force jets continued to circle overhead, and though I knew they were on our side, their presence made me feel even more under attack.

As soon as we got to Queens, people started giving us bottles of water. We were terribly thirsty and dehydrated. Buses were lined up at the curb; we hopped onto one of them. "I'm going to Continental Avenue," the bus driver said and the ride was free! My cell phone worked on the bus. By the time I got to Continental Avenue, my mother had arranged for my friend Gwen to pick me and two sister sojourners up.

Home, home, home. Family, family, family. My sister was in Atlanta on a business trip. On the phone I told her that I was so happy that she was down there because when I was in the bombing of the World Trade Center in 1993, she came looking for me since she also works in lower Manhattan. This time if she had come looking for me she might have died. My mother and my uncle, who had left for Canada, turned around and came back when they heard about the catastrophe. They were there, fussing over me. I remember sitting in a chair and taking off my shoes because I had done so much walking and my feet were so tired. You know I was in shock because it took my mother saying, "Oh my God look at your feet!" for me to realize that they were swollen. I had sprained my left foot, and my right foot was full of blisters. Shock kept me from feeling the pain.

At my mother's house I found out that my entire family was affected by this tragedy. My cousin worked across the street from the Pentagon; her husband worked at the Pentagon; my other cousin worked in one of the Federal buildings near the Pentagon; and my uncle worked in a chemical plant in the South and was sent home early. I could not believe the magnitude of that particular day on my family. The telephone kept ringing until early morning hours. I told my story over and over and over. I also remember the hideous sight on television when every station kept showing the planes flying into the building. I could neither eat nor sleep. I was completely drained.

The following days were agonizing. I was exhausted, but could not sleep. I had continuous muscle spasms in one of my thighs that were very painful. The blisters on my feet were healing, but I could not wear any shoes. Believe it or not, I went back to work the following Monday, but it was very difficult. I had, though I didn't call it that then, posttraumatic stress syndrome. I use Pennsylvania Station in New York and the crowds of people made me very uncomfortable. I had to take deep breaths every time I rode the subway. If there were delays while I was on the subway, I would become very anxious. My heart would beat very quickly and I could barely breathe. Anxiety attacks became a part of my life. Things I did easily before September 11th, like taking public transportation, made me nervous. I am a seasoned New Yorker and I was suddenly tense in huge crowds of people.

One night I had to attend a business dinner. I was walking across 34th Street to the east side of Manhattan. As I approached the Empire State building, I began to have an anxiety attack. I could not walk fast enough to get away from the building. What if a plane flew into the building and it fell over? There was a time when I wanted to be on a higher floor at the World Trade Center in order to get a better view. September 11th changed all that. Now I want to be on a lower floor so I can leave the building quickly in case of another emergency. I am so glad that I took advantage of looking at the breathtaking views from the World Trade Center windows, especially, the sunsets and nor'easters as they approached Manhattan from the west. I'm so glad I was blessed to experience all that beauty. Along with the memories of the horror of September 11th, I have sweet memories too.

At first I was just so joyful to be alive, trivial things diminished for me and my relationships with people changed. I had (and still have) no time for nonsense and drama. I'm re-committed to using my energy positively, and I value life even more than I did before because I have seen for myself, not once but twice, that at the blink of an eye my entire life could have come to an end.

LATER

These past few months have been unimaginably difficult. It's not just that I sleep erratically. There's a lot of talk about getting back to normal, getting closure, and plans to build on the site, which I see as a cemetery. I'm still attending funerals and memorial services. People I know have had heart attacks, panic attacks, nervous breakdowns, and severe depression. Some have just gotten out of the hospital and are beginning a lifetime of physical rehabilitation. Every time somebody tells me to get over it and move on with my life, I get angry. September 11th didn't just change New York City's skyline; it changed those of us who were there—forever.

I believe I was spared for a reason, and part of that reason was to tell my story. As time has passed and the sheer euphoria of being alive has ceased to dominate my days. I've started to see things differently. According to an African American Vietnam vet, who has been of great help to me in my recovery, I do not look the same. I have "a look of sadness and emptiness" in my eyes.

My mind zooms back to the bombing of the World Trade Center on February 26, 1993 when the counselor my organization brought in was himself a victim of the attack. Security was tightened. In the back of my mind, I always thought the World Trade Center would be attacked again because the work that was begun had not been finished. If these were my thoughts, what did the professionals and those who occupy the seats of power think?

Now I ask myself, "Did September 11th really have to happen?" With all the intelligence the United States has, this country must have known it was going to happen. "My country 'tis of thee" seems willing to risk a few thousand lives as "collateral damage" to become involved with a wartime conflict and really devalues those lives if they're Black. I don't have any proof. I do have a background in telecommunications, twelve years at the Port Authority, years of experience in corporate America and the same intuition that got me safely home from the devastated World Trade Center in lower Manhattan to my family in Queens.

Everything fits into a pattern too well. Like an unfinished jigsaw puzzle, some pieces are still missing. How were the "terrorists" "found" so quickly after the attacks? How do you account for the many trades on Wall Street prior to September 11th? Someone benefited financially from those stock trades. We, the citizenry of the United States, who go to work everyday and pay our mortgage notes, are expendable to the people who control this country. What happens to us, especially if we're African Americans, is "collateral damage."

Sometimes I think, "If I see another American flag, I don't know what I'll do." African American history and my own personal history make me disbelieve that "United We Stand" includes us: we've never really been included before. Television coverage of September 11th focused on Euro-Americans, and ignored the heroism of African American security guards, police officers and fire fighters. People didn't write stories about the Black man, a Panamanian, who took over managing the offices of the Port Authority of New York and New Jersey when the head of that company was killed. In the middle of the chaos, he made sure we got paid on time that Friday and expertly re-located our offices to 18th Street. Comments about "losing our freedoms" grate on me because Black people have never really had freedom in this land. Never. And September 11th won't change that unless we continue working to bring about the necessary changes.

CHAPTER TWO

Dateline: 9/11/2001

Dateline: 9/11/2001

I was sitting at my desk on September 11th, piddling with my keyboard and watching the cable stations rerun the tape of a plane flying into the World Trade Center, struggling with a sense of ennui when an unexpected call came. Raoul Dennis, the Editor of the National Newspaper Publishers Association, the organization that provides editorial content for black newspapers in the United States, was on the other line. "I am calling commentators for reaction," he said. I exhaled the column, "Toppling Towers, Tested Power," that appears in this section. When I say exhaled the column, I mean that his request for reaction was release for me. I realize that writing is one of my most natural modes of expression, that possibly I was put on this world to write. My fingers hit the keyboard like a runner hits the street, and before I knew it there were about 750 words on the page. I let it sit, let it simmer, tweaked the words until they blended together in a way that reflected my feelings of anger and resignation about the toppling towers and our nation's tested power. As soon as I e-mailed it out, I breathed a sigh of satisfaction.

Days after the tragedy, I joined the nation in feeling a need for spiritual solace. I can't prove it, but I bet you that church pews were more full than they ever were on the Sunday following the terrorist attacks. I needed something spiritual, but also nationalistic, of God, but in the African American tradition. Like a firefly drawn to light, I stumbled into Union Temple Baptist church, parched for wisdom, aching to hear from the Rev. Willie Wilson. Rev. Wilson is an author, thinker, nationalist, and activist. He is one of the most genuine spiritualists that I have been exposed to in my life. I was drawn to his church for the nourishment I craved, and Rev. Willie Wilson did not disappoint. An edited version of his sermon is included in this section.

—J.M.

TOPPLING TOWERS, TESTED POWER
Julianne Malveaux

Every morning I have an inner battle with myself. Will I walk, or will I chill? Move my body or my mind? At least three mornings a week my body has to win the battle. This morning it did, albeit on a delayed basis. So I had to walk back into my house and pick up a ringing phone to learn that terrorists had aimed a plane at the two Word Trade Center towers, and that thousands of lives were put in jeopardy as those buildings toppled. This was a day that was predestined to spiral downward. At least two more planes were hijacked and crashed, one into the Pentagon. It was rumored that Camp David was attacked. Lower Manhattan was evacuated as was the White House and just about every office building in downtown Washington. The United States had not been attacked on its own soil since Pearl Harbor more than 60 years ago. We've never had war or this kind of uncertainty on our own land. Now, we are feeling what Brits felt during World War II, the fear and the uncertainty of random attacks.

I am first chilled by the magnitude of this damage. The death toll is high, and it will climb. There were hundreds of people on the planes that crashed, thousands working in the office buildings in the World Trade Center. My mind reviews my rolodex, calling up the names and faces of friends who work in lower Manhattan. My heart stops when I think of them, their families, and the devastation that may be caused if they are hurt by an attack. I try to call out, but circuits are busy. I hold my breath.

My second reaction is a stunned outrage. Whatever happened to U.S. intelligence? We spend billions of dollars annually spying and interfering in the operations of other countries. How could we have known nothing about this? President Bush has said we need more money for the military. This attack will make the appropriation of more money a cakewalk. At the same time where are our accountability standards? Does the military do the best it can with the money it has? Why did we know absolutely nothing about such a comprehensive, well-executed, coordinated attack?

As outraged as I am, I am also reconciled to the fact that this attack, despicable as it is, was also provoked. The United States has insisted on playing 700-pound gorilla with the rest of the world, failing to cooperate with inter-

15

national treaties, to participate in international conferences. Our message has been "our way or the highway," and it seems that such a message begs someone to humble us. Our grandmas used to tell us that the bigger you are the harder you fall. No one hoped that the World Trade Center would come toppling down, but many wondered how the hubris the U.S. has showed the world would play itself out. You can't be the biggest, the baddest, the strongest, the mightiest without having a corner of compassion, cooperation or humility. Your opponents will look for cracks in your armor. In a sad but startling way, it looks like they found ours.

Finally, I realize that these attacks are an explicit declaration of war against the United States. What does war mean for black people? It means the declaration of martial law, and regular rules (already unfair) may be bent because we are living in a state of emergency. If our last wars (including Vietnam and the Persian Gulf) are any indication, it means that black troops will serve harder, at a greater risk with less protection and remuneration than other troops. It means that folks who seem or look "suspicious" will be treated suspiciously. It means that, because we, too, sing America, we will be expected to stifle any complaint and swallow any ill treatment in the name of the "greater good."

Since Afghanistan, the Taliban, and other Middle Easterners are suspects for this terrorism, those African Americans who have expressed some sympathy with these causes will be suspect as well. Those progressives who have not deified Israel, but instead brought balanced focus to Middle Eastern matters are likely to find their words and their work scrutinized. Our collective horror at the toppling of the twin towers is likely to howl back at those who put these tragedies in context. We won't necessarily tie yellow ribbons around trees, or wear symbols on our chests, but this crisis will engender a loyalty test that some will not be able to pass. If they have one strike against them because they are black, they'll get another for failing to toe a rabidly nationalist line. The tenor of discourse is likely to be tempered by grief and conformity.

W. E. B. DuBois talked about the duality of our African American existence of "two warring souls in one black body": even as our American nationalism and outrage at this sneak attack angers us, our African identities must allow us to put this foul attack in context. We cannot condone the hijacking of airplanes, the bombing of buildings, and the loss of innocent life. But we must acknowledge that our nation's own hubris may have pushed others into testing our power and exposing our vulnerabilities.

This essay was originally filed with the National Newspaper Publishers Association on September 11, 2001, and published in the Richmond Times-Dispatch, the San Francisco Sun-Reporter and other papers.

USING YOUR SPIRITUAL RESOURCES
Rev. Willie F. Wilson with Andrea Benton Rushing

Transposing an oral art form, like an African American sermon, into the written word is a formidable undertaking. James Weldon Johnson's "God's Trombones", a magnificent volume of poetry based on style and substance of the African American vernacular, teaches us that it can be done. There are so many elements of this genre of art, delivered to a congregation and enclosed in music and prayer that the written word cannot capture. Readers miss how the church looks, the body language of the preacher and the congregation, and the call and response. Church congregations are accustomed to the poetry of the form with its use of simile, metaphor, understatement, hyperbole, paradox, proverbs, and allusions to the Bible. Readers of sermons may not know of the immense body of African American spiritual and secular music, and the shared experiences of the congregations. They know how brilliance can pop up like a jack-in-the-box from a few lines of text. The preacher's voice, which James Weldon Johnson compared to a trombone, cannot be captured in prose. We miss the pauses, changes in volume, timbre and pitch, and tones of voice of that magnificent instrument. We miss the rich repetition, the rolling emphasis that lightly touches some syllables and places a hard edge on others. What written transcription can give us are words spoken in the most powerful institution in African American communities, communities whose origins lie in the power of the spoken word in West Africa and its coded power in the Americas begun during slavery and continuing until today. The African American church is where preachers say they empty themselves out so God can speak through them. "Prepare for a sermon," the saying goes, "as if there is no such thing as the Holy Spirit, and then preach it as if the Holy Spirit is all there is." That's what the Rev. Willie F. Wilson has done a mere five days after the events of September 11th while most of us were still speechlessly chained to re-runs of television footage. What he delivers is neither a pie in the sky sermon, nor a hell and damnation message, so often the stereotypes of African American sermons. Instead he skillfully uses the tools of his art form to take an ancient Biblical story and apply it to a contemporary catastrophe. He preaches boldly speaking truth to and about the mighty. He breaks down, analyzes, local, national, and international economic, historical, political, and social problems with uncanny insight and a deft juxtaposition between his congregation's personal problems and world-rocking events.
                                                                    –Andrea Benton Rushing

September 16, 2001
Union Temple Baptist Church

We've read our scriptures, but I want to read to you from the New International Version. These several verses from II Kings verses 4 and 8 because the word of God is so dynamic and so powerful that, if we read it metaphorically, it has an inimitable nature that speaks to us across thousands of years to offer us universal truths that are just as contemporary as if they were written today.

This is a teaching sermon, and I take my text today from an ancient story about the great Old Testament prophet Elijah, starting at the II Kings: 8. All of us over the last several days beginning on September 11th, have witnessed what has aptly and rightly been described as a horrific attack on the United States. And many of us here in southeast D.C. today are grieving over our own loss of an innocent teacher and her students.

Over and over again, we saw the tape on the television screen telling us of the estimated thousands dead; heard constant accounts about the last phone calls that individuals were able to make from their cell phones; witnessed graphic pictures of the destruction of buildings and bodies. And these turbulent times have induced a mass attack of disillusion and despair and have distilled anger out of the collapse of hope at a time when what we have seen over and over again seems so surrealistic.

But we are not dreaming. What happened was real. Everybody's looking for relief, looking for solutions, looking for answers. Many of us feel hopeless, helpless, in turmoil and in crisis. We need some resources. We need a place we can go that can supply us, give us some strength, give us some power for these hours. Having resources means having assets to change our condition in the face of catastrophe and great oppositions. That's what power is. It's not enough to have the resources. We have to be able to identify, organize, and use them. If you have resources and can't use them, you don't have any power.

You can have resources but, if you don't have the ability to organize your resources, if you don't have the ability to take the assets that you have and make them work for you and organize them in the face of whatever you are dealing with so that you can overcome and be victorious, then you have no power. You got resources, but you don't have any power.

19

We know about this when we look at the continent of Africa. Look at Africa. More natural resources than any continent in existence, but because Africa cannot organize its resources, cannot identify that in unifying themselves and organizing those resources and controlling those resources, and then being able to use those resources they have no power.

As African-Americans, we have mental resources. We've got some brilliant minds in our community. We've got black scientists and black engineers and black architects and black doctors and black dentists. In every kind of field that you can imagine, we have experts in those fields. But we don't have power. That crab in the barrel mentality Booker T. Washington talks about keeps us divided and keeps us pulling each other down, and so, even though we have intellectual resources, we don't have any power.

We are told over and over again, if the collective 500 plus billion dollars in disposable income in our community was organized, was identified and organized and controlled by us, we would be the seventh richest nation on the earth, but because we have not been able to organize these resources, because we have dealt with this $500 billion as disposable income where we simply dispose of it. It goes into our hands and passes out of our hands before eight hours pass by. We've got plenty of money, we've got economic resources, but we don't have any power.

In the face of the catastrophe, the mammoth problems, the gross uncertainty we've faced in these past five days, and the aftermath that lies ahead, I want to talk about spiritual resources. In times like these the song teaches us, we need help from God. We need some spiritual resources. Everybody in here needs the Lord. My sisters and my brothers, I'm talking about a fountain you can go back to over and over again, any time of day, any time of night, and find it full. In this crisis there is a resource available, no money down, no degree required, no matter what we've done and whom we've been, available full and free to us all.

Now, let me take you back to my text to Elijah's story in II Kings. The thing I especially like about this lesson from the Hebrew Bible is that Elijah demonstrates that, if you've got your spiritual resources working for you, you have the ability to deal with anybody, anything, any time, anywhere. Then, no matter what the opposition is, no matter what the problem is, you can deal with it.

Elijah is a prototype of how we, as believers ought to act. He walked with the upper crust, and he ministered to the downtrodden. And that's not all; Elijah was not afraid to say what folk needed to hear—whether or not they liked it. He wasn't scared to speak truth to power.

Look at this text. "God gave Israel, you know Biblical history. God gave Israel kings because they asked for kings," because they said, "Oh God, we need kings to rule over us." So God gave them kings, but the kings were not God's spokesmen. They were secular leaders. So God also sent, I hope you understand me today, prophets to be God's own spokespeople.

George W. Bush stole the election, so he's the president, but he's not speaking for God. And some prophet, some woman or man of God needs to tell George W. Bush as he begins to organize a army to go after someone who he doesn't even know he's going after, that the weapons of our warfare are not earthly arms but spiritual might that can pull down strongholds of evil.

God sends prophets to speak to worldly leaders. In Bible times, back in Elijah's day, the king of Syria was warring with Israel, planning attack after attack, and every time he planned one the king of Israel finds out about the attack beforehand. The king organized ambushes, and the king of Israel escaped every one. The Syrian king begins to think there's a spy in his camp, somebody telling the Israelites what our war plan is. "There's some treason in this camp, and I want to know who is doing it! Check things out and let me know!"

His warriors and counselors are worried and scared, but they have to tell the truth. "Oh, King, ain't nobody in the camp spying, ain't nobody in the camp committing treason, it's that prophet, Elijah. The prophet Elijah, even while you laying on your bed, God is showing him what you trying to do, and God gives him the information and then he tells the King of Israel."

Hear me using ancient history to talk about current events. The King of Syria sends his entire army after the prophet Elijah. Here we are in the year 2001 and the President of the United States is getting ready to send an army to find one man.

It's dawn. Elijah is inside of his tent. His servant gets up, looks out, and he sees all these Syrian horses and chariots about to surround them, and he panics. Back in the tent he wakes the prophet up. "Elijah! Elijah, the army of Syria with its horses and chariots is surrounding us. Elijah, we are doomed!"

Now, when you look at this situation, you can't help but think about how many of us feel today when we look at what's going on, what has happened in our midst. I don't just mean horrific world events. I mean in your personal life. Some of you are up against the wall right now. You're dealing with a circumstance in your family, on your job, and you just don't know what you're going to do, and you saying in your mind, "It's over. Nothin's gonna work. I'm doomed."

But I've got good news today. The Bible tells us over and over that there is something powerful beyond what our eyes can see, there's something that we can do. When our natural resources are depleted we've got some spiritual resources. It might look like you're defeated, but you have some spiritual resources!

When his servant wakes Elijah up, Elijah is cool. He says, "Fear not. For them that are with us are more than them that are with them." You got to have a spiritual eye to recognize your spiritual resources. You cannot focus on what you see with your natural eyes. You know the statement, "What you see is what you get." For the people of God, that ain't true! For children of God, it's a whole different situation. You see, God don't need no money to give you what he need to give you! I know I have some witnesses in here who know that God blessed you when you didn't have anything. God blessed you with some things that you didn't buy, things that didn't require no money. God came and blessed you from some unlikely places that you never thought help would come from. God don't have to fill your pocket with money. God will bless somebody else to bless you with some things that you ain't got to pay a dime for. There's somebody in here right now who got some stuff that you didn't have no money to buy, you got some stuff that didn't come from nobody else but God!

You got spiritual resources. You got some pantries that are overflowing. You got some closets that are full of stuff. You got some spiritual resources. You've got access to spiritual power that will keep you in your right mind when you ought to be crazy; give you peace of mind when you ought to be upset; give you guidance when you're about to lose your way. In these disastrous moments, these trying and turbulent times, you need to remember, that the same God who gave Elijah power thousands of years ago, can give you some today!

You have spiritual resources, if you don't use them, you ain't going to have no power. Listen to the three things Elijah did that brought power from the spiritual resources of God.

First of all, he had to make a spiritual decision, so he prayed. Prayer activates your spiritual resources. His prayer begins "Lord, let him see." That needs to be your prayer. Don't pray that God keeps bombs from falling, keeps planes from going into buildings. Your prayer needs to be, "Lord, let George Bush see!" You need to get on the telephone in your bosom and talk to God. The United States government needs to see. Instead of plotting it needs to be praying because when you pray you get insight, you see what you haven't seen before. The government of the United States will not use this resource. African-Americans can tell George Bush that what he's planning is not going to work. Can I be like Elijah and prophesy today?

Let me prophesize to you and tell you, if George Bush organizes and mobilizes the armies of the United States and attacks, he's dooming himself and the United States. And he needs to see it.

The United States needs to understand the reason for all of this. This didn't just start. The United States has stolen from Native Americans, Africans, African Americans, and Asians all over the planet. Stealing and killing and lying, messing over folk and disrespecting folk all these hundreds of years. In the name of democracy if you please. The United States has been a wicked oppressor all over the world! That's why she's hated.

Don't you get caught up in the hype of "Let's get revenge." You see how they are programming this thing? They are showing you some clippings of what they say are Arabs in the streets, cheering. You don't know when that tape was made. You don't know what they're cheering about! They are orchestrating this thing, programming this thing, so that they can go on and attack. What happened on September 11th is a catastrophe words can't describe. All of us feel the pain. Are we big enough to feel the same pain for humanity? Can you feel the same pain for the mothers and the babies by the thousands who, over the last 50 years, have been killed in the Arab lands by American-backed, American-financed weapons that have destroyed, just last month, 500 women and children killed in Israel, the thousands upon thousands of women and children and babies killed in Iraq! And because the media is controlled by those who want to perpetrate this kind of evil, you don't get the daily reports of those thousands that are being killed.

This is not to condone what has happened, but we have to understand and you have to feel other people's pain. But America has felt no pain. They've felt no pain for us black folk over the last 15 years as thousands of our young men and women have been killed in the streets. So we know about the pain. We tried to tell them, "You gotta do something about this gangbanging!" There is no difference between an international gangbanger and a ghetto gangbanger. You know, fly by night shootings in the air is the same as drive-by shootings on the ground!

Then you gotta ask yourself, you gotta ask yourself, "Well, why are they going to attack them?" First of all, they don't know who to attack. Do you know that Osama bin Laden was an ally of the United States and the bunkers that he is hiding in were built by the United States government when they were fighting against Russia in the 1980s ? Later Osama bin Laden said, "I ain't going to let you do to my people what you're doing to these people", that's not justifying what he did. What he did was evil, but you've got to understand the reason!

If it's about fighting terrorism, the United States government can forget that. Because you're dealing with people that don't fear no death. So dropping some bombs on them ain't going to stop them, it's just going to make them more angry! And then if you're going to bomb, you need to start in the United States. They are embedded in America; they are here; they're there; they're everywhere! If you talking about ridding the planet, you might as well blow the whole planet up!

After Elijah prayed, "Lord let him see," he used spiritual discernment. The servant went back outside. He saw the same army, but he also saw that the chariots and horses were surrounded by fire which represented the presence of God. Elijah didn't get disturbed because he had the spiritual discernment to see not only that God was with him, but also that God was more powerful than the enemy was.

Finally, like Elijah, you must take spiritual direction. He asked God to blind the enemy and their horses." God did it. Then Elijah led them right into the Israelite camp. He prayed again, "Lord, now let them open up their eyes and let them see where they are." Since the Israelites had them surrounded, the King of Israel said to Elijah, "Shall we kill them? Elijah, following God's direction said, "No. Don't kill them. Spread a table and give them some bread and some water."

The Bible tells us that they never attacked each other again. Instead of mobilizing the army, they broke bread. They had fellowship. That's the crucial word in this message. The arrogance of white supremacy won't allow the government to do this. What it really needs to do is find Jesse Louis Jackson, find Minister Louis Farrakhan and say to them, "Will you go and break bread and see if y'all can negotiate some peace, cause we can't do it! We are too arrogant. We think we're so much. We don't have to have the humility to do this, but would you all go and break some bread and bring about some peace?" The Bible says, "When they broke bread, y'all, they went into negotiations and they didn't ever attack each other again."

We as people of African descent are uniquely endowed. We know what it is, to be afraid to go out in the streets! We know what it is, to see killing going on all around us, and because of that, we've got special responsibilities. Don't join the bandwagon. Don't say, "Let's get revenge." Dr. Martin Luther King, Jr. said a long time ago, "If you go by the philosophy of an eye for an eye and a tooth for a tooth, after awhile, there ain't nobody gonna have no teeth, and nobody ain't gonna have no eyes either." People of God, you need to stand up, call the White House, call the Congress, tell them it ain't no time for more fighting, ain't no time for more gangbanging. It's time to break some bread and drink some water. It's time to come to a positive resolution that will end the pain, killing, and dying. That will take the kind of spiritual direction, spiritual discernment, and spiritual decision Elijah demonstrated when Israel was in crisis. You've got to have spiritual discernment. You got to make a spiritual decision. And when you make that spiritual decision, I don't care what's going on. I don't care what it looks like. I don't care what it feels like. God will make a way out of no way. God will open up a door that you thought was a stone wall.

Let's use our spiritual powers. Let's pray that those in leadership will see, that somebody with sound reason will be able to sit in the midst and bring about some peace.

CHAPTER THREE

I Pledge Allegiance?

HUEY SQUEALS TO THE FEDS' TERRORISM HOTLINE ...

WHY DO YOU KEEP HANGING UP ON ME? I'M TELLING THE TRUTH!

THE **CIA** TRAINED OSAMA BIN LADEN IN USING TERRORISM AGAINST THE SOVIETS DURING THE REAGAN-BUSH ADMINISTRATION. THEY GAVE THE AFGHANISTAN REBELS COUNTLESS AMOUNTS OF COVERT FUNDING!

10/5

DON'T YOU HAVE BETTER THINGS TO BE DOING?

BETTER THAN FIGHTING TERRORISM? HECK NO! WE'RE AT WAR!!

I Pledge Allegiance?

I pledge allegiance to the flag of the racist states of America, and to the division for which it stands, an imitation of a nation under somebody's God, divisible, with liberty and justice for some.

I don't pledge the flag, can't do it, can hardly take my hand and let it cover up my heart when I go to public occasions where I am not trying to be an issue. I can't offer allegiance to a nation that does not offer allegiance to me and mine. I understand the difference between ideals and reality, but somehow pledging the flag is like swallowing bile. I won't do it, can't do it, and cannot fathom doing it.

I wish I could. When I see unmarked young faces at a 5th grade promotion ceremony where I am highlighted as the speaker, I wish I could just pledge the flag and utter the darn words, ducking questions from observant youngsters about the words I did not say. When a young man in my neighborhood passes out flags the day after September 11th and my refusal to take one makes his face collapse into itself, I wish I could reach my hand out if only for the sake of peace. Can't do it. Some of us can, and some of us must. For some of us the flag is as much a part of us as our sepia skin, our slave experiences, our survival.

Cheryl Poinsette Brown is a military daughter, a passionate patriot, a soccer mom and wife whose flag-waving patriotism challenges my antipathy. At the same time she challenges the patriotism of those who would embrace the Confederate flag, arguing that they have turned their back on the tenets of our nation that she embraces, and their allegiance to the confederacy is a corrosive component of our civic life. Brian Gilmore, a D.C. writer, scans his landscape with a critical eye, and offers his perspective on the ambiguity of flag-waving. Haki R. Madhubuti is our nation's best kind of patriot, a critic who challenges our nation to honor its promises. His discussion of his evolution to an appreciation of America is a poignant meditation on black people's changed status. Askia Muhammad has shared the meaning of jihad in his essay, revealing the layered challenges that African American men face in white America, especially those men who embrace a Muslim culture, but who sing themselves American. They pledge allegiance iconoclastically, but loyally, eschewing those battles that violate their firm and unwavering beliefs.

Must we pledge to the flag to sing America? The writers in this section fully, firmly, and patriotically explore the question.

-J.M.

PATRIOTISM COMES IN BLACK
Cheryl Poinsette Brown

When my neighbor, with her Georgia twang, expressed her indignation to me about how many American flags were suddenly flying in our neighborhood on cars, on lapels, on television ads and logos, post 9/11, she concluded with "Y'all shoulda been patriotic all along!" I stopped her right there, telling her, "We, whomever you mean by that, were patriotic all along. We just didn't know we had to fly the flag outside our doors to prove it."

In the end I realized that I agreed with my southern belle/steel magnolia neighbor that we should all be patriotic although for reasons which might surprise her. When I look at the flag, I cherish it as a representation of the values that make America strong and that stand in stark opposition to our nation's enemies — those within our borders as well as without. From my perspective, in their opposition to the values for which the American flag stands, al Qaeda, the KKK, neo-Nazis, and the militia movement have much in common, they are all enemies of true American patriots.

Initially it was the litmus test for loyalty implied by my neighbor's comment that disturbed me the most. I bristled at the suggestion that if one did not fly the flag before 9/11, one wasn't "really" a patriotic American. More than that, in the days and weeks following September 11, 2001, I was unsettled by the frothy notion that one's patriotism could be judged by the churn of views being spun on television and the Internet. Where I live, I saw people subjected to scorn, at a minimum, and even suspected of terrorist sympathies for choosing not to fly or display the flag. One of my neighbors was even supported by the majority when he "reported" to the F.B.I. that another neighbor, who I am told is a banker, should be investigated-after all, some argued, he looked Arab and is hardly ever seen; it is better to be safe than sorry. In the aftermath of the destruction, and as details began to come out of who were the perpetrators and how they had infiltrated our society, these were disturbing sentiments yet hard to argue.

It was in this environment that my husband and I had to ask ourselves: do we fly a flag outside our home or not? By doing so, we did not want anyone to think that we were bowing to pressure to prove we were "good" Americans; we did not wish to join what felt like a mob mentality. On the other hand, we sincerely wanted to show our commitment and solidarity with other Americans and to demonstrate our staunch resolve to prevent further such attacks on our soil, our way of life and the welfare of our children. Moreover, we considered whether our flag-waving show of support was in any way inconsistent with our belief that first and foremost America is about freedom of thought, diversity of viewpoints and individual choice.

The funny thing is that my husband talked about putting out a flag when we first bought our home. Like so many things that need to be done around a new house, it got postponed. More than any other reason, we never got around to it because we make it a family tradition to spend the time of year when the flag is most celebrated (at least prior to the tragedy of 9/11), in my husband's Midwest hometown. In Grand Rapids, Michigan the neighborhood parades are complete with kids on rollerblades and bicycles waving to their families lining the sidewalks, fire engines blaring and local and state politicians smiling. There are plenty of flags flying too.

In the end we acknowledged our convictions and followed our own hearts. We now have an American flag outside our door. In the struggle incited by the declaration of war al Qaeda made on September 11, 2001, we know which "side" we are on and we are comfortable with our decision.

As African Americans who question what our government and leaders do, who see the injustices that keep our nation from reaching her heights, who put truth to freedom of speech and thought, who attempt to live as Americans ought rather than just parrot patriotic words; we also fly the American flag. We are voices of discord but not of dissent. We do not dissent from our country's legitimate efforts to protect the way of life we all enjoy. However, especially in this sobering time of global terrorism, it is crucial to the future direction of our nation and its place in the world that our national leadership hear, understand and finally, finally respond to the perspectives represented by America's internal voices of discord. Truly, it is only an America that allows and encourages dialogue, discord and free speech that is worth saving.

Understand that as Langston Hughes said, we, too, sing America. We also are all too aware that there is a discordant note in our national song. "My country 'tis of thee," I sing. It is a bittersweet land of liberty.

The lyrics continue, "land of the Pilgrim's pride." Our national mythology ignores that for many of us the Pilgrims and their descendants have much of which to be ashamed. I think sometimes of what my father-in-law taught his sons when he took them to visit historic Plymouth Rock, "They should have stopped them right here. Instead they felt sorry for them and got took with treachery." In any case, the Indians did not stop the Pilgrims right there. Fast forward to the here and now. History proceeded as it did. For better or worse, the descendants of those Indians, Pilgrims and the enslaved Africans forced onto these shores, along with the diverse immigrants who have come since, live intertwined lives in a nation indivisible.

As the horror of the World Trade Center tragedy played itself out, the media frantically found what faces it could to tell the tales of human loss. Sadly, minorities were well represented in that number. As time passed and the smoke cleared, the media spun its usual patterns. It became clear that the media, culling through the family tales to select its choice cuts, was looking for those deemed most worthy of reporting. Inevitably, it was the blonde, blue-eyed and slender among us. The rest of us, along with our stories of heroism and patriotism, faded into the background, silenced once more.

Long before September 11th I was angry about attempts to define our national life and experience in ways which silence and erase so many of us. I was as angry as my neighbor at "those" people who do not realize the importance of Old Glory and all that it stands for. Anyone who would abandon Old Glory in favor of another flag is not worthy of the freedoms of the very nation that allows them to flaunt her flag. "Those" people who do not line up behind the stars and stripes forever are not, in my opinion, worthy of the citizenship they claim. I think they are ignorant, probably uneducated and, indeed, a blight on humanity.

Who are 'those' people? I am talking about 'those' who display the Confederate battle flag, a sign of treason against the United States of America and the ideals for which Old Glory stands. Because I live in a southern state, every day I am inundated with images of the Confederate emblem. It appears on the front tags of cars and trucks, in front of homes, on hats and shirts, even once on the inside ceiling of a pickup truck parked next to me. Kiosks in the shopping malls specialize in confederate souvenirs and clothing.

Where is the outrage of my neighbor and fellow Americans when confronted by this symbol of treason and hate? It seems to be 'only' a matter of commercial democracy yet this emblem can be found in shopping malls

31

crowded with Americans of all hues. On the other hand, the stars and stripes of the United States of America were not available at every grocery and drug store counter in all manner of shapes and sizes before the attacks of September 11, 2001— so much for the "new" South.

And so my reaction, also long before 9/11, was not to turn away from the flag as some would argue, but to turn toward the stars and stripes, the pledge of allegiance and other symbols of the American ideal. Years before the Twin Towers toppled I taught my then two year old son to recognize the American flag. He would proudly proclaim to me his recognition. "Mommy, the United States of America!" I did so because he is the grandson of an American soldier who resolutely endured taunts because of his uniform during the Vietnam years. I did so because my father's 30 year military career put food in my mouth and I honor the way he chose to make his living. I did so because I sought to begin early my son's tutelage in the values he will need to oppose the Johnny rebs. To this day whenever we are driving and the flag is waving in front of banks, shopping malls, fast food restaurants and grocery stores, he still recognizes the United States of America. His two year old sister now joins in, excitedly pointing and yelling out "the 'merican flag, Mommy, the 'merican flag!" We count the number of flags flying, look for the biggest one, and since 9/11 count the car decals. My children recognize the red, white and blue symbol of their country just as they know that kente, the cloth of kings, comes from Ghana in Africa, land of their ancestors. We have both throughout our home and our children understand them as touchstones of their heritage, symbols of pride in who they are.

I've not yet explained the Confederate symbol of hate to them. Before I do, I want them to be firmly rooted in who they are, to be filled with the truth that builds up in them and learn — as too soon they will — the lies that will try to tear them down, the lies they must oppose. My children will one day take up the torch for liberty and justice for all and be charged with carrying out the mission to help lift this nation to her highest self.

Even so, whenever I see the Confederate emblem, I tense with a flow of adrenaline and get ready for battle. I read its message clearly: "You should still be a slave. You are not worthy of equal citizenship or opportunity in this nation." I know, as does any aware American, that this would not be the great nation it is without the contributions and the hope that its loftiest ideals can be worked out, even if only bit by bit, time after time, by all people who made it to these shores. The contributions of the enslaved Africans who came to these shores have been critical to developing America "as we know it." Slaves built the U.S. Capitol, after all, and slave labor kept the southern economy afloat for decades.

We are the descendants of people who were taken from the birthplace of humanity, forced into airless, sunless holds of ships, brought against their will across the Middle Passage, who died in untold numbers, who survived to build the economy of a nation that became the world's sole superpower. We are the descendants of people who, even though excluded in every way possible, made a life under Jim Crow laws, segregation and ever present racism to send their sons and daughters to participate, fight and die for the rights which they were so often, and so readily, denied.

My brothers, Kenneth and Raymond, like our father before them, are men who served in the U.S. military. Both are graduates of service academies. Kenny graduated from West Point and served more than his required term in the Army; Ray graduated from the Naval Academy and served in the Marine Corps, also more than the required five years. Both served during Desert Storm. Kenny was an officer in the 101st Airborne Division. He was in the midst of conflict during his Desert Storm tour. He continues to serve in the reserves now and could be involved in fighting again. Back then I wore a yellow ribbon for each of my brothers. If they are told to return to duty, I will stand with them again.

Thus it galls me to be regularly confronted by a symbol of treason. It is a betrayal of my ancestors' sacrifices and contributions, an attempt to deny my American inheritance, the rights my forefathers and fathers earned. As Maya Angelou so fittingly said "the price has already been paid."

I felt the power of my ancestors and the price they paid most poignantly while standing in Elmina Castle, the very first slave fort built on the African continent. Built in 1481 in Ghana (the first African nation to free itself of slavery's resultant colonialism), Elmina Castle perched on a beautiful white sand beach, its back to the ocean, its cannon facing the continent, testimony that the captors did not rest easy. There, in the place where the trans-Atlantic commerce in human beings began, I watched the timeless movement of the ocean's waves, heard its hush, felt its calm breeze and ached for the suffering and searing rage, pain and grief endured by my ancestors as they faced that same ocean, heading into the unknown "new world."

I also felt the victory. My ancestors had no idea, could not possibly imagine what their children's children would become part of. They could not know there would be Mahalia Jackson and Aretha Franklin, Jacob Lawrence and Paul Collins, Alvin Ailey and Judith Jamison, Scott Joplin and Louis Armstrong, Sojourner Truth and Condoleeza Rice, Nat Turner, Benjamin O. Mays, Jr. and Colin Powell, Garrett Morgan and Charles Drew, Jack Johnson and Muhammad Ali, Tiger Woods, Venus and Serena Williams. They could not know what they would endure and what we would create. The blues and jazz men and women, the Pullman porters and maids, teachers and preachers, insurance men and "washer women," doctors, lawyers, fire and police chiefs we would become.

Would the ancestors think the sacrifice of their lives, the lives of their African families, the more than 10 million who died in the Middle Passage and the economic development of a whole continent for generations still yet to be born, worth it? I don't know. I do believe they would be proud and amazed at what we, the children of their Diaspora have become. We more than survived; we created a new world of our own. I do not believe they would deny, nor will I let anyone else deny, that our threads are inextricably woven into the fabric of the American flag inextricably as any.

Also knit into the fabric of my American heritage are the lives of my own ancestors. My mother picked cotton and tobacco in North Carolina when the segregated public schools were closed so black children could be sent instead to the fields. Before school integration black children attended public school almost 30 fewer days than white children to accommodate the agricultural calendar. As a girl she loved playing basketball in the Tar Heel state long before Title IX and she made the best cornbread, roast turkey and pound cake anyone ever tasted. On my father's side, my grandfather was a "race man" in central Florida who worked for a municipality. In the hushed family lore, my elders talked about how he was probably killed for it. My grandmother was a "washer woman" whose labor provided the kind of ease and leisure white women used to foment the feminist movement.

My father served in the U.S. Army for more than 30 years. He could make a better life serving his country in the military than he could in the post - World War II South. Like many military men, he took his family with him abroad. As a child I lived in Europe and Asia on military bases where I received an integrated education long before the civilian courts resolved the issue in "the States" as we Army brats fondly referred to home. Through it all I learned early that I am an American. To this day I never feel more American than when I am abroad. Not only do I feel it, I am reminded of it by citizens of any country I visit. As a child I figured out what a big and diverse world we live in; I also learned how small and the same everyone is—children everywhere love to play and laugh and all parents love their children and want the best for them.

I am no different. As the mother of two American children of African descent, I want for them the best in life, and then some. I want them to be the beneficiaries of their grandparents' efforts and mine. What was the civil rights movement for if not for my children to have a better life than the lives of those who came before? I realize that as Americans we live in ways built, in part, on exploitation and over-consumption. I want my children to be a part of taking this country and the world further along the path of justice and prosperity for all. I do not want our way of life blown to bits and destruction in the process.

The people who took down the Twin Towers did not stop to draw any distinction between those Americans who are the descendants of slaves and the descendants of slave owners. It seems all the white people in the world are getting together (did you see how fast British Prime Minister Tony Blair made it to the White House?) and the fact that I'm going to have to side with them is annoyingly ironic. However, al Qaeda has forced me into this position.

Many African Americans can sympathize with the plight of the Palestinian people, wonder why we must have a base near Medina, a holy site of Islam, and have real concerns, as should we all, about our continuing dependency on Middle East oil supplies. No matter what my views on the Palestinian situation and the Middle East problems were before four airplanes were used as weapons of mass destruction, the perpetrators of the attacks on New York and Washington, D.C. threaten my children's future and therefore are my enemies. Until that threat is extinguished, the debate has to wait.

Flying the flag was our choice and we are proud of it. I don't believe I should have to justify that choice to any American, black or white. Yet there are those who question why a black family would choose to fly the flag, and the biggest one we could find at that, when so much of our own country's energy has been directed at keeping us from full enjoyment of the rights of citizenship. I remind those naysayers of what the federal system of justice, enforced when necessary by federal troops, meant for black people seeking equal protection under the law during the civil rights era here in the South. May I also point out that if they were face to face every day with reminders of America's enemies within they might think differently about what "Old Glory" means as well.

"We" *are* America. Our blood is in the land and we claim it for our own. We claim it for our children. This is what I choose when I salute the flag, when I wear it on tee shirts, stick it on my minivan and fly it outside my home. My people have earned the right to do so, paid for it in blood, sweat and too many tears. No one can tell me this is not mine. While it is true that I mourn the outrage, the crimes against those who came before me and fear what may await my children and those of whom I will be an ancestor, I always hold to the sentiments expressed by Blanche K. Bruce, the first black man to serve a full term in the United States Senate. Born into slavery, Senator Bruce escaped during the Civil War. Elected to the Senate by the Mississippi legislature in 1874, Senator Bruce said:

> "I have confidence, not only in my country and her
> institutions, but in the endurance, capacity, and des-
> tiny of my people...we will not forget our instincts for
> freedom nor our love for country."[1]

If a man who *was a slave* can make this profession of patriotism, who among us has either the temerity or stupidity to say that black people are not American patriots?

Senator Bruce was snubbed by the state's other senator who refused to escort him to the podium to take his oath of office. As he began his walk down the Senate aisle alone, New York's senator, Roscoe Conkling, joined him. I choose to remember Roscoe Conkling who took a stand and joined a former slave on his historical walk to the rostrum of the United States Senate, not the man who chose hate over duty and courtesy.

And that is the essence of the choice African Americans must make when deciding whether to salute the flag, pledge allegiance or sing of America. Do we focus first and foremost on the good or the bad and the ugly?

We decided to fly the flag because we will not concede the flag or this nation to anyone. There are black men and women serving this country all over the world. I am proud of them. If for no other reason, I would fly the flag in their honor and in honor of all those who share the values the flag stands for.

What is my response to terrorism from within and without? The message is the same. To anyone who cheers the deeds of September 11, 2001 and plans for more, I say Americans of all colors will defend against you and, if we can, destroy you first. To those who fly the Confederate flag and support its racist history, I say the same. To all enemies of America and our flag I say: This is my country. This is the country the slaves built, and it is the country my children will inherit. If you don't like that the American flag stands for me and mine, that we own America as much, if not more, than anyone, having paid for it in blood, sweat and lives; if you don't like that "we" are here, then you leave.

Note

1. Bruce, Blanche K. Speech before the U.S. Senate, March 31, 1876, reprinted in the Congressional Record, March 31, 1876 (44th Congress, 1st Session), pp. 2103-2104.

STAND BY THE MAN
Brian Gilmore

"I pledge my loyalty and allegiance, without mental reservation or evasions, to America. I shall through my writing seek to rally the Negro people to stand shoulder to shoulder with the Administration in a solid national front to wage war until victory is won."

—Richard Wright (December 16, 1941)

On the morning of September 11th, I was driving down R Street in Washington on my way to a local foundation where I was working as a writer when I saw a huge cloud of smoke off in the distance. I had already heard that two hijacked planes had crashed into the twin towers of the World Trade Center in New York City. When I saw the huge cloud of smoke rising into the sky, I kind of figured it wasn't someone's house on fire. No more than a minute later the radio reported that a plane had hit the Pentagon. I immediately pulled over and went inside the Washington Legal Clinic for the Homeless where I once worked. Everyone there was distraught. Some people began crying. Others were speechless. Then the newscaster announced that the towers had collapsed with possibly thousands of people trapped inside. I told my former co-workers I was leaving.

"Where are you headed?"

"The racetrack," I answered.

My answer was knee-jerk but honest. I wasn't at all surprised at what happened that day because I have always suspected that there are people and nations and factions that do not like America. Oftentimes, Black America does not like America, but, for the most part, many of us remain quiet. We go along for the ride because it is what we are accustomed to doing. Our interests are tied to America. And if you want to know the most poignant truth of all: We really have no choice in the matter. Where are we to go? We are, though some of us forget sometimes, American, perhaps more so than anyone else.

That is, of course, part of why I was headed to the racetrack. I wanted to pretend that the bombing hadn't happened. I also knew that all of us—every black American—would be called upon (like every other American) from that

38

day forth until we were instructed otherwise, to stand by our man—Uncle Sam. Support the war unconditionally. One shouldn't even question the approach to solving the problem (as if there is only one way to fight this battle). Any other conduct during the war would be deemed un-American.

For black Americans it has always been that way no matter our position in society. We would be asked to do what we had always done without any promise of future benefit to prove our unconditional love and loyalty for America. Drop any grievances or problems we have with our American condition for the time being, or maybe for a generation or so. I didn't want to deal with the bombings, and I definitely didn't want to deal with the culture of violence that the bombings had spawned.

I preferred simply to go look at the horses.

Days after the bombing with all of those thoughts of my American self still bearing down on me, I read Richard Wright's statement on World War II that appears above. I found it in Michel Fabre's celebrated biography of Wright, *The Unfinished Quest of Richard Wright* (University of Illinois, 1993). I had been in search of statements by authors, black authors in particular, following Pearl Harbor. I wanted to know what they had to say as that attack became part of us. This was war, and that was war back in 1941, and I knew they found themselves in a difficult spot. Before that war, Roosevelt had expressed some interest in being a friend of Black America, but he hadn't really gone that far. Most people even forget that Black America had planned a March on Washington in 1941 that was canceled at the last minute. The argument by black Americans that fighting against tyranny will make democracy for blacks more possible in America was strong even before the Japanese bombed Pearl Harbor; afterwards, it was overwhelming.

Before the September 11th attack, Black America was even more frustrated. The election and subsequent decision by the Supreme Court that propelled George W. Bush into office still burned in the souls of many black folks. In fact I can't remember a day that went by in the last year that at least one of my black American friends or acquaintances didn't bring up the vote count irregularities among blacks in Florida and how they couldn't wait to vote Bush out of office in 2004.

Even more painfully, our issues, the issues that at least were on the table during the Clinton years (despite his failure to address them), weren't even being discussed anymore. The country was talking tax cuts; we were asking about job cuts. The country was talking education reform; we were asking about just getting an education for our children. Then there were the bigger fish that Clinton turned and ran from for eight years: reparations, racial profiling, police brutality, reforming "drug war" sentencing guidelines, black men disproportionately going to jail.

But when those planes plunged into the World Trade Center and the Pentagon on that blue, blue morning of September 11, 2001, not only was the black agenda taken off the table for the foreseeable future, the table itself was taken down.

That is why Richard Wright's statement struck a chord in me. I finally began to think clearly for the first time about the September 11th bombing. I began to put the attack into some sort of context without being "upset" or "angry" or full of guilt about my initial reaction of wanting to go to the racetrack. I finally knew where I was at that moment, right after I read that quote. I was where the average black American always seems to be in America—in that tragic Duboisian state of double consciousness.

What did the average African American say about the attack and what we should do? This is what I was hearing:

It was an awful thing.
Evil.
Kill the bastards.
Crush them.
Bomb them.
Kill them all.
Profile them Arabs.
Deport them all.

(Note: It was especially vexing to hear black people come on the radio following the bombing and basically call for racial profiling of Arab Americans and deportation. I assure you, this view was rampant. On one radio program based in Washington, D.C., caller after caller, black Americans stated that "profiling" of Arab Americans was, in fact, needed and had to be done for the good of the nation.)

But that is just one side of the black American experience. Here is the other that I began to hear:

Don't we bomb people all the time?

And look how they treated us for so long.

Slavery.

Lynchings.

Second-class citizenship.

Segregation.

Not to mention the same old bullshit

we still got to put up with in daily life.

We are arguing over an apology for slavery.

How can we forget any of it?

We the ones who are going to be over there fighting, too.

And after this war, what then? The same?

Two peoples always, it seems.

I could not get it out of my head that Wright had felt a need to make a statement in support of World War II. For one thing, he was a pacifist. Prior to December 7, 1941 he was badgering America about the need for social justice and equality for the Negro in society. He was against any involvement in the war; he was more interested in addressing America's racial policies. Months before the war on June 6, 1941 at a League of American Writers Council meeting, Wright delivered a speech entitled "Not My People's War" that basically stated World War II was not a war black people should participate in because of how they are treated in society. Even after America's entry into that war, Wright remained focused on the improvement of conditions for America's black citizens.

Though he eventually volunteered to contribute to the war effort through writing, Wright's ambivalence was obvious. He supported the war for essentially the same naive reasons Frederick Douglass asked black people to fight with the Union in the Civil War. It was a chance for freedom and democracy. How could they continue to hold us down if we fought beside them against the true oppressors?

Though I was sure something drastic had to be done against terrorism, I couldn't support America's call for war against Afghanistan. I was against terrorism and violence, for sure, with every bone in my body. I abhorred the actions of the suicide bombers, which were so sick and so terribly destructive. Yet, I was sure that bombing a country that is hopelessly stuck in the medieval age would not solve anything. I was sure that as America began dropping bombs, we would become even more unsafe. I was more concerned about civil defense than revenge. I also could not get all that history out of my head about America and its black American people.

Still I wondered. Why wasn't I deeply depressed? This was a tragedy of epic proportions. The loss of human life was unfathomable. We were all attacked that day — Black America as well. Osama bin Laden issued a *fatwa* (holy war decree) years ago, and he said all Americans should be killed. Not white Americans, but all Americans. That meant me and my wife and my daughter and the rest of my family and Americans of every race and ethnicity.

This wasn't the Iranian hostage crisis of 1979 and 1980, when the captors in a clever show of political solidarity released the black American hostages from the U.S. Embassy. Whoever was responsible for the crashes of September 11th didn't give a damn who you were as a person; this was an attack on America. If the bombers of September 11, 2001 were acting upon bin Laden's *fatwa*, or whoever's order, black America was also a target.

A very good family friend, a schoolteacher, Lizzie Jones, a black American woman who was like a second mother to me, lost one of her best friends in one of the suicide crashes. Her friend was a schoolteacher. They had known each other for more than thirty years and had talked right before the bombing. Her friend was taking a student on a study trip sponsored by National Geographic. She told Ms. Jones she would be back on Saturday, and that she would tell her all about it. Her friend did not come back. She is gone. I saw Ms. Jones on television on the news speaking to her lost friend in spiritual phrases. I felt nauseous.

I am afraid for my daughter. She does not need to live in a world that is full of violence, death, and chaos. My sincere hope is that all of us now understand the real horror of mass violence of this magnitude. I know I do. No way should anyone suffer as we did on September 11, 2001. The frantic phone calls looking for friends and family members, the e-mails seeking out answers, the devastation, the catastrophic grief.

Chilean writer Ariel Dorfman refers to America now as "Unique No More." Dorfman says this is so because America has finally experienced what "so many other human beings" in "faraway zones, have suffered." Yes, we have felt it.

I am pretty sure that Richard Wright anguished over writing all the other words he wrote supporting entry into World War II. But he felt America in 1941 was still his country. America is my country, too, but it is much more complex than that. I don't mean just the place where I was born, but a place that is unequivocally my land and the land of my people without the enormous contradictions that create a strange dialogue, which can be summed up like this:

"But we ended slavery."
"But you allowed it to be legal for hundreds of years."
"We conquered Jim Crow and segregation."
"But it was legal for most of the twentieth century, and we had to almost burn the country down to get you to do it."

Today, I marvel at my friends who talk of their families coming to America from India or Nicaragua or my law school classmates who speak about their grandfather or grandmother's journey to America from Italy or Ireland or Greece in search of a better life in America. It is a magical story I don't have. That's why black Americans can never be whole in America, no matter how hard we try. How can we? We don't even have a past that can be defined, and the part that we know, the story that is passed to us regarding our country's relationship to us, is a complete tragedy. America is my country, yet my country, it seems, has never wanted me.

They were blowing their car horn. They were drunk. I was in Georgetown, and several young, white youths were hanging out of the windows of the car with a sign that read: "Honk, If You Love America." It was cute in a way to see such brash patriotism. Drivers began honking in response to the sign. This was September 16th, and everyone was still in immense pain. The young drunks were trying to make themselves feel better and everyone else at the same time. I didn't honk my horn. I was in the Georgetown traffic jam, frozen and unable to do anything. I began looking around and realized that no one really would notice because so many cars were honking. Most of the people I saw honking their horns were white. I didn't see any black people around. I didn't honk. It was a disturbing moment for me because I was not standing by my man in one of his toughest times. I realized again (as I have been reminded many times since) that though I was and am an American, I didn't have what most Americans feel—that unique sense of belonging. The tragedy was a part of me but it was mostly about the victims, the injured, the dead. I knew I wasn't alone, either.

On the radio in the days after the bombing I heard many black Americans state that they felt bad for the victims, they felt violated, and they felt that America had to do something, but then some would add at the end of their comments statements about not feeling that deep sense of patriotism that most Americans feel. The kind of emotion that pushes you to put your hand over your heart, take your hat off when the National Anthem is played. The "God Bless America" brand of patriotism. They were Americans, but not quite as American as white Americans. They cried for the victims, but, not necessarily, for America.

In the days following the bombing I was asked several times with strange looks: "Where is your flag?" I told some people I didn't have a flag. I told others that I simply could not lie to myself. It never dawned on me that I should fly a flag. I felt terrible for the victims, awful. If the flag was for the victims, it should be flown, but I didn't fly a flag because I remembered the victims in other ways. For me simply to resign myself to flying the flag was not enough. It was superficial, and it took the focus away from those who had died.

I spent much of my time in the days following the bombing riding through the city, looking at flags. I wanted to see who was flying them, and who wasn't. It would tell me something about America. I rode to upper Northwest first. This is the area of Washington where the affluent live, and I saw the American flag waving on nearly every street. On some streets you could tell that the neighbors probably had talked to each other because nearly every house had a flag out front. There was a pride there that was impressive. Cars had flags, too. It made the streets look like there was going to be a July 4th parade.

Then I rode to my old neighborhood where I grew up. The families there are less affluent, but they are doing fairly well, at least most of them. They've always wanted to be American. Black Americans live there mostly, some middle class, some working class, but the neighborhood has only small pockets of despair and is usually quiet except on hot summer nights. There were

American flags flying up here, too, but not as many as in upper Northwest. My mother, who still lives there, had a tiny flag on her front door. You could barely see it. She said someone gave it to her.

Finally, I rode through the most economically depressed areas of Washington: the hood—Northwest, below Howard University, but above downtown—streets where crack and heroin continued to be sold and used as the tragedy unfolded. Drunks were laid out in the gutter, children ran the streets late at night, addicts came up to my car trying to sell stolen items. There was hardly a flag in sight.

HARD TRUTHS:
September 11, 2001 and
Respecting the Idea of America
Haki R. Madhubuti

I do not wear an American flag on my collar, nor is there a flag on my car or on a window in my home. For those who proudly display the flag I feel that it is their right to do so, just as it is my right not to join them. I am a veteran, volunteering and serving in the United States Army between October 1960 and August 1963, discharged honorably and early to attend college on the G.I. Bill of Rights. The military was my way out of debilitating poverty and I will never speak ill of it. However, I am wise enough to not send my sons when the option of a first class university is there for them (two of them attended Northwestern University). On the road to becoming a poet, I have learned to love America. Coming to this feeling was not easy or expected. On my many journeys, if I've picked up anything, it is to question authority.

For me, the attack on the World Trade Center was personal because my daughter's workplace is a short block and a half away. She was en route to work when the first plane hit. Just before the second plane exploded she was on the phone talking to me with tears clearly interrupting her speech.

I was literally shaking in Chicago as I told her to immediately take the safest route out of town and go home. Because roads were blocked, traffic was jammed, and public transportation was not accessible, she had to walk. She was twenty-five and ended up taking off her cute pumps to walk in her bare feet from lower Manhattan to Brooklyn where she lives. Like most citizens of the nation I was enraged and angry. And while viewing man-made mass destruction on innocent people in New York, the one city in the United States that best represents the possibilities of true multi-culturalism, I, too, was ready to fight. However, for me the critical question was not how 9/11 happened, but why?

As a poet, educator, publisher and cultural activist I have had the privilege to travel and interact with people in nearly every state in the United States. I have served on the faculty of major universities in Illinois, New York, Washington D.C., Ohio, Maryland and Iowa. Between 1970 and 1978, I commuted by air each week between Chicago and Washington D.C. to teach at Howard University. In the early eighties, I drove each week between Chicago and Iowa City for two and a half years to teach and earn a graduate degree at the University of Iowa. These commutes and other travels nationally and internationally over the last three decades have enlarged me in unexpected ways. The United States is a very large and beautiful country. Its population is reasonably well-educated and is highly diverse — racially, ethnically, religiously, economically and culturally. This reality gives me cause for hope.

This hope has helped me to escape the trap of accepting simple generalizations about racial and ethnic groups and narrow assumptions about their political positions. Serving in the United States Army as a very young man, taught me that close quarter living, serious open-minded study, daily conversation and interaction with people of other cultures can do wonders in eradicating stereotypes and racial and ethnic pigeonholing.

My work over the last thirty-nine years has been confined almost exclusively to the African American community, the same community where I live, work and build institutions. As a result, I have few white, Asian, Latino American or Native American friends or associates. I am quite aware that there are literally tens of millions of "good and well" meaning people of all cultures doing progressive political and cultural work every day. I say this because it is very easy to take the negative acts of some people and assign them to all people of a particular ethnic group, race or culture. But the plain truth is that we are all individuals. It is best to accept or reject people based upon their individual talents, gifts, intellect, character and politics. America's many cultural and ethnic groups share the English language, public education, popular culture, mass media, and the powerful and effective acculturation into Western civilization and culture. In essence, if we are honest, we are more alike than many would admit.

I wrote in my book *Enemies: The Clash of Races* (1978), that I loved America, but loathe what America had done to me, my people and other non-white citizens of this country. I still stand on these words. We must never forget that America's "democracy" was built on the destruction of the hearts, minds, souls, spirits, bodies and holocausts of the Native peoples and Africans. This fact is not taught in the nation's elementary, and secondary schools, or universities although it remains the secret behind the enormous economic success of the United States. The nation's inability to honestly come to terms with its own bloodied past with public debate, acknowledgement and restitution remains at the heart of the centuries-old racial divide. The sophistication of today's oppression of Native peoples, Black, Latino and poor people is much more insidious, institutionalized and thereby excused by media, politicians, and corporate America as something of the past.

At the same, time, we must acknowledge the vast changes in voting rights, employment, housing patterns, political representation, legal and health care structures, access to secondary and higher education and the creation of a large, yet fragile Black middle class. None of this would have come about, if not for the many Black struggles over the last one hundred years, that forced the powers that be to accept their own laws, and not discriminate against people purely on racial or ethnic differences.

Our struggles here for full citizenship, equality, fair access to all the opportunities afforded white citizens remains at the core of progressive Black struggle. Our right to be politically active is fundamentally what democracy is about. This is no small right. My work of writing, teaching, editing, publishing, traveling to speak, organizing conferences and workshops and other cultural and political activities that I and other like-minded people of all cultures are involved in, in the United States could not be done in Afghanistan, China, Nigeria, Haiti, Iraq, Liberia, Uganda, Sierra Leone, Libya, Colombia, Kuwait and most of the member nations of the United Nations.

In the early seventies, I often thought of migrating to Africa. However, after visits to many African nations, discussions with African Americans who have migrated and returned, and my non-romantic assessment of the African continent economically, politically and culturally, I decided against it. I realized after a great deal of soul-searching and private and public debate that I could help Africa and its people (us) more by working hard to be a success here and like the Irish, the Jewish and other ethnic groups reach out to my people abroad. This decision remains critical in my thinking and actions today.

My focus in this book, *Tough Notes*, is to let young, and not so young, brothers know that we do have realistic options in America. It is my responsibility to communicate to you that our ancestors' centuries old bloodied fight for human, economic and political rights in the United States has not been in vain. Our people, against unrealistic odds, have taken the dirt, crumbs, scorn and ideas of America and secured a tangible future for generations of Blacks to compete and make their own statements about success and attainment.

Yes, there is still much more to do. I have tried to give some insight into the politics of that work in this book. However, many (not all) African Americans have more freedoms, prosperity, liberties and possibilities in the United States than Black people any place in the world today. Of course, those of our people in this category are still a fragile minority. As contradictory, inconsistent, racist and unfair as America continues to be, it still is a nation that does afford a chance, an opportunity to those who are intelligent, organized and strong, focused and bold, serious, hard working, and lucky enough to make their statements heard.

I can state unequivocally that my publishing company, Third World Press, published only the books that I and its editorial staff agree upon. Yes, there has been political and economic pressure on us to not publish certain books. However, these pressures did not directly come from the United States government. The two African-centered schools I co-founded, New Concept preschool and the Betty Shabazz International Charter School likewise continue to exist without open opposition from the government. For 21 years, myself along with other conscious and committed young brothers and sisters operated multiple bookstores in Chicago and only closed them in 1995 because of serious competition from the super chain bookstores. But that, in the United States, I and millions of others have been able to fight for our space even in often difficult political and economic structures is a comment on the possibilities of this country. That I have never had the economic resources to really compete with the major or midstream publishing companies is also a comment on the work that still needs to be accomplished in this nation.

A central part of the responsibility of an informed citizen is to question our government, especially its foreign policy which helped to create an Osama bin Laden, al Qaeda, corrupt monarchs in Saudi Arabia and key nations all over Africa. As the nation grieves and buries its dead, we must not allow ourselves to just automatically buy into the answers from our government.

The larger question from us must be why, after investing over thirty billion dollars of our taxes a year, with few questions asked, is it that the Federal Bureau of Investigation (FBI), Central Intelligence Agency (CIA), the

National Security Council and the Defense Department didn't have a clue to what was happening? And, now a week after 9/11 there is a call from those agencies for people who speak the indigenous languages of Afghanistan and others. Could racism be the reason for a lily white, angel bread security force who can't currently find its way out of a computer program? Most certainly these people could not get back in the field where the real dirty work of human intelligence is being done. Thirty billion dollars for what? This is the type of gross incompetence and racism that Black folk and others have to deal with daily.

So, young brothers, I want you and young people of all cultures to know that the idea of America can become a reality, can become the visionary eye in the center of the storm, the organic seed growing young fertile minds, can be the clean water purifying the polluted ideas of old men fearful of change, can take democracy from the monied few to the concerned majority if we believe in its sacred potential and the potential of the twenty-first century's coming majority of Black, Brown and locked out white people. The best of you must rise. This eminent majority must not have the white supremacist mindset of the founding patriarch or the "superior" souls of the current "rulership." Those among this coming majority must be nurtured and educated in the essential tenets of democracy. Many of you have tasted the debilitating effects of being denied your birth rights. So when the time comes for you to lead, you must be able to look your children in their eyes and state with firmness and clarity that you do believe in democracy and fairness for all people and not just the monied few and numerical majority. We, too, stand and will fight for the historical ideas of the Declaration of Independence, United States Constitution and its Bill of Rights. Finally, we must take ownership of ourselves, our families, communities and this vast and beautiful land. In doing so we will be making the most profound statement on our citizenship, and in the words of the great poet Langston Hughes, "We too Sing America."

TERRORISM, MUSLIM PROFILING AND THE "ENEMY"

Askia Muhammad

A "funny thing" happened to me on the way back from the Third United Nations Conference on Racism, Racial Discrimination, Xenophobia, and Related Intolerance in Durban, South Africa.

Only nobody was laughing.

I thought Durban was the most important place in the world for a "wannabe black intellectual" to be during early September 2001. And it was.

South Africa, was the perfect venue for that kind of meeting because of its own history concerning race relations: apartheid, a violent liberation struggle, followed by a controversial, three-year healing process — the Truth and Reconciliation Commission — championed by former President (who is now virtually a saint) Nelson Madiba Mandela.

Mandela was jailed for 27 years for no other reason than to stifle his political dissent. After his release he led his people to rise above racial recrimination and retaliation and South Africans — indeed, all Africans and all those interested in racial healing — are the beneficiaries of his generous spirit.

Sadly, race still informs the South African social order from the ground up. In the old racial paradigm, white privilege was everywhere and dominated everything.

In those days, non-South African black entertainers or athletes appearing there were given "honorary white" status by the otherwise segregated system in order for them to be accommodated in the manner to which they'd grown accustomed.

"Just think, ten years ago under apartheid, you would not even be permitted to look in my face," a white South African told a black American during my flight from Johannesburg to Durban. In September 2001, I noticed the black South Africans I passed on the street did not look directly in my face. Class status and our relative wealth have rendered black Americans equal to white Americans as far as black South Africans are concerned.

The big drama at the conference was that the Palestinian delegation and its allies over-played their hand, and the American administration sadly under-played theirs.

The Palestinians, with their bullying tactics and their noisy, sometimes twice-daily marches and rallies dominated the agenda of the NGO Forum the week before the official meeting. They probably alienated as many potential allies as they gained for their cause, and they absolutely overshadowed the stories of the real-life, desperate conditions in which most of their people live under brutal Israeli occupation.

The United States could have been the meeting's hero instead of its goat if President George W. Bush had permitted Colin Powell, his African American Secretary of State, to lead his country's delegation instead of California Congressman Tom Lantos, a Holocaust survivor. Powell could have told the delegates just what he told the Republican National Convention just one year earlier that his very presence and status was proof that his party (country) had made great racial progress, despite the fact that there was still much work to be done. In that context, the eventual American walk-out from the conference with the Israeli delegation would not have seemed so much like the act of a couple of petulant children leaving a playground when they could not have their way with the other kids, especially considering the U.S. boycott of the two previous U.N. anti-racism conferences altogether.

So there I was on my way home, reflecting on the mirror, no, the parody of American life which is modern South Africa. I was constantly amused at the ways advertising, sloganeering, and American-type icons dominate there. There are "Supa Quick" and "Wheel 'n Steel" auto repair shops "Pick 'n Pay" shops, and "Loco Liq" liquor stores for example. I was sitting in BJ's at the Johannesburg airport that's tucked between the "Juicy Lucy" and the "Chicken Licken" franchises when I saw and heard something on a nearby television monitor that made me spring to my feet.

It was Monday about 3:30 p.m. local time, 9:30 a.m. Eastern Daylight Time, Tuesday, September 11, 2001. Over and over again CNN was showing an airplane crashing into the World Trade Center. Panic and confusion were the order of the day.

The White House and the U.S. Capitol were being evacuated. Another airliner crashed into the Pentagon. My flight scheduled to leave for New York four hours later was canceled.

Disbelief swept through the Jo'burg airport as all TV monitors in the place were switched to CNN. In that twinkling of what could have been a movie special effects artist's eye, the world, as I had known it, was turned upside-down.

For the next four days hundreds of us in Jo'burg, and thousands of others at airports all around the world were stranded in the limbo-world of security, diplomacy, official ignorance, suspended commerce, and increasingly scarce hotel rooms as more and more passengers piled into international transit hubs while no one already there was permitted to travel to the United States.

As I stood for hours in lines, "queues" as they are called abroad, I realized we were the lucky ones. We were looking for our luggage, not lost loved ones. We were trying to find out when we might fly home, not lined up to get into a homeless shelter in Manhattan.

There was much gnashing of teeth then, as Americans came to grips with the enormous losses from the deadliest terror attack in U.S. history. But there was also the loss of a certain naiveté, a certain innocence, and a certain security that previously had come from America's geographic isolation from the rest of the imperial world. There was also a huge loss of prestige.

Heretofore protected from potential European or Asian adversaries or competitors by Earth's two largest oceans, the Pacific and the Atlantic, the American corner of the world had been an impregnable fortress.

Politically, that fortress was defined in 1823 when President James Monroe invoked the "Monroe Doctrine," which said in effect, the U.S. would be the sole "colonial" power in the Western Hemisphere, and that the crowns of Europe's monarchies were unwelcome here.

The bloody World Wars of the twentieth century were fought on some-one else's soil, in the skies above other countries, never in Fortress America. As bad as the Vietnam debacle may have been to the image of American invincibility, the napalm, the Agent Orange defoliant, the chemicals, the bombs, the land mines, were all left behind to wreak havoc on Asian land.

But this World Trade Center thing hit Americans literally "where we live." In New York, New York, the city so nice they named it twice, its twin tallest buildings, packed with innocent workers in their offices, crumbled in a fiery heap along with a great deal of our pride.

How could anyone get away with such an audacious attack against

Fortress America, and in broad daylight at that? Who would dare perpetrate such a hateful act against the world's only remaining superpower?

Why "Islamic fundamentalist terrorists," of course. Maybe they were. Maybe they corrupted the teachings of the Holy Quran the way Christian terrorist Timothy McVeigh corrupted his understanding of the Bible. By singling out our Islamic enemies, we could collectively explain away all lapses in security, all the provocations we might have committed against the Palestinian poor and downtrodden. Those provocations might have inspired, even though they never justified, such a horrible retaliation.

In the blood of the innocent dead, men women and children of all colors, all religions; of 62 nationalities including hundreds of Muslims, and on the gallows of the notion of "Islamic terrorism," those who are responsible for our safety and for our government's policies abroad could wash their hands of every hint of culpability. We could blame radical Muslims and there would be no political price to pay, no important constituency to offend here at home.

I was not in the country that stress-filled week, but I am not surprised to learn that soon after the terrorist attacks, Muslims were singled out and themselves made the objects of open reprisals all around the country by the types of characters who normally prowl at night in drunken coteries, hiding their faces while hunting unsuspecting, defenseless targets who fit certain "profiles" in their xenophobic minds.

Another casualty that certainly resulted from the September 11th sneak attack was American civil liberty itself. In the past the targets of this same mob mentality have been African Americans, some who fought for this country in World War I and World War II only to come home and sometimes be lynched while still wearing their military uniforms, and Latinos who were attacked on the streets of Los Angeles in the 1940s by sailors in uniform just home from war in what were called the "Zoot Suit Riots."

This time around thousands of Arabs and various others with Islamic nationalities were first secretly rounded up and detained without charges for questioning concerning the terrorist attacks. Secret charges may or may not have been filed during secret proceedings where neither defendants nor their attorneys are permitted to even know the evidence, or the witnesses against them! Whew!

After that, all Americans can kiss the Sixth Amendment goodbye.

Then came legislation giving the Attorney General broad new powers: a freer hand in obtaining subpoenas and court orders to conduct searches and to eavesdrop on any phone a suspect might possibly even look at, let alone use. In a classic example of Orwellian "doublespeak," that law was dubbed the "Patriot Act."

The Attorney General announced that previously privileged conversations between these nameless national-security-detainees and their attorneys would be monitored. So much for the canon law privilege that is older and more sacred even than spousal privilege!

Big Brother's on a roll here.

Next came an Executive Order by the President establishing military tribunals for foreigners charged with acts of terror. These military trials can be held in secret with military officers sitting in the place of judges and jurors, and they don't even require a unanimous verdict in order to impose the death penalty let alone to convict the defendants!

It all reminds me of an African proverb: "In a court of birds, the bug never wins his case."

I'm afraid that all the Muslims I know who never met a conspiracy theory they didn't like, may be right about America's intentions towards the larger Muslim world. "You'd better memorize all your Islamic lessons," they warn, "because one day the government will raid the homes of the Muslims and confiscate all our literature."

"Homeland Security This." "War Against Terrorism That." It is as though Muslims in America are already living under martial law, except dusk-to-dawn curfews haven't yet been imposed.

As for those who defend this latest murder of civil liberties, citing Presidents Abraham Lincoln and Franklin Roosevelt as "good presidents" who enacted similar unconstitutional measures, the Supreme Court later rebuked both of those presidents.

More recently however, another former Supreme Court Justice issued an even more timely warning concerning the threats to civil liberties in times like these. On Dec. 22, 1987, in a speech at the Law School at Hebrew University in Jerusalem, Justice William Brennan cited five examples of: "the shabby treatment civil liberties have received in the United States during times of war and perceived threats to its national security."

They are: the Alien and Sedition Acts of 1798; President Lincoln's suspension of the Constitutional guarantee of habeas corpus which resulted in the detention of 13,000 during the Civil War; the Espionage Act prosecutions of anti-war sentiments during World War I; the internment of 110,000 Japanese on FDR's watch during World War II; and finally the Cold War Communist scare.

To Justice Brennan's list I would add that after World War I ended, that "national security" scare continued for years. In January 1920, Attorney General Mitchell Palmer authorized raids in 33 cities in which federal agents arrested 4,000 suspected Bolsheviks for deportation. And who can forget J. Edgar Hoover's notorious COINTELPRO campaign against militant black activists in the 1960s and 1970s, not to mention his FBI's spying and illegal disruptions among those in the much tamer civil rights movement.

So what's a self respecting Muslim to do? One that is not an unpatriotic "Fifth columnist," working secretly to aid America's enemies?

To Osama binLaden—who calls President George W. Bush "the head of the world's infidels," and says "every Muslim should rush to defend his religion"—I say: your fight is not in my name, Sir.

To my President—who said in his address to a joint session of Congress soon after the attack: "Every nation in every region now has a decision to make: Either you are with us or you are with the terrorists"—with all due respect I say: This may very well be my country, but this is most certainly not my war.

No. As a Muslim American, I find myself conflicted in the same way Dr. W.E.B. Du Bois described African Americans nearly a century ago. "One ever feels his twoness," he wrote in 1903 in *The Souls of Black Folk*, "an American, a Negro; two souls, two thoughts, two unreconciled strivings; two warring ideals in one dark body."

I come from the Islamic tradition in this country, which for 70 years has recruited young men and women to step forward and take faith, and belief in the higher power, and in the inevitability of freedom and justice for all, as reasons to live and to build better communities, not as a cause for which to die.

As unforgiving as was the Nation of Islam's Elijah Muhammad of the sins of America's "blue-eyed devils" against my foreparents who were kidnapped and brought here from Africa and made slaves, the message I learned from him was that Allah (God) and Allah alone would bring about that judgment, that universal peace wherein all people could at last live together.

Instead of recruiting young men and women to step forward to die for a cause, Mr. Muhammad found his followers in a state of lethargy — mentally "dead" for all practical purposes — and raised us to want to live so that we could put forward an earnest effort to influence and mold for the better, our own downtrodden and neglected Black communities.

Black Americans who were converted to Islam walked away from crime and drugs and alcohol and death, into energetic lives with only their wits, and the message of Islam, Peace, Submission to the Will of Allah, as their weapons. Others who also followed that same call to faith that I heard 30 years ago, walked into lives as contributing members of the society. America is a better place because they made that change.

In a hostile America when activists for racial equality were being routinely beaten and murdered, "Black Muslims" went forward in safety, with not so much as a penknife in their possession and Black America—all of America— is a much better place thanks to the presence of Black Muslims in the last half of the twentieth century.

Then, Americans reviled their Muslim population as "The Hate That Hate Produced," and the Arab world, the orthodox Muslim world dismissed them as not being "real Muslims."

I am proud that I was on the steps of the U.S. Capitol on Oct. 16, 1995 when more than 1 million, mostly Black, mostly men reaffirmed that same "life" tradition by answering Louis Farrakhan's call for a Holy Day of atonement and reconciliation at the Million Man March.

America could end its announced war against terrorism with a resounding victory in a New York minute if this country's policymakers would take just one day for solemn prayer, reconciliation and atonement. But I digress.

I learned during my orientation into the faith that the most often used word in the Quran, the Muslim scriptures, is not "jihad," which is mistakenly construed to mean "holy war," but rather "raheem," which means "mercy." I, for one, am quite content to worship a God who is more merciful than warlike.

Jihad actually means "striving unceasingly toward self-purification in the path of Allah by the individual, and the collective struggle of a community

57

against all forms of corruption, injustice and tyranny" while the Arabic word "qitaal," is the word that means fighting.

Members of the Nation of Islam are taught a simple lesson concerning fighting for the "cause." That which is right cannot go to the aid of that which is wrong, so the lesson goes. Therefore, Nation of Islam members, as all sincere Muslims, are instructed to strive for moral rectitude in all their conduct, to obey all laws, never so much as even jay-walking.

"Don't do anything to anyone that you would not have them do to you," this benediction begins at Nation of Islam meetings. "We are instructed to never be the aggressor, but if you are attacked, you are to fight like hell with those who fight with you, and Allah will bless you to be the winner."

Soon after the 9/11 attack, a group of Muslim scholars replied to a request from Muhammad Abdur-Rashid, the senior-most Islamic Chaplain in the U.S. Armed Forces about the permissibility of Muslim military personnel participating in America's fight against Islamic countries.

Well, I don't care what the scholars or the chaplains say.

I say again, what I said in a letter proclaiming my status as a Conscientious Objector to the Chief of Naval Personnel on May 20, 1969: "I believe, as one who has declared himself to be a righteous Muslim, that I should not participate in any wars which take the lives of humans. I do not believe that this nation should force me to participate in such wars."

What I say is: As-Salaam-Alaikum.

I say: Shalom. I say: Peace be unto you.

I refuse to call those Sept. 11th murderers "martyrs." My dictionary defines martyrs as those who are "punished with death for adherence to their cause." As those who "submit to death rather than forswear their religion."

While it does take a certain "bravery" for people to calmly, resolutely and intentionally take their own lives, Kamikaze-style, in pursuit of a stated goal, or principle, or religion, no way are those acts to be confused with martyrdom.

While I don't hate those who go forward with good intentions and end up doing bad deeds on either side, I do reject the nihilistic path that condemns all who hope and struggle for a change for the better in this wretched world. And I reject the war-mongering, imperialistic American foreign policy path that got us to this point in the first place.

I saw a feature on a TV news magazine in which they delved into the psyche of suicide bombers. They interviewed two would-be suicide assassins whose bombs failed to detonate, and two psychiatrists, a Palestinian, the only Arab shrink in all of Palestine, and an Israeli who has studied every single suicide bombing since 1983.

The program reported that after these men were given their final instructions and the actual bombs they were to explode, they were not at all gripped with fear, but with a surprising sense of calm.

I have never entertained the thought of committing an act of violence against any innocent strangers. But as I went with the TV hosts into the minds of the suicide bombers, I realized that I too have walked the streets with that same deadly resolve, convinced and prepared for anything.

It was in Los Angeles, Thanksgiving week, 1985. My mother, Nola Mae Canteberry, had died on Saturday, November 23rd. I'm an only child and she had no surviving brothers or sisters. Her only cousin had died a few years earlier. Though my father and some of his siblings were alive in the area, my parents had never been married, and there had been a bitter court battle over my paternity when I was a baby. I was there alone to arrange her funeral.

She did not own a car at the time of her death. An itinerant, "freelance" journalist living then in Washington, I had no means to rent a car. I don't even remember how I managed to pay for my airplane ticket. The slow-running bus portion of the L.A. "Rapid Transit District" was my only reliable means of transportation.

Mama Nola did have burial insurance, and two paid-for plots at Inglewood Memorial Park, but the insurance policy would not pay until several weeks after her death. I desperately needed two thousand five hundred dollars for the funeral to proceed. My son's grandparents agreed to loan me the money. They wired it immediately.

Looking in the Yellow Pages, the only Western Union outlet I could identify which I could reach conveniently by bus was located dead in the heart of Watts.

When I moved east from California 15 years earlier, I was glad to be gone. I never really wanted to go back to Los Angeles with its thuggish gang life and materialistic culture. By the mid 1980s, the crack-cocaine explosion had transformed that place I already despised into a real-life "New Jack City." Only this place was no Hollywood movie set. Random violence and utter disrespect for life were the rules of the street.

I took the bus to the Western Union outlet and retrieved the cash. When I left that place, unarmed, and with all that money, I was resolute. I had determined that nothing or no one would stop me from taking the money in my pocket to that funeral home to arrange for the burial of my mother. I was in some kind of an otherworldly "zone."

If I had encountered a would-be assailant, then bad news would beat him home that day, because I was prepared to fight like hell, and win. I would have just as soon been dead that day, than to have lost the money I borrowed to bury my mother.

I didn't feel invincible. I just felt that the successful completion of my mission was inevitable. So, in early December 1985 we did bury my mother. May Allah (God) be pleased with her.

Now, back to the future.

In 1813, ten years before President Monroe articulated the Monroe Doctrine—that was as much a casualty of the murderous September 11th attack as the thousands of innocent lives that were lost—Commodore Oliver Hazard Perry sent a message after his victory over the entire British fleet in the Battle of Lake Erie: "We have met the enemy and they are ours!"

More than a century later, cartoonist Walt Kelly who drew the "Pogo" comic strip, modernized that famous quote in a way that can be applied to the bigots as well as to those well-meaning policy wonks at John Ashcroft's "Just-Us Department" who have used the World Trade Center crime as an excuse to lash out at people who are different—this time Muslims and Arabs and those who look like them.

"We have met the enemy and it is us," said Pogo in the comics.

Funny thing though. I'm still not laughing.

CHAPTER FOUR

Lift Every Voice

Lift Every Voice

The question of voice was an important motivator in putting together this volume. Who gets to talk, when, where and how? Who has the privilege of having their voice heard? Who determines which voices are heard? And does the recognition of, projection of voice have anything to do with the distribution of power in our society? If there is no African American perspective highlighted, does that mean that none exists? Is the "pale, male talking head" the only perspective there is?

The Negro National Anthem begins with the words, "Lift every voice and sing." It sounds good set to music, but it is a call to arms, a call to participation, a call to the actualization that comes from raising, expressing, our views. Too many folks don't lift their voices, some because they think they won't be heard, others because they have discounted themselves. There should be no discounting of voice and views. We must lift every voice and sing, till earth and heaven ring, ring with the harmony of liberty. The words of the Negro National Anthem take on an urgency after September 11, 2001, an urgency that speaks to the necessity of our participation in civic life.

Aaron McGruder, the sardonic cartoonist whose Boondocks characters lend a hip-hop flair to hundreds of our nation's newspapers, has been a courageous, edgy, and witty addition to our social commentary. His comic strips have been so pointed that they've incited small protests, even before September 11th. In the wake of attacks on our country, his voice (and Huey's) have also been attacked, with some newspapers pulling his strip for a few days, and with McGruder parodying his critics by using the American flag as a voice for some of his strips. We offer his commentary, through his comics, as a perspective on the war on terrorism.

Congresswoman Barbara Lee had special courage in putting her dissenting voice out there when she took to the Congressional floor and refused to vote war powers to President Bush. We have reprinted her statement both because of its eloquence, and because it is important to note how quickly free speech principles yielded to thuggery when Lee's voice motivated death threats and hostility. Barbara Lee spoke truth, and she deserves our applause, but also our perusal of her words.

Roland Martin is one of those "brother men" who breaks it down, telling his colleagues that their views on diversity "suck." His essay *Whitewash* reminds us that "normal" commentary mostly excludes African Americans, and that such exclusion reminds us of the work we have to do. Similarly, Tamara Wilds and Melanie Campbell use ethnographic methods to collect the voices of seniors and youth, to take us past "official" aspects of the spoken word. The people whose voices they include in their essays are not well-known or famous, but they represent through echoes in call and response, the "Re! Re! Re!" in Aretha's "Respect," the trill in make it real. They are the people who lack representation despite the fact that many purport to represent. In separately insightful pieces, Tamara Wilds and Melanie Campbell offer up the raw voices of those who ache to be heard.

Opinion polls are the antithesis of raw voices, and political scientist Karin Stanford offers a perspective of black American voice from her combined view of history and the opinion polls. Lest we think that the voices Tamara Wilds and Melanie Campbell offered are unique, Stanford suggests that many African Americans look askance at this administration and its goals. Her careful analysis of polling data, combined with her astute interpretation of history and context, are an important component of our conversation about black folks and the war on terrorism.

–J.M.

By September 2001, many young black activists had filed to run for public office, including Congressional seats and big-city mayoral seats from New Jersey to Michigan. Hundreds attended the U.N. World Conference Against Racism in South Africa just days before 9/11. The sheer strength of hip hop culture has helped to create a new generation of black activist leaders comfortable with themselves and the culture which has influenced them over the past decade.

It is unfortunate that many of these leaders fail to take into account the struggles and successes of civil rights movement. An embrace of the power, the history and the contributions that has made this generation the "Hip Hop Generation," has come perilously close to a denial of the activist leaders on whose shoulders we stand. Insofar as 9/11 affected every American in some manner, what were the effects of 9/11 on the political ideology of black youth? Did the terrorism perpetrated against our forefathers and foremothers-and parents and grandparents-seem real? Did we gain a new appreciation for those who fought domestic terrorism before us? Did it reinforce an appreciation for the civil rights movement and the advances gained during that era? Did it help black youth develop a model of success for its generation?

Surely it did draw attention to political races across the country as terrorism, defense and the Middle East became hot topics in areas across the country. In much the same way as a rising tide lifts all boats, young, black political candidates experienced a rise in their visibility post-9/11—and they certainly took advantage. The essay in this section by Melanie Campbell explores the political ideology of black youth and the effects September 11th may have had on it.

–R.G.

YOUNG BLACK AMERICA'S RESPONSE TO SEPTEMBER 11TH
Black Youth Continue to Define Their Political Ideology
Melanie L. Campbell

On September 10th many Black leaders had just returned from the World Conference Against Racism, Xenophobia, and Related Intolerance's in Durban, South Africa. The Conference had declared *"slavery was a crime against humanity."* It appeared that Reparations was finally going to be addressed for Black Americans and the entire African Diaspora. Early the next morning the United States was under attack. New York City's venerated World Trade Center, the heart of Wall Street, had been demolished and the symbol of our previously impenetrable defense, the Pentagon, had suffered a direct hit. The world as we knew it changed in a matter of minutes.

In the wake of the attack the Black community joined in the national display of patriotism. As you walked the streets there were American flags on our cars and in our yards too. Brothers were wearing red, white and blue bandanas on their heads and singing God Bless America. Everyone rallied around the President; he became the "man of the hour." Many of our Black elected officials helped to give the President a blank check to pay for the "War on Terrorism." For a brief moment, America appeared to be one America. Then, the voices of young Black America helped to remind us that we are not one nation, but one global village. Young America's voices of dissent rang out on the Internet, on the radio, on the college campus and on the street corners. You could even hear it in their music and in their poetry. Hip-hop artist Nas raps:

> There's Asia, Africa, Europe, France, Japan
> Pakistan, America, Afghanistan
> There's Protestants, Jews, Blacks, Arabs
> Call a truce, world peace—stop actin like savages
> No war. We should take time and think.
> The bombs and tanks make mankind extinct.
> But since the beginnin' of time it's been men with arms fightin'

Lost lives in the Towers and Pentagon, why then
Must it go on?
We must stop the killin'
Tell me why we die, we're all God's children
So move over Colin Powell or just throw in the towel.[1]

After 9/11 domestic issues were sidelined. According to the media, the only issue was the "War on Terrorism" and anyone talking about anything else or criticizing the government response in any way were quickly labeled bin Laden sympathizers or "unpatriotic."

I remember as we watched these horrific acts, almost immediately racism and bigotry reared its head against Arab Americans. Hate crimes, which are acts of terrorism against anyone who looked like they were Middle Eastern, were being reported all over the country. Racial profiling of Middle Easterners and Muslims became acceptable practice in airports and civil liberties had taken a back seat in the name of "national security."

For Black America racial profiling is an all too familiar practice that we face every day when we walk the streets or drive our cars or ride in an elevator and some white lady grabs her purse for fear of being robbed. Then, the irony of it all is that up until September 11th, many Arab Americans were just as guilty of racially profiling Black Americans as white people. In D.C., where I live, many Arab American taxi drivers still will not pick up a Black person, assuming they are going to the "wrong" side of town or won't pay.

After September 11th, there has been a plethora of surveys that conclude that young people are more positive about politics and the government since the tragedy. Further, surveys show that young people's attitudes toward public service, politics and community involvement were also positively impacted. These surveys however do not reflect the deeper concerns expressed by Black youth about the issues that were already impacting their generation, such as: racial profiling, expansion of the prison industrial complex, lack of quality education, lack of quality health care, economic opportunity and environmental justice.

Everyday in my capacity as Executive Director of the National Coalition on Black Civic Participation I work with young Black leaders, scholars, organizers and activists through our Black Youth Vote leadership development program. We talked about this issue and I asked some of them to share their thoughts about how September 11th affected them. Their words speak volumes on how our young people have been deeply moved by these events. Eric Irving, a 21 year old budding activist shares his thoughts on September 11th and its aftermath:

> We have long felt insecure in our own homes and in our own communities. It was why we could view the horrors of September 11th and still go to sleep that night. It is why we are not among the loud voices for constructing this massive security society.

This new security state which has been created, with random searches, intrusive authorities and racial profiling, has evoked a frustrated and outraged response from the mainstream. But how is it different from what young black men and women have grown up in all their lives? What young black man doesn't have a story of a random and unnecessarily intrusive search as a result of racial profiling? The term "Racial profiling" was invented to describe what has happened to black people...especially young black people. Why should we be outraged or even surprised that America has found another minority group to villainize and oppress?

Silently, groups of young black folk have been suspicious about the events of September 11th and its consequences. But on that day we didn't care about the age or race or gender of the people inside, just that some God, any God, could deliver us from all this horror. On that day despite all of the injustices afflicted upon us by other Americans, young blacks realized we were ALL in the same boat. These terrorists did not care about the race of the passengers of those flights or of the workers in the towers. We now understood that the rest of the world saw us as Americans and nothing more. James Baldwin spoke, fittingly, in *The Fire Next Time* about how the fate of black America was inextricably linked to that of white Americans and vice versa. We now have burned in our psyche an unforgettable reminder of just that fact.

As young people we now have experienced a benchmark moment in history, one that we can carry for the rest of our lives. Like the assassinations of Martin Luther King and JFK, we can tell our children where we were and what we were doing during this moment in history.

Jennifer Walker, a 24 year old from Alexandria, Virginia weighs in on the U.S. role in the September 11th terrorist attacks:

> In the immediate hours before patriotism shot up out the ground like water gushing from a newly discovered well, I found myself in a very melancholy and reflective mood. I was grateful for the lives of my loved ones and sympathetic to the loss of so many innocent folk. For me, the whole surreal scene of planes crashing into buildings, people tossing themselves to the streets in one last feeble attempt at preserving their life or ending their pain, was eclipsed by this sad sense that these events fit neatly in line with a chain of things that had been occurring throughout our world.

The United States of America had just walked out of a conversation in Durban, South Africa that addressed some of the sadness that served as fuel for this atrocity. We had failed to own up to this country's legacy of corrupt and manipulative foreign policy practices.

I ached inside after September 11th, but I did not adopt the broad-sweeping patriotic ideology that overran the nation. To me, it simply spoke to an entire nation's underlying fear of dying a violent and unexpected death. The United States still was a macrocosm of so many binding economic, social and cultural inconsistencies that I couldn't buy into it. Instead, I found myself feeling guilty for failing the world. If there was a people who were in the geographical, political and spiritual position to combat oppression exerted outwards from the United States, wasn't it those people who had suffered most from its internal atrocities. So, after September 11th, I felt ashamed that, as an African American woman, I had not stepped up to the plate more and demanded that the United States do some soul searching on the inside so that "we" could not project our demons to the rest of the world.

Ms. Walker and Mr. Irving, members of the hip-hop generation, agreed on several issues, such as the U.S. role in fomenting the anger that precipitated the terrorist attacks, the knee-jerk reaction of scrapping civil liberties and squashing civil rights and, certainly, the blind patriotism that, to use Ms. Walker's words "overran the nation." Other members of their generation feel the same and they are spreading their words in savvy and economical fashions.

The Hip-Hop Generation Gets the Message Out Their Way

Black youth are using the Internet, hip-hop magazines and urban radio targeting the hip-hop market to receive or dispense their messages about their issues of concern. Many black web sites are owned and operated by young African Americans including Urban Think Tank, Davey D's Hip-Hop Corner and Dogonvillage.com. Young people have embraced new technology as their means of communicating and getting their messages out.

Members of the Hip-Hop Generation are the muses and the products of the Information Age. We are a profilers dream says Jeff Chang. The issues of profiling and privacy are intertwined. We are America's post-boomer cohort, the most diverse generation in U.S. history. Many in the hip-hop community express concern that their generation will become innocent victims since the passage of the 'Patriot Act' which has unlimited powers under the guise of 'domestic terrorism' which gives the federal government, specifically the FBI power to further harass hip hop activists.[2] It was only 35 years ago when the FBI, under J. Edgar Hoover's COINTELPRO, abused their powers by eavesdropping and profiling Dr. King and many civil rights leaders unjustly.

It is even more imperative that Black youth are educated on the political process, including foreign policy and how it impacts their daily lives. It is another way that the older generation and our young people can work together to insure that our voices are not silenced and that the "War on Terrorism" is not turned on Black people or any other community. We too sing America, we too believe in protecting our families and loved ones. As in the wars of the past, it is our Black young men and now young women who are also on the front line of this war. The Black community's history and struggle for the past 450 years gives us reason to be concerned about allowing our rights to be set aside.

New Generation of Black Political Efficacy: Are Black Youth Defining The New Political Power Structure?

Nine months after September 11th, the 2002 primary elections demonstrate that Black youth political activism has not been muted. Young people are not waiting for the passing of the baton, they are running for office and defining their own political ideology. Black youth are challenging seasoned Black politicians and are raising the necessary campaign funding to be serious challengers.

In Detroit 31 year old state Senator, Kwame Kilpatrick beat 69 year old City Council member Gil Hill in the November 2001 election. Hill made an issue of Kilpatrick's age, saying voters should choose an "experienced driver at the wheel, not someone with a learner's permit." Kilpatrick, who served as the head of the Michigan Legislative Black Caucus won his race; voters evidently wanted a change.[3]

In New Jersey Corey Booker, a young Oxford graduate, ran against incumbent Newark Mayor Sharpe James. Booker lost by a slim margin of six percent, with Sharpe James carrying fifty-three percent of the vote. In Alabama, 60 year old Congressman Earl Hilliard, a five-term incumbent, lost his bid for re-election in a primary runoff to 34 year old Harvard graduate and criminal defense and workers' compensation lawyer Artur Davis. Davis carried the election with fifty-six percent of the vote, beating Hilliard by a decisive eight percent.

On the surface, this is a long-awaited occurrence that takes place between generations. However, when you hear comments made by some of the young aspiring politicians, one questions whether they are running against the civil rights movement, running with a sense of responsibility to the Black community or, whether they have bought into the notion that racism is no longer an issue for their generation and we are living in a "color-blind" America. Is it that "today's Black voters are becoming more independent and are looking for results rather than inspirational messages of taking over the political power structure? In the Detroit race, one of the knocks against Hill was that he was too connected to the city's power structure, dating back over 40 years."[4]

Yvonne Bynoe, co-founder of Urban Think Tank, wrote of what she calls the new breed of black politicians. "When 33 year old Cory Booker decided to challenge 66 year old Sharpe James to become mayor of Newark, he became one of the most visible, national symbols of the changing of the Black political guard. James, a product of the Civil Rights era, is a politician who emerged out of the 1967 riots to lead a devastated city. Booker, a son of the suburbs and Ivy League institutions, by contrast represents the fruits of The

Dream. James ran a simplistic US vs. THEM message that resonated with older Black voters.[5]

The Hilliard race was an upset that had many implications, from the power of money to the shake up of the Black political power structure in Alabama to the impact of the Middle East conflict to whether or not there is a changing of the guard taking place. Davis previously challenged Hilliard and lost by 24 percentage points, as well as lost in raising money. In 2000, Hilliard raised $483,046 to Davis' $84,872. In 2002, Davis not only beat Hilliard by a significant margin at the ballot box, but he raised $879,368 to Hilliard's $550,808. Davis received 82 percent of his individual contributions from out-of-state donors, mainly from the New York Jewish community. Hilliard raised a significant amount of his funds from the Arab American community. Many reports speculate that Hilliard's support of the Palestinians cost him his election.

When reporters asked some Alabama residents why Hilliard lost, the Middle East conflict was not the central reason conveyed. D. Linell Finley, an adjunct professor of political science with Auburn University at Montgomery said that he didn't think the out-of-state donations fazed Alabama voters. He believes the out-of-state money leveled the playing field for Davis.[6]

Alabama A&M Associate Professor of Political Science, Ron Slaughter, believes the Black community is becoming more independent politically. "The perception of the black community as a monolithic voting block is changing. People are challenging others and are voting for people not just because of their race, but because of the issues."[7] Perry County Commissioner, Albert Turner, Jr. concurred with Slaughter in his analysis. "No longer can you say you marched on the Selma Bridge and that gets you in office and keeps you in office. The day of who's the blackest is over. It's about production now."[8]

Davis appears to believe it was about issues as well as a changing of the guard. *The Birmingham News* quoted Davis at his victory celebration saying, "If we think that this is simply a victory of one person, then we fail to realize the larger message of this candidacy and this campaign victory tonight. I have a great deal of respect for all of the organizations in this state and I look forward to working with them. But the day of their controlling who wins elections is over."[9]

In order to bridge this divide between our generations, we must provide vehicles for our young people to gain insight from our past struggles and connect the dots as this relates to the political process and their legitimate concerns about the state of Black America. NNPA Editor-in-Chief George Curry states, "It's not enough for older adults to tip their hats in the direction of young voters. Rather, the young people must be included in all aspects of the political process, including being supported for public office. In short, they want to be full partners."[10]

Hip-hop impresario, promoter and philanthropist, Russell Simmons, has stepped up to help fill this void to ignite and engage young people in the political process. In May 2002, Simmons worked with a coalition in New York City — Hip-Hop Summit Action Network, Alliance for Quality Education and United Federation of Teachers — and mobilized over 100,000 students, parents, hip hop artists and community leaders at City Hall. Despite criticism by mainstream media that young people only showed up to see a free concert, Simmons believes youth of New York are not stupid and they care about getting a quality education. Simmons has also partnered with Columbia University professor Manning Marable to establish a hip-hop think tank and with civil rights groups to get young people to vote and establish a national literacy program. Marable believes "hip hop truly represents the voice of a new America, continuously defining and redefining the politics of America."[11]

The Joint Center for Political and Economic Studies reported the new racial scope of the new generation on its Youth NABRE On Line Chat on Race and Ethnicity. "Today's youth have experienced extreme shifts about the future outlook of this country, from the optimistic dot com millionaire dream, to the shocking 9/11 nightmare. America's racial identity is also shifting; today's 15-25 year old youth are part of the most racially mixed generation that this nation has ever seen. A third of this generation is non-white, and the Census projects that by 2050 there will be more non-white than white Americans, and most of this population will be Asian, Latino and Black."[12]

Today's Black Youth cannot be defined as the "modern day civil rights generation." Mainstream America attempts to define youth in many terms, from Generation X to Generation Y. Many African American youth choose to define themselves as "The Hip-Hop Generation." One thing is certain, this is not a monolithic group ideologically, politically, economically, educationally, socially or spiritually; it is the generation however, that will lead thecAfrican American community in the twenty-first century.

Black Youth Are Poised To Lead

Dr. Ronald Walters and Dr. Robert C. Smith, noted scholars and political scientists write in their book, *African American Leadership*, that "It is important for the future of the Black community that efforts be directed toward creating an independent student and youth leadership formation. The Student Nonviolent Coordinating Committee (SNCC), was critically important in the civil rights movement in terms of bringing to the fore new ideas, tactics and strategies and generally serving as the movement's frontline 'shock troops.'"[13]

Black youth are lighting their own torches for economic, political and social justice. There are many examples that dismiss the myth that young people are apolitical, apathetic, singularly focused on self-gratification and wealth. Black youth are establishing their own community organizations to address social justice issues and some traditional civil rights organizations are opening their doors for new leadership or at least adding a few seats for young people to have a voice at the leadership table. Across the country, from the West Coast to the East Coast, down in the Black Belt of Alabama, to the birthplace of Hip-Hop, New York City, Black youth are utilizing a more localized approach than previous generations to address issues they care about.

Conclusion

September 11th is the defining moment for this generation, just as the assassination of Dr. Martin Luther King, Jr., Malcolm X, President John F. Kennedy and his brother Bobby Kennedy were the defining moments for our parents and grandparents. The question becomes will young Black America rise to the occasion. Will we be the voices of reason and dissent where it is needed or be silenced for fear of speaking truth to power? Will we do what many young people accuse our progenitors of doing or will we assimilate? Will we lose our culture and sense of history as Black people in this country or will we be the bridge builders to help America embrace the global community, to teach ourselves about our neighbors outside our borders, to truly celebrate diversity, not just in America or Europe, but also in Asia, Africa and the Middle East?

This generation will have the responsibility for how race relations will be addressed in this country that has not faced up to its past and desires to be a society that is no longer based on "black and white." The September 11th tragedy brings with it a window of opportunity to bridge the racial and cultural divides in America and abroad.

Black America must embrace our youth, our most precious resource, to lead a new fight for human rights and global justice. It is time to celebrate a new generation of leadership and as today's patriarch of the Civil Rights Movement, Dr. Joseph Echols Lowery has said many times, we must embrace justice and "Redeem the Soul of America."

Notes

1. Youth Outlook, Hip Hop Responds to 9/11, January 2002.
2. Chang, Jeff, Styling & Profiling: Privacy &
   The Hip Hop Generation After 9/11,
   Davey D's Hip Hop Corner, March 24, 2002
3. Hubbard, Lee, Hip Hop vs. Civil Rights,
   Hip Hop News, Davey D's Corner, May 20, 2002.
4. Hubbard, Lee, What Does "The Black Vote" Mean Today?,
   Africana.com, December 13, 2001.
5. Bynoe, Yvonne, Esq., UrbanThinkTank.com,
   The New Breed of Black Politicians, May 2002.
6. Reeves, Jay, Associated Press Writer, Yahoo! News, June 27, 2002.
7. McClure, Vicky and Gordon, Tom, Davis'
   Win Seen As Sign Voters Are More Independent,
   The Birmingham News, June 27, 2002.
8. McClure, ibid.
9. McClure, ibid.
10. BlackPressUSA.com, OP-ED,
    Preparing Now for the Fall Elections, George E. Curry,
    NNPA Columnist, June 22, 2002.
11. Simmons, Russell, OP-ED, Hip-Hop's Fighting For Better Schools.
    www.Allhiphop.com. May 2002.
12. JCPES, The Network of Alliances Bridging Race & Ethnicity,
    Trends and Attitudes
    of the Next Generation on Race and Ethnicity,
    Highlights from Youth NABRE/NABRE's
    Online Chat, December 5, 2001.
13. Walters, Ronald H., Ph.D., and Robert C. Smith, Ph.D.,
    African American Leadership State University of New York: Binghamton.
    1999. Page 235.

SPEECH BEFORE THE U.S. HOUSE OF REPRESENTATIVES–SEPTEMBER 16, 2001
Congresswoman Barbara Lee

Mr. Speaker, I rise today with a heavy heart, one that is filled with sorrow for the families and loved ones who were killed and injured in New York, Virginia, and Pennsylvania. Only the most foolish or the most callous would not understand the grief that has gripped the American people and millions across the world. This unspeakable attack on the United States has forced me to rely on my moral compass, my conscience, and my God for direction.

September 11th changed the world. Our deepest fears now haunt us. Yet I am convinced that military action will not prevent further acts of international terrorism against the United States.

I know that this use-of-force resolution will pass although we all know that the President can wage a war even without this resolution. However difficult this vote may be, some of us must urge the use of restraint. There must be some of us who say, let's step back for a moment and think through the implications of our actions today—let us more fully understand its consequences.

We are not dealing with a conventional war. We cannot respond in a conventional manner. I do not want to see this spiral out of control. This crisis involves issues of national security, foreign policy, public safety, intelligence gathering, economics, and murder. Our response must be equally multi-faceted.

We must not rush to judgment. Far too many innocent people have already died. Our country is in mourning. If we rush to launch a counterattack, we run too great a risk that women, children, and other non-combatants will be caught in the crossfire. Nor can we let our justified anger over these outrageous acts by vicious murderers inflame prejudice against all Arab Americans, Muslims, Southeast Asians, or any other people because of their race, religion, or ethnicity. Finally, we must be careful not to embark on an open-ended war with neither an exit strategy nor a focused target. We cannot repeat past mistakes.

Speech Before the U.S. House of Representatives

In 1964, Congress gave President Lyndon Johnson the power to "take all necessary measures" to repel attacks and prevent further aggression. In so doing, this House abandoned its own constitutional responsibilities and launched our country into years of undeclared war in Vietnam. At that time, Senator Wayne Morse, one of two lonely votes against the Tonkin Gulf Resolution, declared, "I believe that history will record that we have made a grave mistake in subverting and circumventing the Constitution of the United States. I believe that within the next century, future generations will look with dismay and great disappointment upon a Congress which is now about to make such a historic mistake."

Senator Morse was correct, and I fear we make the same mistake today. And I fear the consequences. I have agonized over this vote. But I came to grips with it in the very painful yet beautiful memorial service today at the National Cathedral. As a member of the clergy so eloquently said, "As we act, let us not become the evil that we deplore."

WHITEWASH
Roland S. Martin

After the devastating and catastrophic events of September 11th, America was in constant analysis, deep thinking and soul searching, all in an effort to understand and comprehend how less than two dozen individuals could plot and plan a catastrophic event that would eventually kill more than 3,000 people.

Much as it has done for years, the American media went into a frenzy to give listeners, readers and viewers a perspective into what happened. Many of us on that fateful day were all considered Americans. Never mind Bull Connor and his tactics; forget the Tulsa Race Riots of 1921; excuse the Rodney King beating and the massive racial profiling that has been happening in this country since the beginning of slavery. That day we were all Americans and met at the cross section of pain and suffering.

But just a few weeks later President George W. Bush called for America to return to normal. And it didn't take me long to do so. To my friends in the mainstream media—you continue to suck when it comes to diversity.

"Suck" is a strong word to use, but I couldn't find any other word to express my anger and complete disdain at the lack of diversity of talking heads in the wake of the September 11th attacks on the World Trade Center and the Pentagon. Even a year later we're given a steady diet of intellectuals and analysts who look remarkably familiar.

Heeding the call for unity and healing, I have tried to stay away from writing about racial issues in the wake of this attack that killed thousands, injured thousands more and caused mental anguish and pain to millions without regard to race, religion or sex. The brother has been patient. After watching *Nightline* along with all of the cable channels and networks since September 11th, trying to be Job-like (as in Job from the Bible) has gone out of the window.

Nightline focused on the stifling of voices in the wake of the tragedy. After a fine report by one of its reporters, Ted Koppel convened a roundtable to discuss how the tragedy has caused journalists to be careful.

I turned to my wife and said, "God, I hope there are some black journalists on this roundtable." Her response? "Yeah, right."

Yep, she was right. We were treated to three white guys, including a Texas columnist who was fired for criticizing the president, and a white woman. Again, no diversity of thought or opinion on this subject.

You name it, there has been some white guy talking about how this tragedy affects America. The subjects are so varied: terrorism, biochemical attacks, safety, transportation, Islam, Christianity, intelligence and racial profiling.

Attempts have been made by several outlets to mix up their talking heads, but about the only person who consistently has supported diverse viewpoints has been Bill Maher, host of the show *Politically Incorrect*. As a whole the industry has not done well. I have personally communicated with black reporters and producers at several networks who have privately complained that they are having difficulty in getting their respective booking departments to include more black, Hispanic and Asian sources.

There have been a plethora of stories from college campuses regarding this issue, but have you seen a report from a historically black college campus? It doesn't have to come from a black angle. It would simply be nice to see such a campus chosen as the source of a report.

I viewed a network report on what Christian ministers were saying about the attack. Guess what? Three white guys. It is true that Bishop T.D. Jakes and the President's spiritual adviser, the Rev. Kirbyjon Caldwell, have gotten some face time. But it has still been unequal.

We have seen nearly every person who once served in a presidential Cabinet being interviewed. But it's amazing that people like former Transportation Secretary Rodney Slater, former Labor Secretary Alexis Herman, former United Nations Ambassador Donald McHenry, former Assistant Secretary of State Susan Rice, former Secretaries of the Army Togo West and Clifford Alexander, and so many others have not been seen. The current U.S. Surgeon General, Dr. David Satcher, is a brother, yet we keep seeing other folks talk about the mental health of America! Can we at least see the nation's top doc discuss this issue? Noted psychiatrist Dr. Alvin Poussaint has also been noticeably quiet, and I'm sure not by his own choosing.

It's not hard to find such sources. The week of the attack, I was on the *Tom Joyner Morning Show* and nearly all of these folks I've mentioned were interviewed. Then again, Joyner is a nationally syndicated morning show host who has a predominantly black audience. He's made the effort to have their phone numbers.

Let's get some other names on the table. ABC, to their credit, had poet Maya Angelou on September 14th, and she was so wonderful! Aside from appearing on *Oprah*, she hasn't been seen since. Andrew Young is a former big city mayor and ambassador to the United Nations who has extensive experience dealing with the Israeli-Palestinian conflict (he lost his UN job after it was reported he was meeting secretly with Palestinians). He also was one of the co-chairs of a commission that released a detailed report on the threat of terrorism in America earlier this year. I recall only seeing him on the day of the national prayer service.

Dr. Cornel West of Princeton and Dr. Michael Eric Dyson are two wonderful voices that could speak on the religious issue. Have they been on the boob tube? Hardly.

Roger Ferguson, the number two official at the Federal Reserve, was the person who quickly stabilized the financial markets in the aftermath of the attacks because his boss, Alan Greenspan, was out of the country. Has anyone given him credit for moving so fast and tried to talk with him?

Each network has former military officers as experts. Yet I cannot recall seeing a single African American in this position. Not one! What gives?

Nearly every person serving on the Senate and House intelligence committees have been talked to. But I don't recall seeing Rep. Alcee Hastings of Florida and Rep. Sanford Bishop of Georgia being asked their opinion on the perceived breakdown in intelligence.

Top editors at *Fortune* and *Forbes* have been mainstays on the business shows regarding the turbulence in the financial markets. Don't you think the folks at *Black Enterprise* are equally adept at discussing such issues?

Airline pilots were sought out when stories emerged about cockpit safety. But did anyone reach out to the Organization of Black Airline Pilots? They even lost one of their own: Leroy Homer was one of the pilots on the United flight that crashed in Pennsylvania.

Many columnists have been interviewed on a number of roundtables. But where are James Campbell of the *Houston Chronicle*, the *Miami Herald's* Leonard Pitts, Bette Baye of the *Louisville Courier-Journal*, Gannett's DeWayne Wickham, Derrick Jackson of the *Boston Globe*, and Rochelle Riley of the *Detroit Free Press*? (If you want a list of other black columnists go to www.trottergroup.com).

I know some of my non-black colleagues may see this as a call for quotas and me being far too sensitive on this issue. If so, they miss the point. This is simply about journalists and news executives doing their job and doing what is right.

Much of this issue stems from the American media's refusal to recognize that it is part of America and is just as racist and insensitive as other industries. I've always found it ironic at how we are so good at covering the troubling racial and gender problems at Fortune 500 companies, but when that same pen, pad and camera is turned towards our own, folks clam up and give that famous comment that every editor and news director hates to hear, "No comment."

My media comrades are such wimps at confronting themselves. When portions of this essay were placed on a media website, I received a number of hateful e-mails from individuals in the business. These are the folks who are the assignment editors, news directors and producers who have it as a part of their job to cover the news from a balanced perspective. They hate it when called on the carpet to admit to their failings.

The issue as to who should serve as analysts — in the biz we call them talking heads — is often left in the hands of those in charge. In this business, minority journalists are certainly not at the top of the ranks. History tells us that when you have a person of conscience, or better yet, a person of color, at the top, then things are and will be different. Staffing will be diverse; stories not normally covered will find themselves in the paper, magazine or on air; and the individuals who are covered will reflect that community.

That was the case a few years ago when Gannett mandated that staffers at their respective newspapers, television and radio stations interview a predetermined number of people of color. Photos in the newspaper were to reflect a multicultural view, and the bonuses of the bosses were tied to such coverage. The whiners and complainers, which included the folks who decry diversity and multiculturalism as political correctness, yelled and screamed. Gannett was serious about the effort because the man at the top, CEO Al Neuharth, made it clear that he wasn't kidding. When some managers balked, they were rightfully fired.

There are a few Al Neuharths who have the understanding that, if some sector of the community isn't being covered, then we are at a disadvantage. A stroll through the ranks of the major media companies finds that Richard Parsons at AOL Time Warner is the only African American sitting at the top. No African American, Hispanic or Asian runs any of the other major media companies (black-owned Radio One, which is radio-focused, is excluded). This lack of diversity at the top always shows up at the end, which is your newspaper, television newscast or radio broadcast.

According to the 2001 Radio-Television News Directors Association/Ball State University Survey, whites held 92 percent of all news director jobs in the country. In radio, they held 95.6 percent, which is an increase of nearly 4 percent from 1994. The facts are just as sobering in the newspaper industry. Minorities make up 11.85 percent of all newsroom jobs in the U.S., including 9.7 percent of newsroom supervisors.

What all of this data means is that the people in control often don't look like the rest of America. As a result, when decisions are made as to what to report, whom to call and interview, the folks doing the decision-making are overwhelmingly white. This consistently causes a lack of thoroughness because as we all know, we are more comfortable with who we know as opposed to going beyond our borders and reaching out for a different voice.

Some companies are making an effort to change. ABC is the most recent company that has mandated the compiling of a list of several hundred sources that can be called on for interviews. News President David Westin has made it clear that he wants ABC to be diversified in its coverage. Good. I'm finally glad he came around because I was appalled during the network's 2000 election coverage to see a sea of white faces commenting on the presidential debates. Not one–I repeat, not one–individual who served as an analyst or reporter was a person of color. It didn't get any better as I flipped over to NBC, CBS and CNN. I kept seeing the same things over and over. When this happens, we don't get the varied perspectives on important issues that are often overlooked.

Consumers should make the effort to call, fax, e-mail and essentially harangue these news outlets for their obvious failures. Organizations such as the National Association of Black Journalists, the National Association of Minority Media Executives and others have made it their mission to increase the ranks of those in management. Their hard work, as well as the years of work put in by individual journalists, has led to people like Gerald Boyd assuming the post as the number two person at *The New York Times*. Greg Moore is the editor at the *Denver Post*, Ken Bunting is the top person at the *Seattle Post-Intelligencer*, and Gilbert Bailon is the executive editor at the *Dallas Morning News*. There are countless others who are making inroads in the newspaper industry. Mark Whitaker is the editor of *Newsweek*, the first African American to hold the lofty position. But on the television side, that nut hasn't been cracked. No minority is president of a network news division, and that has trickled down to the various talk shows, where few minorities sit in the position of executive producer or booker, the two critical individuals who determine who gets on a show.

At a time when there are more minority journalists and pundits who are at the disposal of media outlets than at any other time in history, it's amazing how we can still act as if this is 1902 rather than 2002. There is no excuse, justification or explanation that can be used to deflect attention from this rather troubling issue. While we think times have gotten better, they have gotten worse.

Take late night television for example. If you turn on your television any night of the week, we will be fed mostly white faces on Jay Leno, David Letterman and even the vaunted *Nightline*. Although they are more often than not better than the other fare, the lack of consistent faces of color are evident. Now that ABC cancelled Bill Maher's *Politically Incorrect*, even fewer voices will be heard.

Yet at the same time the cable networks are quickly moving away from news to more talk. It seems that each passing day finds someone at FOX, CNN and MSNBC getting their own show. As usual, they are retreads of mostly white faces (Connie Chung is the noticeable exception). The increase in these shows has only increased the number of voices, which only increases the anger of seeing few people of color.

This Ferris wheel continues to go round and round and nothing changes. As long as we continue to see mostly white faces, we will not be able to further the conversation and open up the floor for different viewpoints and perspectives on the terrible and senseless tragedy of September 11th.

Then again, I guess the lack of diverse voices shows that at least the American media has returned to normal.

DO YOU SEE WHAT THEY SEE?
DO YOU HEAR WHAT THEY HEAR?:
Two Black Women Share Their Candid Views on September 11th and Its Aftermath
Tamara A. Masters Wilds

I was mortified by what I saw on television in my university office the morning of September 11th. The weeks that followed were unforgettable. Like many others, I was torn between staying in front of my television to remain connected to the rescue and recovery efforts in New York and at the Pentagon, and turning it off to avoid crying yet again as a reporter interviewed a dazed mother or fianceé of a victim. Yet, as a historically and politically aware Black woman, even as I prayed and grieved for the mourning families, I became increasingly frustrated with the spontaneous and deafening patriotism that swept the country. Posting a flag on the rear window of my car was never an option. It seemed too much like some ridiculous signal to others that I was on the "right" side of this catastrophe, 100% in support of my blameless and "free" country. I understood that a flag wouldn't stop some racist police officer from pulling me over for driving through a "nice" neighborhood in which I couldn't possibly reside. Likewise, the call for immediate and deadly revenge on the terrorist organization and leader responsible for the attacks seemed a hasty and too simplistic of a response to such a complex crisis. Slowly, I began to find out that I was far from alone in my views. Yet, no one seemed to be discussing these "alternative" perspectives during the countless September 11th specials that aired on national television. According to the mainstream media, all Americans not only saw the same thing on September 11th, they also held the same views about what happened. There was no critical dialogue about September 11th and no one bothered to acknowledge the various cultural, racial and class-based perspectives being discussed in households and over phone lines across America. The following discussion is my attempt to both acknowledge and explore some of those perspectives. I sat down with two Black women, one "seasoned" and one young, to discuss their reactions to what took place on September 11th and its aftermath. I chose an elder woman and a young woman because I knew that their distinctive experiences would provide interesting perspectives. I chose these two women in particular because they agreed to talk to me. Several young and older women that I approached shuddered at the thought of having to speak about such a horrible turn of events, while others were uncomfortable with having their thoughts tape-recorded and in print. These two women were bravely willing to share their views, many of which they knew would be criticized as cynical and unpatriotic. It is difficult to determine exactly how representative their opinions are of the "Black perspective." Yet, they live and function in familial and social circles that heavily influence their synthesis of information and resulting perspectives; they are not alone in their thinking. Their voices have not been heard, primarily because America is clearly not interested in listening to what they have to say. As the anniversary of September 11, 2001 approaches, their opinions and views, whether they infuriate us, make us uncomfortable or validate our own views, must be added to the stories being told.

Rabiah and Lillie have never spoken or met each other. Although both women come from middle class families, they live very different lives separated by two distinct generations. Rabiah is 20 and a rising junior at a historically black university on the east coast. Lillie is 76, a mother of four and grandmother of ten. As a college student, Rabiah's life is filled with activity and people. Lillie spends most of her days in a comfortable room in her daughter's home. She keeps the television on all day, and it provides her with most of the information she knows about current events. It was this habit that was responsible for Lillie witnessing the happenings of September 11th "almost as if she were there." Rabiah found out about the Pentagon and World Trade Center from fellow students because she didn't have a television in her room. On her way to class she was promptly told that all classes had been cancelled and why. She immediately called her mother.

My conversations with Rabiah and Lillie, Black women separated by two generations, evoked these specific memories, but they also revealed several common themes and sentiments. Both women were devastated by the day's events and the aftermath. Like most Americans, they were overwhelmed by the magnitude of what transpired in less than two hours. It is important to recognize that even as they formed many of their opinions about September

11th, they continued to grieve for the families who lost loved ones. In fact, their sorrow surfaced repeatedly during my conversations with them.

However, the passage of time and awareness of their unique experiences living in America as Black women enabled them to separate those emotions from their views.

Although they shared many of the same views, Lillie's collective memory surpasses Rabiah's by five decades. Several of her views are based on lived, rather than learned experience, which resulted in a deeper level of cynicism in her comments. For example, Lillie was not surprised that the events of September 11th took place and was much more skeptical than Rabiah that America would learn the right lessons. Furthermore, Lillie's views were characterized by a certain amount of passivity because as she put it, "I have lived my life." Yet she spoke sincerely about her concern for young people like Rabiah who are just beginning to really live their lives in a country plagued by racial oppression and international chauvinism. Rabiah, who is extremely active on her campus, was frustrated by her inability to make a direct impact on her country's choices following September 11th. Consequently, she spoke very passionately as she shared her opinions and responses to September 11th. Although Lillie and Rabiah had a great deal to say about September 11th, both women made particularly fascinating observations about specific phenomena like "terrorism" and the "patriotism" demonstrated by fervent flag waving. The following discussion is a collection of their thoughts and views on those topics.

The Flag

"Forget a flag; I was hurt for those people."
—Lillie

The hoisting of the American flag at ground zero and at the Pentagon seemed appropriate. It was a sign of solidarity and more importantly, a sign of national mourning for the thousands of families and friends who lost loved ones in the tragedies in New York, Pennsylvania and at the Pentagon. But the patriotic hysteria that arose in the weeks and even months following September 11th was perplexing to Lillie and Rabiah. The American flag was everywhere, on cars, home windows, office windows, tee shirts and billboards. Rabiah remembered her campus becoming a veritable flag fashion show. At her university's homecoming she observed how the flag was represented on the "baby" tee shirts of co-eds strutting through the stands of the football stadium.

Rabiah felt no need to wear a flag tee shirt or display flags in her room because she believed that most of the time "a flag is supposed to be raised on a flag pole." In Rabiah's mind, her decision not to display the flag or wear it across her chest made her neither more nor less patriotic. She explained that her decision was rooted in her refusal to recite the pledge of allegiance during her junior year of high school. Just as she balked at the hypocrisy of the pledge's words in high school, something about the proliferation of flags following September 11th was just too contrived and "engineered."

Like Rabiah, Lillie didn't wear or post flags following September 11th. Furthermore, she emphatically stated that she would not have accepted one even if someone had arrived at her doorstep and tried to give her one for free. Here, Lillie explains why she felt that the flag was secondary to the pain and suffering that thousands of people experienced as a result of what happened in New York and at the Pentagon:

> "I don't believe in the flag. I guess all of the sudden, you know everybody's patriotic. I didn't look at it like that. I was hurt, I was just hurt. Forget a flag; I was hurt for those people."
> —Lillie

For Lillie, belief in the flag is equivalent to a belief in America's founding principles of "liberty and justice for all," which she believes have never been fully applied to Black people. Thus, even before September 11th Lillie didn't believe in the flag and felt that it would have been dishonest for her to conveniently begin displaying one because so many others chose to. Both Lillie and Rabiah were cognizant of the contradictions present in the flag and the solidarity it was supposed to represent, a convenient solidarity, which neither of them could stomach long enough to even consider buying one. Most white Americans would be astounded to hear Lillie and Rabiah's opinion of the flag. The fact that many African Americans displayed flags in the aftermath of September 11th would probably add to their confusion. Yet, Lillie and

Rabiah's refusal to display the flag was representative of a good number of African Americans who feel that the flag, as the most recognizable symbol of America, represents all that is American. It encompasses the good and the bad experiences that this country's diverse population has experienced. Racism and discrimination have played an unfortunately key role in that experience and therefore could not be separated from such a strong symbol, or ignored because of the devastating tragedies of September 11th.

Subjective Terrorism

"I guess there should be a war on terrorism, but then if there's a war on terrorism, there's a war on us just the same."

—Rabiah

Americans have been inundated with the word "terrorism" since September 12, 2001. America enlisted the assistance of allied nations like Britain in bringing those who were supportive of those terrorists to justice. Yet, the definition of the word seemed limited to those people or groups that were remotely involved or supportive of the September 11th attacks, even when the Bush Administration was obligated to address the simultaneous violence occurring in Israel and Palestine. Thus began the war on terrorism with its vague, yet lethal language aimed at anyone thought to be contributing to it in any form.

When asked whether she thought we could or would win the war on terrorism, Lillie replied, "No, I certainly don't...and nobody else will win it. That's a hard thing to win." Lillie's general mistrust of the government and her specific suspicion of the Bush Administration led her to believe "that there is just a whole lot of mess going on that we will never know about." Having lived through World War II, The Korean War and Vietnam, Lillie went on to explain that she felt the war on terrorism was at its root, another example of the United States' obsession with maintaining power over other nations. September 11th exposed weaknesses in America's coat of armor that rendered it vulnerable to other attacks. Lillie believes that the war on terrorism is really America's way of flexing its military muscles to prove to other nations that it is still the most powerful country in the world.

Rabiah and Lillie felt that the administration offered a grossly oversimplified "good versus evil" explanation of the war on terrorism. Al Qaeda leader, Osama bin Laden and his followers were portrayed as the sole offenders, excluding mention of America's prior relationship with the leader. Furthermore, both women discussed America's use of its role as a super power to "terrorize" other countries. Although Rabiah and Lillie did not name specific countries, they were most likely referring to America's military "intervention" in the internal conflicts of other nations such a Vietnam, Central America, Somalia and the Persian Gulf. Lillie and Rabiah were quick to point out America's hypocrisy in its international affairs but they were equally disgusted by its failure to see its role in committing terrorist acts against its own citizens.

Lillie and Rabiah both vehemently discussed the fact that Black Americans have experienced terror in this country at the hands of white Americans since their arrival on the continent as slaves, a fact that was ignored by the mainstream media in the months after September 11th. The media's repeated reference to September 11th as the first time that Americans experienced such terror at home, negated the experiences of Native Americans and Black Americans, just two of the groups who suffered greatly at the hands of America's great white forefathers, sons, grandsons and now distant ancestors. When Lillie exclaimed that, "Black people cannot get all worked up and scared and stuff because we have been terrorized all our lives," she located terror as a consistent part of the Black experience in America. Racism or the "double standard," as Lillie refers to it, has been the major source of oppression for Black people since they arrived here centuries ago. Lillie spoke with a certain sense of irony that the terrorism that happened on September 11th, which many white people were experiencing for the first time, was a common occurrence for most Black people who "live it every day and look at it and are surrounded by it."

Rabiah remembers hearing her father respond in a similar fashion to a newscast about the war on terrorism, snapping back at the television that "they can be terrorists...when you lynch people and then you put out flyers for people to come to the lynching for fun and bring the whole family like it's the circus. That's terrorism". Like Lillie, Rabiah's father was referring to the unprovoked violence visited upon Black people in his lifetime, "not so long ago."

While she has no direct memory of such atrocities, through comments like this, Rabiah's father and other family members have kept such horrible memories alive for her. To them, and to her, enslavement, economic and political oppression, and violent subjugation of Black people in America is just as real and wrong as what the victims of September 11th suffered: You cannot completely ignore the former and acknowledge the latter as if America has never played a role in causing similar pain and suffering to its own. For Black men and women, terror is always lurking in the shadows. It threatens to appear every time a police officer pulls a young Black man over, or a skin-head spots a young Black woman walking alone. For Black people, terror is as old as slavery and as new as James Byrd being lynched in Jasper, Texas at the turn of the century.

Unlike Lillie, Rabiah mentioned another present day example of such racial oppression and terror in the form of racial profiling of Arab Americans that followed September 11th. Arab Americans became easy targets, suspicious to many by virtue of sharing the same skin tone or religion of the terrorists. To Rabiah's dismay, some African Americans joined in on the guilt-by-same race targeting and suspicion of Arab Americans and East Indians. Here, Rabiah talks about her disgust with some of the Black people she encountered who expressed such views:

"What got me the most was so many Black people who were doing the same thing...who started in on the whole, "Oh! America said they were terrorists so they're all terrorists." It's amazing because people do that to us and everyone's so upset, but it's like now that they're doing that to somebody else, it's okay. It's never gonna be okay for you to put one group of people in a box and say we hate them or we're scared of them. People used to say that when Black people came down the street; they can't be in this neighborhood, or they need to leave, what are they doing over here? It's the same exact thing."

In spite of Rabiah's astute observations, America's subjective definition of terrorism and unfortunate mistreatment of Arab Americans has received little attention in the mainstream media. Consequently, Arab Americans continue to be harassed and racially profiled as other people of color and white Americans remain cowardly relieved, erroneously believing that their civil liberties are safe from violation.

Get-back

"Some people truly believe that America should never ever
get back anything that we have ever given out to anyone
else."

–Rabiah

Very few Americans have been willing to openly discuss the possibility
that America was not completely innocent on September 11th. Interestingly,
Rabiah and Lillie did not hesitate to speak frankly about their amazement that
that America "had it coming." For them, America's hypocrisy is deafening and
its position as an international super power is necessarily linked to its domination of other countries and other people over the last century. In the name
of preserving democracy Lillie maintains that America has sought to control
too much:

If you don't do what these people here in this country say, you done
messed up. You have to do exactly what they say do. And I guess it is the most
powerful country. I do believe that. But they want to be in control of everything and everybody and every country. That's why they're always dipping
their nose in other people's business. But it's all distorted. The whole system.
Whatever the United States says, that's what you better do. Cause they'll get
you. And they're powerful, but they are slowly but surely coming down.

For Lillie, September 11th was a clear indication that America is "coming
down" from its reign as an unstoppable international "bully." Here, Rabiah
speaks of the arrogance of Americans, many of whom believe that America is
invincible:

It's like nobody should ever do anything to us when we do this to everybody else. I'm not gonna say that America didn't deserve it, but I'm not gonna
say that those people deserved to die. Just the same as no one else who
America has gone and bombed or fought in their country, those civilians and
those people didn't deserve to die either.

Rabiah went on to explain that while those who died were innocent victims, as a powerful nation, America was far from innocent and must accept
responsibility for its role in helping to create an environment in which such

91

violence and hatred could thrive. Like Rabiah, Lillie also isolated the September 11th victims from the nation as a whole. For Lillie, America's proverbial chickens came home to roost and its citizens endured an awful tragedy as a result. It was a classic example of "the good suffering with the bad because innocent people are always getting caught up in other people's mess so why should we be any different?"

Lessons and Legacies

"The only thing I know is for us to do the right thing, because that will prevail."

—Lillie

"I'm an optimistic person, I always wish for peace."

—Rabiah

Lillie and Rabiah hoped that America as a nation would be humbled by September 11th, a tragedy that most Americans thought could never happen on this soil. Lillie believed that a significant lesson to be learned from September 11th is the fact that America is "not above terrorism." Rabiah agreed, offering the perspective that "that's the biggest thing about September 11th, you never know what can happen regardless if you think you know everything that can happen." In their minds, America is neither invincible, nor perfect in its dealings with other nations. Perhaps this catastrophe might help some Americans understand the extent to which many other nations have suffered as a result of America's "intervention" and domination.

Death and mourning were the ultimate equalizers on September 11th and Lillie believed that America missed a true opportunity to take advantage of that common ground rooted in sorrow, to unite around issues of racial inequality. Referring to the various images of Americans of all colors "pulling together" Lillie observed that, "it looked like this would, you know with all that hugging and kissing and them flags, and all that stuff it looked like that would kind of help them to really realize what we've been going through." Rabiah remarked that any positive changes in race relations that occurred as a result of September 11th were brief and drowned out by the immediate focus on visiting revenge upon those who were responsible. Consequently, a lot of hatred and prejudice was displaced rather than eradicated as many Americans "decided to just go from hating one group of color (Black people) to hating another group of color (Arab Americans)."

Neither Lillie nor Rabiah lost friends or loved ones during the tragic events of September 11th. There are those who might say that their views would have been different had the tragedy been made more personal to them. But perhaps they still would have been able to separate their mourning and sorrow for their lost loved ones from their general belief that America was not free from blame. Rabiah ended our conversation with these words about the very real sorrow that thousands of Americans are still experiencing as a result of September 11th. Her words demonstrate the extent to which the human sadness connected to the lives that were lost, is the common denominator for most Americans, regardless of their views:

I'm just happy that none of my family or close friends happened to be affected and that was a blessing to me just because I still got one more day to talk to them and one more day to call them and one more day to laugh with them and I know those other people are wishing the same thing that they maybe had one more day with those same people who they don't anymore.

Division Among Us

"I don't think you really want to hear what I have to say."
—Lillie

For months, Lillie watched television and saw few faces that looked like hers analyzing what happened. Furthermore, everyone seemed to have the same script, and it didn't sound like hers at all. Likewise, Rabiah began to realize in the months following September 11th that her opinion was the exception, not the rule. During my conversations with them, both women were aware that their observations and views were different and therefore controversial. Lillie even turned the tape recorder off a few times until she became comfortable with the fact that I wanted to hear her honest opinion. Despite the two generations that separate them, Lillie and Rabiah were equally suspicious of nearly everything they observed after September 11th and were weary of their country's leadership and its response to the horrific events. The mainstream media did a terrible disservice to the nation in the months following September 11th, with their antiseptic treatment of that day and its aftermath. Americans were pacified rather than engaged in critical analyses of what happened and why. Yet somehow, with limited information, Lillie and

Rabiah were able to construct intelligent and intense opinions about all that took place.

Lillie and Rabiah's remarkably similar views on September 11th and the war on terrorism provide a fascinating example of the diverse African American perspectives that have been avoided or ignored until now. Both women have similar family backgrounds and have lived all over the country. But their shared middle class economic status and exposure to various regions of the country does not account for their parallel views on so many of the same topics related to September 11th. It is their experiences as Black women connected to Black families living in America that have clearly resulted in skepticism towards their country and its leadership, which neither of them care to hide. Our continued effort to make some sense of what took place must include the voices of those who both force us to look beyond and critically question what has been presented to us so neatly by our government and the mainstream media. Their voices, opinions and perspectives matter and to acknowledge them is to honor the lives of the thousands of culturally, racially and economically diverse people who lost their lives on September 11th.

THE WAR WITHIN:
African American Public Opinion on the War Against Terrorism
Karin L. Stanford

It is a peculiar sensation, this double-consciousness, this sense of always looking at one's self through the eyes of others, of measuring one's soul by the tape of a world that looks on in amused contempt and pity. One ever feels his twoness,—an American, a Negro; two souls, two thoughts, two unreconciled strivings; two warring ideas in one dark body, whose dogged strength alone keeps it from being torn asunder.

        –W.E. B. DuBois, *The Souls of Black Folk*

In 1903, W.E.B. DuBois eloquently described the duality that has characterized the history and ideological tendencies of African Americans. Double consciousness has become an essential aspect of the African American personality and manifests itself in the methods and tactics used in response to their unique history of enslavement, discrimination and denial of basic human rights. Although integration has by far been the dominant strategy, nationalist and separatist politics have also emerged as a response to continued discrimination in America. The internal dilemma existing within the African American community is ever-present, but often lays dormant during times of optimism. It often emerges when the United States is engaged in military conflict.

As in the case of strategies to eliminate discrimination, double consciousness often distinguishes African American public opinion from that of other Americans. The distinctiveness of the African American experience also explains why certain issues, such as race and ethnicity, patriotism and foreign affairs have become hotbed issues for its community.

The ever-present quandary of African American double consciousness resurfaced once again after the September 11, 2001 terrorist attacks on the World Trade Center and the Pentagon. In their roles as American citizens the

African American community participated in high-visibility acts of patriotism, engaged in fervent flag-waving and provided public support for President George Bush's ensuing war to capture the culprits. The irony of this manifestation of broad-based support for President Bush's subsequent declaration of "war on terrorism," is that he only received eight percent of the African American vote during the contentious 2000 presidential election campaign. After the September 11th crisis, approximately 50 percent of the African American community expressed confidence in the President's ability to handle the catastrophe. A Zogby International Poll conducted on September 20, 2001, indicated that a whopping 94 percent of African Americans rated President Bush's handling of the terrorist attacks as "excellent, good or fair."[1] The polls suggested an endorsement for a President in whom 92 percent of African Americans had little confidence 10 months prior to the attacks.

Historically, African Americans have attempted to demonstrate loyalty to their country by ignoring recurring grievances, ranging from economic and wealth disparities between African Americans and white Americans, to unjust sentencing and racial profiling. The disparities are striking. For example, as recent statistics indicate, 23.6 percent of African Americans are living in poverty compared to 7.7 percent of white Americans. In 1997, African American owned businesses averaged only $86,500 in receipts, compared with $410,600 for all U.S. firms. Data from the 2000 Census showed that African Americans comprise a greater share of prison inmates than they do in the overall population of at least 29 states. In addition, data compiled from the FBI indicated that African Americans comprised 29 percent of all arrests, even though they make up only 12 percent of the U.S. population.[2]

From the perspective of African Americans Candidate Bush's campaign strategy was antithetical to addressing those concerns. Candidate Bush pledged to cut taxes and reorganize Social Security accounts under terms that reward the most successful Americans. Bush also refused to commute the death sentence of Gary Graham, an African American sentenced to death in Texas based on one person's questionable eyewitness testimony. The African American community also felt slighted when Candidate Bush refused to speak out against South Carolina's refusal to stop flying the Confederate battle flag over its state capitol; generally speaking, his apparent lack of support for civil rights and affirmative action did not help his relationship with African

Americans. Most noticeably, the Bush Administration's decision to pull out of the United Nation's World Conference Against Racism held in Durban, South Africa just one week before the attacks proved to the African American community that the administration refused to seriously address their concerns.

Despite continuing assaults on African American civil liberties and life chances, terrorist attacks on the U.S. compelled African Americans to rally around the flag and the president. Immediately after the attacks, African Americans began the process of closing ranks. Kweisi Mfume, president of the National Association for the Advancement of Colored People (NAACP) told African Americans, "The hour is upon us to put aside differences and dissent. This tragedy and these acts of evil that occurred on September 11th must not go unpunished. This is a time for all Americans to stand united and defend the ideas of a free and open society where terrorism has no place".[3] Bishop T.D. Jakes, pastor of The Potter House in Dallas, Texas, said, "I believe [President Bush] deserves our whole support, our complete prayer and consecration because we have never been threatened like we are being threatened right now."[4] Except for Barbara Lee, an African American Congresswoman from California, all other members of the Congressional Black Caucus voted for H.J. Resolution 64, which would have reduced congressional oversight over the executive branch's war conduct, allowing open-ended actions to conduct the "war on terrorism."[5]

Less than one year later, and predictably so, African American support for the President's war effort has declined considerably. African American leadership and its intelligentsia have recently become open and often uncompromising in their criticism of the "war on terrorism." After a trip to the Middle East Reverend Al Sharpton, President of the National Action Network, criticized President Bush for his one-sided view of the conflict.[6] Hugh Price, President of the National Urban League questioned the Bush Administration's decision to limit the civil liberties of all Americans as a response to the attacks and called for congressional hearings on the "appropriateness of the curtailment of our freedoms."[7] African American public opinion has shifted as well. Unlike the 90 percent approval rating in September 2001, eight months later, 34.4 percent of African Americans considered President Bush's handling of the Middle East crisis as poor.[8]

This essay explores African American public opinion on the September

11th attacks and the subsequent "war on terrorism." It seeks to explain the African American perspective on the war and set forth important differences between the opinions of African Americans and white Americans. In particular, it addresses the shift in African American public opinion that occurred within months after the attack. This discussion will examine key issues, such as the importance of foreign affairs to the African American community; job performance ratings of President George Bush; President Bush's handling of the Middle East crisis; homeland security; civil liberties; and racial profiling. Overall, this analysis is positioned as part of a larger dialog on African American patriotism, identity and double consciousness.

Framework for Analysis of African American Views on the War Against Terrorism

Any attempt to explain African American opinion must consider two issues: (1) data collection; and, (2) African Americans' historical involvement in U.S. foreign affairs. Hence, African Americans must be situated within their proper context in American history and culture in order to appreciate their logic and perspective.

Data Collection

Obtaining data on African American opinion on the September 11th attacks and the subsequent War on Terrorism proved to be a daunting task. Because polls only comprise a very small sampling of African Americans, most, to date, rarely provide a racial breakdown of results. In addition, polls often are structured to quantify responses to closed-ended questions, rather than provide qualitative information that could help decipher the meaning of each answer.

Considering those limitations, this analysis will rely heavily on the public opinion polls of Zogby International which are distinguished by the fact that they provide a racial, gender and class breakdown of opinions. When available, other polling sources are used to demonstrate the diversity or similarity of responses. From these polls we are able to assess African American views on the "war on terrorism" and closely related issues. In addition to the polls, this analysis also incorporates the interviews, policy statements and judgments of African American scholars, leaders and elected officials. Understanding the perspective of African American leadership and intelligentsia allows one to put the data in proper context and provides additional insight on African American policy views.

African American Historical Involvement in International Affairs

Despite the popular assumption that African American preoccupation with domestic concerns prohibits an interest in foreign affairs, nothing could be further from the truth. African American activity around questions of U.S. foreign affairs is evident as far back as 1890, when George Washington Williams, an African American historian traveled to Belgium on behalf of the U.S. to investigate charges of Belgium genocide against the Congolese. Booker T. Washington's agitation for reform in the Congo, W.E.B. DuBois' five Pan-African Congresses, Martin Luther King's call for an end to the Vietnam War, and Malcolm X's reports from Africa and Arab countries indicate a history of involvement in international affairs.

African American opinion on international issues is influenced by the uniqueness of African American history. Historical antecedents and recent international activity indicate that African American international involvement can be framed by its quest to link racial, social and economic justice issues within the United States to similar issues abroad. During the height of the cold war, African Americans tended to be more liberal than white Americans on foreign policy issues. Hence, African Americans favored less military and space spending and were less hostile toward communism than white Americans.[9]

In some instances African American public opinion has become a part of the national dialogue on U.S. foreign policy. For example, African American concerns about apartheid helped to support an international movement against South African racism. Other instances occurred in 1991 after General Raoul Cedras overthrew the government of President Bertrand Aristide in Haiti and when African Americans organized to fight against the difference between the treatment of Haitian and Cuban Refugees, both of whom were seeking better lives in the United States. In each of these instances, African American leaders, organizations and individuals protested U.S. policies and actions as well as galvanized African American support to persuade the U.S. to reconsider its positions.[10]

Although African American international interest is primarily focused on Africa and the Caribbean, the Middle East has also received significant attention from African Americans. Most often in support of those considered powerless, African American leaders and activists have become engaged in Middle East politics. For example, members of the Nation of Islam publicly supported Egypt against Israel, the U.S. and several European Powers during the Suez Crisis of 1956. New York Muslims were galvanized by Egypt's show of resistance at a time when pacifism and non-violence dominated the African American civil rights struggle.[11] African American civil rights leaders have questioned the activities of Israel in the Middle East on more than one occasion. During a 1949 summer visit to Israel, NAACP leader Walter White questioned the Israelis about their treatment of Arabs. Regarding segregation in Israel he commented, "I have seen here some evidence of that master-race psychology."[12] During the National Black Political Convention of 1972, African American delegates adopted several resolutions that supported the cause of revolutionary movements in Africa and clarified their position on issues in the Middle East. The convention resolved to "condemn the Israeli government for her expansionist policy and forceful occupation of the sovereign territory of another state and declared support for the struggle of Palestinian people for self-determination."[13] Another incident occurred in 1979, after Andrew Young was forced to resign from his post as U.S. Ambassador to the United Nations as the result of alleged unauthorized conversations with an official of the PLO. As a result of Young's expulsion, several civil rights leaders issued a statement indicating that they would reassess their relationship with Israel, establish closer ties with the Palestinians, and try to force a change in American Middle East policy.[14] Perhaps the most extraordinary intervention by an African American in Middle East affairs occurred in 1984 when Reverend Jesse Jackson, Sr., rescued an American navy pilot who was held hostage in Syria. This act, along with Reverend Jackson's admonishment of U.S. policy, which he considered unbalanced, further highlighted the importance of the Middle East conflict to African Americans.[15]

Most recently African American conservatives have publicly expressed a different perspective from the traditional African American view of U.S. involvement in the Middle East. In an article, "Standing Firm for Israel," television commentator and former presidential candidate Alan Keyes said,

"America's support for Israel is an ongoing demonstration that America will stand with those who champion liberty and representative government, anywhere in the world, especially if they have the courage and integrity of Israel."[16] Shannon F. Reeves, an African American Republican who resides in the congressional district of Congresswoman Barbara Lee, called her vote against H.J. Resolution 64 "partisan" and said that it "lacked conscience and patriotism."[17] While the comments of the conservatives represent a small segment of the African American community, they do suggest the emergence of a new and vocal critique of traditional African American views on international affairs.

African American internationalism manifests a concern for those who are considered powerless and oppressed and it also suggests a propensity to disregard the stated national interest of the U.S., in an effort to set forth its own interest. Given the history of African American international activity, one must note that the opinions expressed about the "war on terrorism" are not those of neophytes to international questions, but of those who have a long history of concerns about the U.S. role in the world. Thus, African American opinions on the "war on terrorism" cannot be analyzed in a vacuum, but must take into account African American past concerns about Middle East affairs.

Fighting the War On Terrorism

On September 20, 2001, President George Bush addressed a Joint Session of Congress and the American people, outlining a comprehensive U.S. and international effort to end global terrorism. He identified Osama bin Laden, a Saudi Arabian Islamic fundamentalist, and al Qaeda, a loose network of terrorist groups, as the prime suspects. The Taliban, a fundamentalist Islamic group based in Afghanistan, was targeted because they allowed the terrorist network to operate within Afghan borders. The military response to the attacks was assigned the name, "Operation Enduring Freedom." The goal of the operation was to destroy the terrorist infrastructure within Afghanistan, capture the al Qaeda leaders and put an end to terrorist activities in Afghanistan.[18]

As the U.S. engaged in war abroad, several domestic changes occurred that purported to help protect American citizens from future terrorist attacks.

Most notably, the Office of Homeland Security was established to develop and coordinate a comprehensive national strategy against terrorist threats. President Bush appointed Tom Ridge, a former Governor of Pennsylvania as the Office's first director. At the federal level a total of $10.6 billion from the fiscal year 2002 Emergency Budget Supplemental was dedicated to Homeland Security.[19]

In addition to founding the Office of Homeland Security, the USA PATRIOT Act of 2001 (Uniting and Strengthening America by Providing Appropriate Tools Required to Intercept and Obstruct Terrorism) was passed by Congress as a means to make it easier for government agencies to track down and capture terrorists. Among other intrusions on civil liberties, the "anti-terrorism act" requires: credit bureaus to reveal private information; schools to hand over education records to the attorney general; monetary institutions to share financial information to U.S. Intelligence Agencies; and communication companies to disclose electronic communications on behalf of consumers.

African American Views on the War
President Bush's Job Performance

Several CNN/USAToday/Gallup Polls conducted in September 2001 indicated that 90 percent of Americans approved President Bush's plan to eliminate terrorism and wage war on Osama bin Laden, the Taliban and al Qaeda. Just before the attacks President Bush's overall job approval rating was 51 percent.[20]

The reasons for such broad-based support were obvious. First, this was only the second time in its history that the U.S. had suffered an attack on its own soil. Second, the number of casualties, over three thousand, was also unprecedented. Finally, the goal of the attack was to destroy the economic, political and military centers of America. By hijacking four commercial jets and using them as missiles to target the home of American government, its military headquarters and financial center, it was clear that the attackers sought to close down the U.S. government and to destroy the country. Notwithstanding the magnitude of the attack, it is common for citizens to support their leaders in wartime. Believing that the president should focus on fighting the war and not on internal dissent, Americans embraced their President's plans and actions.

Almost a year later, however, a Zogby International Poll conducted on June 17-19, 2002 reported a decrease in support for President George Bush. Only 69 percent of likely voters considered President Bush's job performance as positive. Twenty-eight percent gave President Bush a negative job performance rating. The African American community expressed even less confidence in President Bush: only 12.8 percent of African Americans rated Bush's job performance as excellent, while 36.2 percent of white Americans (three times as many) indicated the same. Approximately, 11 percent of African Americans considered President Bush' job performance as poor, compared to 9.7 percent of white Americans. Although most African Americans see Bush's performance as good or fair, the African American/white differential is nonetheless striking.

Overall, how would you rate President Bush's performance on the job?

	Total	Age Group				Race					Gender	
	%	18-29	30-49	50-64	65+	White	Hispanic	African American	Asian	Other	Male	Female
		%	%	%	%	%	%	%	%	%	%	%
Exc	32.7	30.6	34.8	33.6	31.5	36.2	27.4	12.8	19.5	34.7	32.6	32.8
Good	36.4	37.4	34.4	37.6	37.1	35.8	43.1	36.9	55.8	24.6	37.5	35.4
Fair	19.9	22.3	20.9	15.7	21.0	17.5	17.8	36.1	20.5	30.4	18.3	21.4
Poor	9.5	9.1	8.0	12.1	9.0	9.7	5.8	11.2	4.3	10.2	9.9	9.2
NS	1.4	.5	1.9	1.1	1.4	.8	5.9	3.1			1.7	1.2
Total	100.0	100.0	100.0	100.0	100.0	100.0	100.0	100.0	100.0	100.0	100.0	100.0

Source: Zogby International Poll, June 17-19, 2002

It is common for Presidential approval to decline after a threat has been weakened or eliminated. According to Daniel Yankelovich, co-founder and chairman of Public Agenda, there are several stages in the way public opinion forms and solidifies. The first stage is opinion formation, when people's consciousness is raised and they develop a sense of urgency about an issue. The second phase is the "working through stage," which is more complicated. In the second phase, people are confronted with trade-offs, while wrestling with conflicts and values. The final stage is the stage of resolution, where individuals make judgments and eventually make decisions about their position.[21]

Yankelovich's stage analysis explains why overall support for Bush has shifted from 90 percent to 69 percent in less than a year. His comments are supported by a CNN/USA Today/Gallup Poll (May 28-29), which indicated that eight months after the attack, only 9 percent of Americans are very worried about becoming a victim of a terrorist attack and 31 percent were somewhat worried. Over 50 percent of Americans were either not too worried or not worried at all.[22]

The decline in overall public support for the President's job performance can easily be explained by the stage analysis, but what accounts for the differentials between African American and white American opinion? The June 17-19, 2002 Zogby Poll suggested that African American support for Bush less than one year after the attack appears to be lukewarm. Close to 50 percent of African Americans indicated a fair or poor rating, compared to white Americans who provided a combined 27.3 percent poor or fair rating. Viewed another way, African Americans indicated close to 50 percent of a good or excellent rating, while white Americans provided a contrasting 72 percent good or excellent rating.

President Bush's Handling of the Middle East Crisis

Another significant issue is President Bush's handling of the Middle East crisis. Again, a Zogby International Poll indicates more approval from white Americans than African Americans for Bush's performance. Approximately 27 percent of whites, in contrast to 14 percent of African Americans gave Bush an excellent rating.

Overall, how would you rate President Bush's handling of the Middle East crisis?

	Total	AgeGroup				Race					Gender	
	%	18-29	30-49	50-64	65+	**White**	Hispanic	**African American**	Asian	Other	Male	Female
		%	%	%	%	**%**	%	**%**	%	%	%	%
Exc	25.3	24.2	24.9	27.7	24.7	**27.2**	25.9	**14.8**	22.6	14.3	25.9	24.7
Good	35.3	32.1	35.2	38.9	33.8	**36.9**	20.0	**32.7**	43.3	40.8	33.6	36.9
Fair	25.2	28.2	27.6	18.6	26.7	**22.3**	35.5	**36.8**	34.2	31.7	26.8	23.7
Poor	12.0	14.6	10.1	14.1	10.1	**11.6**	15.0	**12.6**		10.2	12.1	11.8
NS	2.3	.7	2.2	.8	4.7	**2.0**	3.5	**3.1**		2.9	1.6	2.8
Total	100.0	100.0	100.0	100.0	100.0	**100.0**	100.0	**100.0**	100.0	100.0	100.0	100.0

Source: Zogby International Poll, June 17-19, 2002

Homeland Security

Although most Americans support the President's war against terrorism, questions have arisen about the Bush Administration's knowledge of the attack before it occurred. A CNN/USA Today/Gallup Poll (May 28-29, 2002), found that only 25 percent of Americans believed that the Bush Administration could have prevented the attacks, while 63 percent did not believe that prevention was possible. On the other hand, 67 percent of Americans believed that the Bush Administration was not paying enough attention to terrorism.[23] Skepticism about preventing the attacks has primarily focused on the federal agencies, as the following chart demonstrates. A Zogby Poll taken June 17-19 showed that 42 percent of white Americans believed that the federal agencies could have prevented the attacks, while 49.6 percent of African Americans feel the same.

Do you agree or disagree that federal agencies like the CIA and the FBI ignored evidence that might have prevented the terrorist attacks of September 11th?

	Age Group				Race					Gender	
	18-29	30-49	50-64	65+	**White**	Hispanic	**African American**	Asian	Other	Male	Female
	%	%	%	%	%	%	%	%	%	%	%
Agree	41.8	46.7	44.7	44.0	**42.7**	55.6	**49.6**	46.1	53.7	40.7	48.6
Disagree	41.1	37.4	37.5	26.8	**36.7**	33.6	**25.1**	53.9	23.6	40.7	30.0
NS	17.1	15.9	17.8	29.2	**20.6**	10.9	**25.3**		22.6	18.6	21.4
Total	100.0	100.0	100.0	100.0	**100.0**	100.0	**100.0**	100.0	100.0	100.0	100.0

Source: Zogby International Poll, June 17-19, 2002

There is also disagreement between African Americans and white Americans on the performance of the Office of Homeland Security. Both groups rated homeland security performance in the mid-range categories, considering most of the agency's actions good or fair. However, in the "excellent" category, white Americans gave the Office of Homeland Security a six percent excellent rating compared to only 1.4 percent of African Americans. A wider disparity is shown in the poor category, with 23.7 percent of African Americans believing that the office performed poorly compared to less than 10.1 percent of whites.

Similar results exist on questions related to the job performance of Homeland Security Director Tom Ridge. Most Americans rate the director's performance as good or fair, with African Americans on the lower end of both. However, there is wider disparity in the excellent and poor categories. Only 3.1 percent of African Americans consider Tom Ridge's job performance excellent, compared to 8.1 percent of white Americans. In the poor job performance category, 13.8 percent of African Americans see Tom Ridge's job performance as poor, compared to seven percent of white Americans.

Would you describe the actions to date of the Office of Homeland Security as excellent, good, fair or poor?

	Total	AgeGroup				Race					Gender	
	%	18-29	30-49	50-64	65+	**White**	Hispanic	**African American**	Asian	Other	Male	Female
		%	%	%	%	**%**	%	**%**	%	%	%	%
Exc	5.2	1.5	7.3	5.1	5.1	**6.0**	4.0	**1.4**		4.2	5.6	4.9
Good	36.6	34.9	38.5	40.1	32.0	**38.9**	11.7	**36.0**	48.8	45.6	35.7	37.5
Fair	36.2	51.1	36.3	31.0	33.4	**33.4**	75.1	**30.9**	33.7	21.9	36.5	35.9
Poor	10.9	5.0	10.5	15.0	10.8	**10.1**	4.0	**23.7**	7.0	2.9	12.0	9.8
NS	11.1	7.5	7.4	8.8	18.7	**11.6**	5.2	**7.9**	10.5	25.4	10.1	11.9
Total	100.0	100.0	100.0	100.0	100.0	**100.0**	100.0	**100.0**	100.0	100.0	100.0	100.0

Source: Zogby International Poll, June 17-19, 2002

How would you rate the overall job performance of Tom Ridge, the director of the Office of Homeland Security?

	Total	Age Group				Race					Gender	
	%	18-29	30-49	50-64	65+	**White**	Hispanic	**African American**	Asian	Other	Male	Female
		%	%	%	%	**%**	%	**%**	%	%	%	%
Exc	7.1	2.0	8.0	9.3	6.7	**8.1**	4.0	**3.1**		4.2	7.7	6.5
Good	37.8	44.0	40.6	37.0	31.9	**38.3**	33.8	**36.7**	54.7	35.5	38.2	37.4
Fair	31.3	45.2	32.2	27.8	26.5	**28.7**	52.6	**34.5**	23.9	30.8	31.9	30.8
Poor	7.1	4.0	4.8	10.3	8.6	**7.0**	1.1	**13.8**	7.0	2.2	8.3	6.0
NS	16.7	4.8	14.4	15.7	26.3	**17.8**	8.4	**11.9**	14.4	27.3	13.9	19.3
Total	100.0	100.0	100.0	100.0	100.0	**100.0**	100.0	**100.0**	100.0	100.0	100.0	100.0

Source: Zogby International Poll, June 17-19, 2002

Support for the Office of Homeland Security suggest that the vast majority of Americans are willing to forego some civil liberties to fight terrorism and that they trust the new government agency to adequately carry out the nation's domestic security programs. It also suggests that African Americans have less confidence in the Office of Homeland Security and its Director than that demonstrated by white Americans.

Explaining African American Opinion

Explanations for African American support for the war, as in the case of white Americans, are fairly simple. Random attacks on civilians place all Americans in jeopardy. Any support Osama bin Laden may have gained from Americans critical of U.S. foreign policy did not occur because random attacks against civilians put even potential supporters and their families at risk. The terrorist attacks are even more egregious for the African American community considering that it won civil rights largely due to the non-violent resistance philosophy espoused by Martin Luther King, Jr.

Certainly socio-economic class and political ideology factored into African American public opinion. Although the pollsters neglect to provide a breakdown of African American opinion by class, it is fair to argue that socioeconomic factors, such as income and education account for the differences between African Americans. That is to say that the higher one's class, the more vested the person is in the country's political and economic stability. Similarly, conservative African Americans and those who are registered Republicans are more likely to consider the job performance of President Bush and his administration as excellent or good.

Accounting for the contrasting opinions between African Americans and white Americans on President Bush's job performance, his handling of the Middle East crisis, and Homeland Security are not as easily explained. Below are several factors that may explain the reasons why African Americans indicate less support for the "war on terrorism" than white Americans.

Historical Treatment of African Americans in America's Wars

African American community support for U.S. military objectives has largely been associated with their hopes of integrating fully into American society. During World War I, W.E. B. DuBois, called on fellow blacks to "forget our special grievances and close our ranks shoulder to shoulder with our own white fellow citizens." Patriotism, he wrote, "would result in the right to vote and the right to work and the right to live without insult."[24]

Nonetheless, African Americans continued to experience segregation and discrimination as soldiers inside the U. S. military and in civilian life. Not only did African Americans have to overcome resistance to their participation, but between 1914-1920 a total of 382 African Americans were lynched or fell victim to race riots. Similar hostilities occurred during World War II. Even after African Americans proved to be loyal soldiers, no branch of the military welcomed integration until President Harry Truman signed an executive order mandating it.[25] Participation in subsequent wars yielded similar results. Hence, one explanation for the ambivalence shown by African Americans for President Bush's "war on terrorism" may be related to the idea that the "war" will not result in a better life for their community.

Closely related to discrimination inside the armed forces is the fear that a sustained war can mean large numbers of African American casualties. During the Vietnam War there was evidence to suggest that African Americans sustained more casualties than other soldiers. In 1968, African Americans made up 9.8 percent of the military forces, but close to 20 percent of all combat troops and 14.1 percent of total U.S. fatalities in Vietnam.[26] As was the case during the Vietnam War, the number of African American fatalities during the Persian Gulf War of 1990 was also disproportionate. During George H. W. Bush's Operation Desert Storm, the American military was not only integrated, but there were a significant number of African Americans in leadership positions. Nonetheless, there were still a higher number of casualties for African Americans. Although African Americans made up only 12 percent of the population of the 266 American soldiers killed in the Gulf War, 15 percent were black.[27]

Effects on the Domestic Economy

African Americans have expressed fear that the war may also result in long-term economic instability within their community. In the Washington Post, Op/Ed section, National Urban League President Hugh Price and National Organization for Women President Kim Gandy set forth the economic concerns of African Americans and poor people. Citing President Bush's support for increased tax cuts for high-income individuals, Price and Gandy argued that the Bush Administration had not paid enough attention to those who have been laid off as a result of the attacks. The article also expressed the concern that resources used for the war would affect programs that had been established to provide a safety net for poor families, i.e. low-income housing assistance, infant and child nutrition programs and job training.[28]

Loss of Civil Liberties

Many African Americans also worry that legislation designed to help capture potential terrorists may produce dangerous results for them. To be sure, it is now easier for the U.S. government to search, seize and detain people on suspicion alone, an issue long regarded as a problem for the African American community.[29] African Americans also believe that the heightened powers given to Attorney General John Ashcroft, a man who many view as anti-civil rights and pro-racial profiling, may result in a major loss of civil liberties for them.[30] The African American collective memory recalls how the FBI-sponsored COINTELPRO (Counter Intelligence Program) disrupted the activities of civil rights organizations and other advocacy groups, such as the Black Panther Party. African Americans fear that without serious checks on government intrusion, history will repeat itself. The "war on terrorism," according to this view, may grow to include harassment of black advocacy groups that take controversial or non-conformist political stances. Dr. Valerie Johnson, professor of political science at the University of Illinois, Chicago, believes that the "war on terrorism" will suffer from the same problems as the "war on drugs"; i.e., having no well-defined enemy, goals or timeline for completion.[31]

In contrast to African American concerns a National Public Radio News/Kaiser Family Foundation/Harvard University's Kennedy School of Government Survey shows that most Americans are willing to forego civil liberties in order to pursue terrorists. Sixty four percent of those surveyed favor military tribunals for non-citizens and 68 percent favor allowing the government to listen in on conversations between terrorist suspects and their lawyers. The survey also found that most Americans are willing to accept significant restrictions on their speech. For instance, a majority believe that someone expressing support for the terrorists should not be allowed to teach school.[32] Unlike African Americans, most white Americans do not see themselves as potential victims of these kinds of repressive and intrusive policies.

Closely related to civil liberties is the issue of racial profiling. Since the terrorist attacks, Arab and Muslim Americans have become the victims of hate crimes and racial profiling. Immediately following the September 11th attacks most Americans approved, at least somewhat, of randomly stopping those who fit the profile of a suspected terrorist.

Surprisingly, most polls indicated a much higher approval rating for racial profiling of Arabs by African Americans. A Zogby International Poll conducted between September 25th and October 8, 2001 showed that African American approval of racially profiling Arab Americans reached a peak of 60 percent on Sept. 30th, compared to 45% among the overall population. A Boston Globe report also showed that 71 percent of African Americans favored more intensive security checks for Arabs, including those who are U.S. citizens before they board planes. A smaller majority of whites said, they would favor such a policy. The statistics later leveled out with African Americans showing a 45 percent approval rating by October 8th, virtually in line with the 41 percent figure of other racial groups.[33]

Determining the reasons for African American views on racial profiling is complicated. Certainly, African Americans have been one of the prime targets of racial profiling and hence, should be more sensitive to its pitfalls. Columnists and pundits have sought to explain African American opinion on this issue. One view is that the response was a knee-jerk reaction to African American's immediate fears about terrorism. As a result, the African American community was prepared to embrace all remedies as a response to the crisis. A second explanation is that African American approval of racial profiling was higher because they feel more vulnerable to danger than others in American society. Earl Ofari Hutchinson points to religious intolerance and ingrained distrust of Arabs within the African American community. "Complex issues such as the presence of Arab-owned convenience stores in predominately black neighborhoods and the tension between the two communities play into this equation as well.[34] Clarence Page admits that there are as "many tensions as well as warm friendships between members of both groups.[35]

Perhaps the primary issue is that of relationships, as with racial profiling in general. An ABC News Poll found that people who say they personally know Muslims are much less likely to support random police stops of Arabs or Muslims. In addition, the poll reports, these people are "also less likely, by 18 points, to express suspicion of Arabs as a result of the terror attacks."[36]

The Perception that U. S. Foreign Policy is Racist

When the U.S. walked out of the World Conference on Racism in Durban South Africa, it confirmed to many African Americans what they had suspected that the Bush Administration had no real commitment to racial equality domestically or globally. As a result, after the terrorist attack occurred, some African American leaders argued that the U.S. was not unjustly attacked and that the bombing was another case of the "chickens coming home to roost."[37] Najee Ali, head of Project Islamic Hope, an African American civil rights organization that fights against poverty and social injustice understands the view held by many African Americans that U.S. foreign policy frequently does not serve the interest of black or poor people. In an interview he stated that the U.S. history of supporting oppressive governments, i.e., Zaire, the Sudan and Angola, is a primary reason why his constituency sees the attacks as a response to racial bias and unfairness in the conduct of U.S. foreign policy. In particular, he added that ignoring the concerns of the Palestinians would most likely lead to more terrorist attacks.[38] Minister Louis Farrakhan shared similar sentiments in a letter he wrote to President Bush on December 1, 2001. He declared that America must "break from the policies of the past...The more fair, just and equitable the solution to the Palestinian/Israeli conflict, the more the anger of those on both sides will subside."[39] Other African Americans question what is meant by terrorism by pointing out that former South African President and ANC leader Nelson Mandela was considered a terrorist by South Africa, Israel and the United States.[40]

As in the case of the ANC, many African Americans see the Middle East conflict, particularly the conflict between the Palestinians and Israel as one between colonists and those who are poor and oppressed. It is not uncommon for members of the African American community to link their fight for justice and human rights to anti-colonialism everywhere.

Conclusion

Similar to the case of other groups, there are several stages in the way that African American opinion forms and solidifies, albeit with some significant differences. Unlike the case for other group's opinion formation, African American opinion is influenced by their history of discrimination and disenfranchisement in the U.S. This accounts for the disparities between African American and white opinion after the stage of resolution, where individuals make judgments and eventually formulate conclusions.

During the initial stages there were similarities in African American and white American's view of the war. Both groups endorsed the President's response to the attacks. The decline in support for the war effort was expected after the initial crisis ended. However, the extension of the "war on terrorism," which included such acts as the passage the USA PATRIOT Act, led to a decrease in African American support.

Viewing the war through the eyes of an American, African Americans supported President Bush's wartime initiatives, albeit with some reservations. However, viewed though the eyes of an African American, an America win or loss of the war on terrorism will not resolve the fundamental problem of race, domestically or globally. Until our nation is willing to expend resources addressing domestic and international racial concerns, W. E. B. DuBois' description of African American duality will remain accurate.

Notes

1. Zogby International Poll, September 20, 2002.
2. U.S. Census Bureau, Current Population Survey, March 2000, Racial Statistics Population Division; U.S. Census Bureau, 1997 Survey of Minority Owned Business Enterprise: Black; Genaro C. Armas, "Census Data On Blacks in Prison," Associated Press, July 18, 2001.
3. NAACP News, "Mfume Calls Again for American Solidarity," www.Naacp.org. September 18, 2001.
4. Martha Simmons and Frank A. Thomas, editors, *9.11.01 African American Leaders Respond to an American Tragedy* (Valley Ford: Judson Press, 2001), 21.
5. Congresswoman Barbara Lee's statement on the vote can be found on her web site at www.house.gov/lee.
6. For the full transcript of Reverend Al Sharpton's address to the National Press Club, see Lakisha N. Williams, "Reverend Al Sharpton Addresses National Press Club," May 4, 2000. www.nationalactionnetwork.org.
7. Hugh Price, "Remember the Error of our Old Ways", *The Black World Today*, December 12, 2001.
8. Zogby International Poll, May 28-30 2002.
9. National Opinion Research Center, 1987 Survey. For an analysis of the survey results, see Robert C. Smith and Richard Seltzer, *Race, Class and Culture: A Study in Afro-American Mass Opinion* (Albany: State University of New York Press, 1992), 41.
10. Bill Nichols, "Clinton Flip Flops on Haiti Issue," *USA Today*, March 3, 1993 4A.
11. Clinton E. Marsh, *From Black Muslims to Muslims: The Transition From Separatism to Islam, 1930 - 1980* (Metuchen, N.J.: Scarecrow Press, 1984), 72.
12. Poppy Cannon, *A Gentle Knight: My Husband, Walter White*(New York: Rinehart, 1956), 96-98, 102, 103.
13. National Black Political Convention Steering Committee, Washington, D.C. March 28, 1972, Statement to the Press.
14. See Thomas Landess and Richard Quinn, *Jesse Jackson and the Politics of Race,* (Ottawa: Jameson Books, 1985) 137.
15. See Wyatt Tee Walker, *The Road to Damascus* (New York: Martin Luther King Fellows Press, 1971).
16. See Alan Keyes, "Standing Firm for Israel," WorldNet Daily, April 29, 2002.
17. Shannon F. Reeves, "The Lone Voice of Dissent," Africana.com October 2, 2001 www.africana.com.

18. There are several web sites that provide details of Operation Enduring Freedom. President Bush's speech can be found on the web site of Global Security at www.globalsecurity.org.

19. See White House, Office of Homeland Security, "Strengthening Homeland Security Since 9/11," www.whitehouse.gov/homeland.

20. CNN.com Interview with Frank Newport, Editor in Chief of the Gallup poll and Vice President of the Gallup Organization based in New Jersey. Interview was conducted on September 17, 2001. www.cnn.com.

21. Public Agenda, Special Edition, Perspectives: Public Opinion Can Be Volatile in Wartime, Interview with Daniel Yankelovich, (2002) www.publicagenda.org.

22. See Pollingreport.com, War on Terrorism, CNN/USA Today/Gallup Poll, May 28-29, 2002.

23. Ibid.

24. W.E.B. DuBois, "The Black Soldier, *The Crisis* July 1918

25. See Gail Buckley, *American Patriots* (New York: Random House, 2001) for an in depth history of African Americans in the Military. Pages 337-41 provide a detailed discussion of Executive Order 9981, which mandated integration in the U.S. armed forces.

26. Ibid. 416 and Peter M. Bergman, Ed. *The Chronological History of the Negro in America* (New York: New York American Library, 1969), 613.

27. Steven A. Holmes, "Military Moves to Aid Racial Harmony," *The New York Times*, April 5, 1994; and Gail Buckley, *American Patriots*, 433-434.

28. Hugh B.P and Kim Gandy, "Don't Sacrifice the Poor," *Washington Post* October 15, 2001, Page A19.

29. HR 3162, USA Patriot Act of 2001 passed the U.S. House of Representatives on October 24, 2001.

30. See Jonetta Rose Barras, "Many Blacks Have Doubts: Here's Why," *Washington Post* October 28, 2001, B03. Barras reports on a Howard University School of Law dialogue on the war, which lays out several reasons why African Americans do not support the war.

31. Telephone interview by author with Dr. Valerie Johnson, June 28, 2002.

32. NPR News, the Kaiser Family Foundation and Harvard University Kennedy School of Government Poll, "Security Trumps Civil Liberties," November 20, 2001. See www.npr.org for polling results.

33. For a compilation of data on African Americans and Racial Profiling poll results see Clarence Page, "Unfair Profiling of Arabs too accepted by Blacks," Zogby International Soundbite, October 5, 2001.

34. Ibid. Sasha Polakow-Suransky, "Racial Profiling Goes Beyond Black and White," Africana.com. October 30, 2001. www.Africana.com.

35. See Clarence Page, "Unfair Profiling of Arabs Accepted by Blacks, Too" Zogby International Soundbite, October 5, 2001.

36. Gary Langer, "Power to the Police," ABCNews.com, October 10, 2001. www.abcnews.com.
37. See Statement of the New Black Panther Party, "Attacks on America: American Must Look Within; War Cannot Solve the Problem." September 17, 2001.
38. Interview by author with Najee Ali, July 6, 2002.
39. See "A Letter to President George W. Bush," the *Final Call* (On-Line Edition) written by Minister Louis Farrakhan, December 1, 2001. www.finalcall.com.
40. Jonetta Rose Barras, "Many Blacks Have Doubts," B03.

CHAPTER FIVE

What is Terrorism?

Editor's Note

"The Boondocks" is being replaced this week with "The Adventures of Flagee and Ribbon," a hilariously patriotic new offering.

Editor's Note (Cont.)

Those of you who have written demanding the return of "The Boondocks," your names have been forwarded to the FBI.

What is Terrorism?

The typical desktop dictionary defines terrorism as violence or the threat of violence, especially bombing, kidnapping and assassination, carried out for political purposes. It says that to terrorize is: (1) To intimidate or coerce somebody with violence or the threat of violence; and, (2) To fill somebody with feelings of intense fear over a period of time. The United States most certainly was on the receiving end of horrific terrorist acts on September 11, 2001, but the dictionary suggests it wasn't the first time that some people in the United States have experienced terrorism.

Ask Donovan Jackson, the 16 year old who had his head bashed into the hood of a police car at the end of a routine traffic stop about terrorism. Ask every African American whose heart leaps to his or her throat when followed by a police car. While all of my paperwork may well be in order, I can't shake the apprehension that descends when I see a police car behind me. It isn't unrealistic to feel fear when so many "routine" police stops have ended so badly, but the police relationship with the African American community has been one that has "filled somebody with feelings of intense fear over a period of time."

Terrorism. Ask Native American people about terrorism. Or, look through history to consider the number of times that our government has coerced others with violence. A consideration of the dimensions of terrorism drives some of the contributions to this section.

John Edgar Wideman's searing prose details the reasons that he sees terrorism broadly, not narrowly. Marcia Ann Gillespie reminds us that there is a gender component to the concept of terrorism, that there are women who always live scared, that fear is such a fabric of their lives that they cannot imagine a world without it. Such stifling space conforms to the dictionary definition of terrorism.

I heard Kimberly Ellis speak at the State of the Black World Conference in Atlanta George in December, 2001. I was as impressed with the content of her remarks as with her presentation, with her stately posture and clear, firm voice sharing the results of her doctoral dissertation research. She told a familiar story, and buttressed it with detail and corroboration about the attack on black people in Tulsa in 1921. She did not use the words "domestic terrorism," but her descrip-

tions of Tulsa incidents stopped me in my tracks. As we mourn the victims of September 11th, Kim's research reminds us that there have been other victims, but that history and racism have attempted to bury them and the details of the terrorism they experienced.

Reginna Green brings incisive eyes to the question of terrorism, using the words of Gil Scott Heron and the Last Poets to fuel her essay. We are bonded by the question, "where were you when," but our bonding begs for context about terms like revolution and terrorism. Reginna asserts that September 11th may have been the beginning of a revolution, and suggests that we can choose how to turn this tragedy into international triumph by reinventing relationships.

—J.M.

WHOSE WAR: THE COLOR OF TERROR
John Edgar Wideman

Nobody asked me, but I need to say what I'm thinking in this new year in New York City, five months after the Twin Towers burned, after long stretches of fall weather eerily close to perfect—clear blue skies, shirt-sleeve warmth—through December, a bizarre hesitation, as if nature couldn't get on with its life and cycle to the next season, the city enclosed in a fragile, bell-jar calm till shattered by a siren, a plane's roar overhead.

I grew up in Homewood, an African-American community in Pittsburgh where people passing in the street might not have known each other's names, but we knew something about each other's stories, so we always exchanged a greeting. We greeted each other because it felt good and also because we share the burden of racism, understand how it hurts, scars, deforms, but yes, it can be survived, and here we are, living proof meeting on the ground zero of a neighborhood street. The burning and collapse of the World Trade Center has conferred a similar sort of immediate intimacy upon all Americans. We've had the good luck to survive something awful, but do we truly understand, as Homewood people are disciplined to understand by the continuing presence of racism, that it ain't over yet. There's the next precarious step, and the next down the street, and to survive we must attend to the facts of division as well as the healing wish for solidarity.

Staring up at a vast, seamless blue sky, it's hard to reckon what's missing. The city shrinks in scale as the dome of sky endlessly recedes. Piles of steel and concrete are whims, the vexed arc of the city's history a moment lasting no longer than the lives of victims consumed in the burning towers. The lives lost mirror our own fragility and vulnerability, our unpredictable passage through the mysterious flow of time that eternally surrounds us, buoys us, drowns us. Ourselves the glass where we look for the faces of those who have disappeared, those we can no longer touch, where we find them looking back at us, terrified, terrifying.

A few moments ago I was a man standing at a window, nine stories up in an apartment building on the Lower East Side of New York, staring out at a building about a hundred yards away, more or less identical to his, wondering why he can't finish a piece of writing that for days had felt frustratingly close to being complete, then not even begun. Wondering why anybody, no matter how hard they'd plugged away at articulating their little piece of the puzzle, would want to throw more words on a pile so high the thing to be written about has disappeared. A man with the bright idea that he might call his work in progress "A speech to be performed because no one's listening." Like singing in the shower: no one hears you, but don't people sing their hearts out anyway, because the singing, the act itself, is also a listening to itself, so why not do your best to please yourself.

And the man standing at the window retracts his long arms from the top of the upper pane he's lowered to rest on as he stares. Then all of him retracts. Picture him standing a few moments ago where there's emptiness now. Picture him rising from a couch where he'd been stretched out, his back cushioned against the couch's arm, then rising and walking to the window. Now visualize the film running backward, the special effect of him sucked back like red wine spilled from the lip of a jug returning to fill the jug's belly, him restored exactly, legs stretched out, back against the couch's cushioned arm. Because that's who I am. What I'm doing and did. I'm the same man, a bit older now, but still a man like him, restless, worried, trying to fashion some tolerable response with words to a situation so collapsed, so asphyxiated by words, words, it's an abomination, an affront to dead people, to toss any more words on the ruins of what happened to them.

I, too, return to the couch, return also to the thought of a person alone singing in a shower. A sad thought, because all writing pretends to be something it's not, something it can't be: something or someone other, but sooner or later the writing will be snuffed back into its jug, back where I am, a writer a step, maybe two, behind my lemming words scuffling over the edge of the abyss.

I'm sorry. I'm an American of African descent, and I can't applaud my president for doing unto foreign others what he's inflicted on me and mine. Even if he calls it ole-time religion. Even if he tells me all good Americans have nothing to fear but fear itself and promises he's gonna ride over there and kick fear's ass real good, so I don't need to worry about anything, just let him handle it his way, relax and enjoy the show on TV, pay attention to each breath I take and be careful whose letters I open and listen up for the high alerts from the high-alert guy and gwan and do something nice for a Muslim neighbor this week. Plus, be patient. Don't expect too much too soon. These things take time. Their own good time. You know. The sweet by-and-by. Trust me.

I'm sorry. It all sounds too familiar. I've heard the thunder, seen the flash of his terrible swift sword before. I wish I could be the best kind of American. Not doubt his promises. Not raise his ire. I've felt his pointy boots in my butt before. But this time I can't be Tonto to his Lone Ranger. Amos to his Andy. Tambo to his Bones. Stepin to his Fetchit. I'm sorry. It's too late. I can't be as good an American as he's telling me to be. You know what I'm saying. I must be real. Hear what I'm saying. We ain't going nowhere, as the boys in the hood be saying. Nowhere. If you promote all the surviving Afghans to the status of honorary Americans, Mr. President, where exactly on the bus does that leave me. When do I get paid. When can I expect my invitation to the ranch. I hear Mr. Putin's wearing jingle-jangle silver spurs around his dacha. Heard you fixed him up with an eight-figure advance on his memoirs. Is it true he's iced up to be the Marlboro man after he retires from Russia. Anything left under the table for me. And mine.

Like all my fellow countrymen and -women, even the ones who won't admit it, the ones who choose to think of themselves as not implicated, who maintain what James Baldwin called "a willed innocence," even the ones just off boats from Russia, Dominica, Thailand, Ireland, I am an heir to centuries of legal apartheid and must negotiate daily, with just about every step I take, the foul muck of unfulfilled promises, the apparent and not so apparent effects of racism that continue to plague America (and, do I need to add, plague the rest of the Alliance as well). It's complicated muck, muck that doesn't seem to dirty Colin Powell or Oprah or Michael Jordan or the black engineer in your firm who received a bigger raise than all her white colleagues, muck so thick it obscures the presence of millions of underclass African Americans living below the poverty line, hides from public concern legions of young people of color wasting away in prison. How can I support a president whose rhetoric both denies and worsens the muck when he pitches his crusade against terror as a holy war, a war of good against evil, forces of light versus forces of darkness, a summons to arms that for colored folks chillingly echoes and resuscitates the Manichaean dualism of racism.

I remain puzzled by the shock and surprise non-black Americans express when confronted by what they deem my "anger" (most would accept the friendly amendment of "rage" or "bitterness" inside the quotes). Did I see in their eyes a similar shock and surprise on September 11th. Is it truly news that some people's bad times (slavery, colonial subjugation, racial oppression, despair) have underwritten other people's good times (prosperity, luxury, imperial domination, complacency). News that a systematic pattern of gross inequities still has not been corrected and that those who suffer them are desperate (angry, bitter, enraged) for change.

For months an acrid pall of smoke rose from smoldering ruins, and now a smokescreen of terror hovers, terror as the enemy, terror as the problem, terror as the excuse for denying and unleashing the darkness within ourselves.

To upstage and camouflage a real war at home the threat of terror is being employed to justify a phony war in Afghanistan. A phony war because it's being pitched to the world as righteous retaliation, as self-defense after a wicked, unwarranted sucker punch when in fact the terrible September 11th attack as well as the present military incursion into Afghanistan are episodes in a long-standing vicious competition—buses bombed in Israel, helicopters strafing Palestinian homes, economic sanctions blocking the flow of food and medicine for Iraq, no-fly zones, Desert Storms, and embassy bombings—for oil and geopolitical leverage in the Middle East.

A phony war that the press, in shameless collusion with the military, exploits daily as newsy entertainment, a self-promoting concoction of fiction, fact, propaganda, and melodrama designed to keep the public tuned in, uninformed, distracted, convinced a real war is taking place.

A phony war because its stated objective—eradicating terrorism—is impossible and serves to mask unstated, alarmingly open-ended goals, a kind of fishing expedition that provides an opportunity for America to display its intimidating arsenal and test its allies' loyalty, license them to crush internal dissent.

A phony war, finally, because it's not waged to defend America from an external foe but to homogenize and coerce its citizens under a flag of rabid nationalism.

The Afghan campaign reflects a global struggle and also reveals a crisis inside America—the attempt to construct on these shores a society willing to sacrifice democracy and individual autonomy for the promise of material security, the exchange of principles for goods and services. A society willing to trade the tumultuous uncertainty generated by a government dedicated to serving the interests of many different, unequal kinds of citizens for the certainty of a government responsive to a privileged few and their self-serving, single-minded, ubiquitous, thus invisible, ideology: profit. Such a government of the few is fabricating new versions of freedom. Freedom to exploit race, class, and gender inequities without guilt or accountability; freedom to drown in ignorance while flooded by information; freedom to be plundered by corporations. Freedom to drug ourselves and subject our children's minds to the addictive mix of fantasy and propaganda, the nonstop ads that pass for a culture.

A phony war, but also a real war because as it bumbles and rumbles along people are dying and because like all wars it's a sign of failure and chaos. When we revert to the final solution of kill or be killed, all warring parties in the name of clan tribe nation religion violate the first law of civilization—that human life is precious. In this general collapse, one of the first victims is language. Words are deployed as weapons to identify, stigmatize, eliminate, the enemy. One side boasts of inflicting casualties, excoriates the other side as cowards and murderers. One side calls civilians it kills collateral damage, labels civilian deaths by its opponents terrorism.

From their initial appearance in English to describe the bloody dismantling of royal authority during the French Revolution (Burke's "thousands of those Hell-hounds called Terrorists ... are let loose on the people") the words terror and terrorist have signified godless savagery. Other definitions—government by a system of coercive intimidation—have almost entirely disappeared. Seldom if ever perceived neutrally as a tool, a set of practices and tactics for winning a conflict, terror instead is understood as pure evil. Terror and terrorists in this Manichaean scheme are excluded even from the problematic dignity of conventional warfare.

One side's use of terrorist to describe the other is never the result of a reasoned exchange between antagonists. It's a refusal of dialogue, a negation of the other. The designation terrorist is produced by the one-way gaze of power. Only one point of view, one vision, one story, is necessary and permissible, since what defines the gaze of power is its absolute, unquestionable authority.

To label an enemy a terrorist confers the same invisibility a colonist's gaze confers upon the native. Dismissing the possibility that the native can look back at you just as you are looking at him is a first step toward blinding him and ultimately rendering him or her invisible. Once a slave or colonized native is imagined as invisible, the business of owning him, occupying and exploiting his land, becomes more efficient, pleasant.

A state proclaiming itself besieged by terrorists asserts its total innocence, cites the unreasonableness, the outrageousness, of the assaults upon it. A holy war may be launched to root out terrorism, but its form must be a punitive crusade, an angry god's vengeance exacted upon sinners, since no proper war can exist when there is no recognition of the other's list of grievances, no awareness of the relentless dynamic binding the powerful and powerless. Perhaps that's why the monumental collapsing of the Towers delivered such a shocking double dose of reality to Americans—yes, a war's been raging and yes, here's astounding proof we may have already lost it. It's as if one brick snatched away, one sledgehammer blow, demolished our Berlin Wall.

Regimes resisting change dismiss challenges to their authority by branding them terrorist provocations. In the long bloody struggles that often follow, civil protests, car bombings, kidnappings, assassinations, guerrilla warfare in the mountains, full-scale conventional military engagements, blur one into the other. At first the media duly reports on the frightening depredations of terrorists—Algerian terror, Mau Mau terror, Palestinian terror, Israeli terror, South African terror—then bears witness as fighters from the Mau Mau, the Palmach, the P.L.O., emerge to become leaders of new states. George Washington, inaugurated as America's first president only a few blocks from the ruins of the World Trade Center, would have been branded a terrorist if the word had been invented in 1775. Clearly not all terrorists become prime ministers or presidents, but, if and when they do, they rewrite the history of their struggle to attain legitimacy. This turnabout clarifies the relationship between power and terror. Terrorists are those who have no official standing, no gaze, no voice in the established order, those determined by all means possible to usurp power in order to be seen and heard. Some former terrorists survive to accomplish precisely that. Others survive long enough to decry and denounce the terrorist threat nibbling at the edges of their own regime.

The destruction of the World Trade Center was a criminal act, the loss of life an unforgivable consequence, but it would be a crime of another order, with an even greater destructive potential, to allow the evocation of the word terror to descend like a veil over the event, to rob us of the opportunity to see ourselves as others see us.

The terror that arises from fear of loss, fear of pain, death, annihilation, prostrates us because it's both rational and irrational. Rational because our sense of the world's uncertainty is accurate. Rational because reason confirms the difference between what is knowable and unknowable, warns us that in certain situations we can expect no answers, no help. We are alone. Irrational because that's all we have left when reason abandons us. Our naked emotions, our overwhelmed smallness.

Terror thrives in the hour of the wolf, the hour of Gestapo raids on Jewish ghettos, of blue-coated cavalry charges on Native-American villages. Those predawn hours when most of us are born or die, the hour when cops smash through doors to crack down on drugs or on dissidents, the hour of transition when sleep has transported the body furthest from its waking state, when our ability to distinguish dream from not-dream weakens. Terror manifests itself at this primal juncture between sleep and waking because there we are eternally children, outside time, beyond the protections and consolations of society, prey to fear of the dark.

To a child alone, startled from sleep by a siren, the hulking bear silhouetted in the middle of the dark room is real. The child may remember being assured that no bears live on the Lower East Side of New York, may know his parents' bed is just down the hall, may even recall tossing his bulky down parka over the back of the chair instead of hanging it neatly in the closet like he's been told a million times to do. None of this helps, because reason has deserted him. Even if things get better when his mother knocks and calls him for breakfast, the darkness has been branded once again, indelibly, by agonizing, demoralizing fear, by a return to stark terror.

For those who don't lose a child's knack for perceiving the aural archaeology within the sound of words, words carry forward fragments, sound bites that reveal a word's history, its layered onomatopoeic sources, its multiplicity of shadowed meanings. Terror embeds a grab bag of unsettling echoes: tear (as in rip) (as in run fast), terra (earth, ground, grave, dirt, unfamiliar turf), err (mistake), air (terra firma's opposite element), eerie (strange, unnatural), error (of our ways), roar-r-r (beasts, machines, parents, gods). Of course any word's repertoire is arbitrary and precise, but that's also the point, the power of puns, double entendre, words migrating among languages, Freudian slips, Lacan's "breaks," all calling attention to the unconscious, archaic intentionality buried in the words.

But the word terror also incarcerates. Like the child pinned to its bed, not moving a muscle for fear it will arouse the bear, we're immobilized, paralyzed by terror. Dreading what we might discover, we resist investigating terror's source. Terror feeds on ignorance, confines us to our inflamed, tortured imaginings. If we forget that terror, like evil, resides in us, is spawned by us no matter what name we give it, then it makes good sense to march off and destroy the enemy. But we own terror. We can't off-load it onto the back of some hooded, barbaric, shadowy other. Someone we can root out of his cave and annihilate. However, we continue to be seduced by the idea that we might be able to cleanse ourselves of terror, accomplish a final resolution of our indeterminate nature. But even if we could achieve freedom from terror, what would we gain by such a radical reconfiguration of what constitutes being human. What kind of new world order would erase the terror we're born with, the terror we chip away at but never entirely remove. What system could anticipate, translate, or diffuse the abiding principle of uncertainty governing the cosmos. Systems that promise a world based on imperishable, impregnable truth deliver societies of truncated imagination, of history and appetite denied, versions of Eden where there is no dreaming, no rebellion, no Eros, where individuality is sacrificed for interchangeability, eternal entertainment, becalmed ego, mortality disguised as immortality by the absence of dread.

Power pales (turns white with terror, imagines its enemies black, invents race) when power confronts the inevitability of change. By promising to keep things as they are, promising to freeze out or squeeze out those not already secure within the safety net of privilege, Mr. Bush won (some say stole) an election. By launching a phony war he is managing to avoid the scrutiny a first-term, skin-of-its-teeth presidency deserves. Instead he's terrorizing Americans into believing that we require a wartime leader wielding unquestioned emergency powers. Beneath the drumbeat belligerence of his demands for national unity, if you listen you'll hear the bullying, the self-serving, the hollowness, of his appeals to patriotism. Listen carefully and you'll also hear what he's not saying: that we need, in a democracy full of contradictions and unresolved divisions, opposition voices.

Those who mount a challenge to established order are not the embodiment of evil. Horrifically bloody, criminal acts may blot the humanity of the perpetrators and stimulate terror in victims and survivors, but the ones who perpetuate such deeds are not the source of the terror within us. To call these people terrorists or evil, even to maintain our absolute distinction between victims and perpetrators, exercises the blind, one-way gaze of power, perpetuates the reign of the irrational and supernatural, closes down the possibility that by speaking to one another we might formulate appropriate responses, even to the unthinkable.

Although trouble may always prevail, being human offers us a chance to experience moments when trouble doesn't rule, when trouble's not totally immune to compassion and reason, when we make choices, and try to better ourselves and make other lives better.

Is war a preferable alternative? If a child's afraid of the dark, do we solve the problem by buying her a gun?

FIGHTING MEN, SILENT WOMEN?
Marcia Ann Gillespie

Why do men carry on as if war and its consequences is all about them, and what makes so many women go along with that fiction even though we should know better? As if women have not led armies and fought in them, nursed the wounded and tended to the dead. As if women and children have not been targeted by the bombs and the bullets, the machetes and spears. As if since time immemorial women's bodies have not been considered spoils of war. As if women lived in glass bubbles shielded from the privation and violence, the pain and fear, the death and destruction, and untouched by the fear, greed and hatred that wars sow. I am not so naïve as to believe that women by nature are pacifists, or that there are not beaucoup women eager to prove that they can wage war as well as, if not better than, men. Since September 11th, I have seen far too many women caught up in patriotic zeal, waving the flag, chanting USA and demanding pay back.

Why do Westerners, most especially Americans dare to presume that the wars we wage with our missiles, smart bombs, and stealth bombers in countries other than our own are somehow more civilized than the up close and personal wars in places like Rwanda, Bosnia, Sierra Leone or Sri Lanka? One might argue that if war is an abomination — and I think that it is — then war waged from a distance is the ultimate obscenity. At the very least those who would make war should be required to walk through the abattoir.

For more than one hundred years this country has engaged in war at arms length. The battlefields, scorched earth, and destroyed villages have been in someone else's country. The grieving, traumatized faces are those of strangers, the keens and wails are from "over there." We are terribly distanced from the pain and suffering, the fear and despair. Having been burned in Vietnam, our government now keeps tight control over what we read, hear, and see when we "engage" in military actions. Post Vietnam the rule has been to make war only when we feel absolutely certain that we can minimize our risks, inflict maximum damage, and win quickly. In Grenada and the Gulf War "we" flexed our muscles, tested our weaponry, and restored the public's confidence in our military and the myth of our invincibility. These wars at a distance have also helped to feed the myth in this country that war is men's business. That of course was before September 11th, before al Qaeda terrorists launched their deadly missions, before we as a nation learned how it felt to be vulnerable.

Today we are engaged in a war of retribution. Our enemies in this war are terrorists whom our government defines as those who have harmed or who seek to inflict harm on this country and its citizens. This vaguely defined war on terrorism can be waged against the government of a country or its leader, a political group or an individual. Its objectives are extremely broad and diffuse, and as a result this war could drag on and on for decades with no end in sight. There are no fixed rules, but if you are an Arab and or a Muslim, you are automatically suspect. In the name of "homeland security" this war targets, detains, and deports certain immigrants. As if those who commit acts of terror in this country against its citizens were always from somewhere else—no Oklahoma City, no men in sheets, no Atlanta bombing as if Muslims were the only religious fundamentalists we need fear. This war deliberately ignores the ongoing homegrown terrorism being waged against health providers who dare to provide abortion services. There's no campaign underway to round up and investigate everyone involved with groups like the Lambs of God and other reactionary Christian fundamentalist groups who are determined to curtail women's reproductive freedom and advocate the use of violence to achieve their goals.

This war carefully parses the definition of terrorism: There is normalized terrorism—the acts of stalkers, rapists, brutalizers of women. Then there is political Terrorism—the suicide bombers, the hijackers. Does Mr. Bush's war against terrorism, recognize domestic violence as gendered terrorism? Of course not. The use of rape to terrorize and demoralize ones "enemy" is now considered a war crime. But in times of war and peace, rape is a terrorist act and rapists are terrorists. Will Mr. Bush declare rape an act of terrorism and *all* rapists, "Enemies of the State"? Don't hold your breath. The fact that terrorism directed against women is commonplace is not the issue in this war, or in any other war, unless of course it serves a purpose. And it does.

One unofficial rule of war is that the enemy must be demonized in order to fuel the public's outrage and ensure support for the war doesn't wane. Atrocity stories become an essential part of the demonization process. Here's where violence against women, and women's oppression by the enemy rises above the mundane and becomes a powerful propaganda tool for the state.

On September 10, 2001, one would have been hard pressed to gain this government's attention about the ongoing plight of women in Afghanistan. For years women's groups here and abroad had been vainly trying to bring the issue to national attention, to little or no avail. Was George W. Bush or any member of his cabinet agonizing about the suppression of women's rights by the Taliban? Hardly. If the Taliban had immediately cooperated with the United States in the hunt for bin Laden, that carefully orchestrated outrage about women's status in that country would never have materialized.

In the wake of September 11th that indifference was quickly replaced with outraged denunciations of the Taliban's treatment of women amidst a barrage of bleak stories in mainstream media detailing their lost freedoms. Using women's oppression to fan the flames, the invasion of Afghanistan was no longer just a man hunt; now it became a liberation. Once couched in those terms, women's groups that had long sought redress for Afghan women, groups that might have seriously questioned/denounced this war kept silent and some turned into hawks.

Now having proven the propaganda value of women's oppression the question is how will it be used to fuel this war against terrorism in the months and years ahead. Will stories about Sadaam Hussein's abuse of women serve as prelude to our second invasion of Iraq? Will women's suffering be served up whenever the public's support of this war seems to be slipping? The obvious answer is, yes.

Far less obvious is why so many women aren't making the connections and challenging the parsing of terrorism. When do we stand up and remind this government that we as women are far more likely to fall victim to homegrown terrorism, not some action from abroad? But the question that plagues me is how do we women move to challenge the status quo when it comes to the larger issues of war and peace and make life difficult for those who would make war on our backs?

As a black feminist, I am only too aware that patriarchy and racism are most rampant during times of war. I've watched and waited with growing rage and despair for Civil Rights activists and organizations to denounce the obvious racism at work in the targeting of Muslims, specifically, Arabs here in the United States. How do we fail to make the obvious connections between the racial profiling of African Americans by law enforcement agencies and the targeting of Muslims and Arabs in the name of "homeland security"? One would think that after Vietnam African Americans would have immediately caught on to the racist acts and assumptions fueling this latest conflict. Instead as a people we seem far more willing to aid and abet the scapegoating of other people of color, as if by doing so we get the monkey off our back. What's being lost in the midst of all this flag waving and nationalistic fervor is the opportunity to build coalitions with other people of color. Coalitions that we will sorely need if we are to truly root racism out of this society. Perhaps far more troubling and telling is the degree to which this conflict exposes, not just the desire to make someone else be the "nigger", but the religious intolerance that runs deep in our community.

The fact is that these organizations and their leaders seem wedded to a 19th century model that tends to dismiss the issues of other groups of color as less significant than our own, and at worst fails to acknowledge the presence of other people of color in this country. Just as they remain wed to the patriarchy. So no, they never seem to get gender issues and remain resistant and often downright hostile to feminism. No, they simply don't get the irony of a war against terrorism that cynically exploits women's oppression and violence towards women for its own ends. Why would they when the oppression and victimization of women within our own community is routinely downplayed or used in an equally cynical fashion when it fits the old "massa" script and the race card can be played?

Do we feminists dare to name the problems and challenge our supposed leaders to confront the issues? This day of reckoning is way overdue. What better time to stand and be counted. The longer that we allow these organizations and groups to operate as old boys clubs, where issues of racial justice are defined almost exclusively as what's in the best interests of men and gender justice is given little more than lip service, the more irrelevant they become in a society and a world where the issues are ever more cleverly cloaked.

We most certainly must challenge ourselves and all other feminists when it comes to the use of women's oppression to advance the cause of war. Have we done our homework by listening to and being guided by the wisdom of our Afghan sisters and other feminists in the region? By not vociferously questioning this war on terrorism, are we representing their interests, needs, and desires or are own? It's clear to me that if we fail to make the connections between the "normalized" homegrown terrorism that distorts and defines women's experience on a daily basis and the terrorism that Bush and company have declared war against, then we allow ourselves to be co-opted.

I hope that you will refuse to be silenced. I have.

ENEMIES, BOTH FOREIGN AND DOMESTIC
Tulsa, 1921 and September 11, 2001
Kimberly C. Ellis

When Vernon Jordan gave the commencement address at Howard University in the Spring of 2002, he issued particular insights eerily appropriate for graduates of an elite, historically Black university. Citing a prolonged history of domestic, racial violence against African American communities throughout the United States, Jordan proclaimed:

> They are not new to us. Slavery was terrorism, segregation was terrorism, the bombing of the four little girls in Sunday School in Birmingham was terrorism. The violent deaths of Medgar, Martin, Malcolm, Vernon, Dahmer, Cheney, Schwerner and Goodman were terrorism. And the difference between September 11th and the terror visited upon Black people is that on September 11th, the terrorists were foreigners. But when we were terrorized, it was by our neighbors. The terrorists were American citizens.[1]

September 11, 2001 was a wake up call for most Americans. Never before had white, male, capitalist society been so painstakingly brought to its knees on American soil. And, although various government pundits censored anyone who dared say that the Islamic militants who committed such acts were not cowards, all eyes were frozen to the television screen by the manner in which the bastion of world exploitation was brought to a stunning halt. Babylon, some said, was finally getting a taste of the terror she had issued throughout the world. Having been temporarily scared straight, mainstream America turned to Ole Faithful—its American Negroes—to sing gospel songs and envelope a spirit of forgiveness, unity and strength. Amazing Grace, the National Anthem, prayer services and Black popular entertainment swept the American landscape faster than Condoleeza Rice could tutor the President.

In May 2002, German magazine *Der Spiegel* reported that at the European Summit, President Bush asked the President of Brazil, the country with the largest African population outside of Africa, "Do you have Blacks here, too ?"[2] Such historical ignorance is typical, not only of a mediocre student with unabashed white privilege, but also of most Americans. Thus, typically absent from mainstream publications, media pundits and water cooler discussions were the reasons why the call upon Black America to provide spiritual leadership and solace during such troubled times had become second nature. Absent still are apologies for slavery and the subsequent century of torture and degradation faced by Africans in America, beginning with the withdrawal of the federal troops and the end of the Reconstruction period in the American South.

Such conversations and references would remain absent except from the marginalized voices of Black American scholars, social and political activists; mainly, but not exclusively, those still seeking reparations for such crimes against humanity. When Congresswoman Barbara Lee issued the only dissenting voice in Congress, to finance an abstract "war on terrorism," she had to acquire police protection twenty-four hours a day; Lee also had to sift through numbers of death threats among her regular business mailings. Much of black America celebrated Barbara Lee's courage and compassion because we knew all too well how abstract a war against "terrorism" is in a country well known for assaulting and terrorizing its own citizens.

But gone from American mainstream discussion were references to such terrorism within its own borders. Instead, Americans were bombarded with war imagery on television, in newspapers and in movie theaters. Regurgitating trite lines of shallow patriotism, President Bush echoed such sentiments with the encouraging, "Let's Roll."

Some Black Americans enjoyed such sentiments of protection from the patriarchal order. Others were far more concerned about an arrogant military posture set to wreak havoc first in Afghanistan and soon across the globe. When would such posturing come full circle and shift its focus upon Black Americans? After all, it was the Black Panther Party for Self-Defense that was listed as "the greatest threat to national security" in America, thereby giving the Federal Bureau of Investigations and the Central Intelligence Agency the freedom to violate the privacy of and terrorize Black Americans. In 1921, the Tulsa race riot provided another opportunity to terrorize under governmental authority.

What is Terrorism?

As African American men continue to be shipped overseas to kill people often referred to as "sand niggers" by White Americans, they will face the same paradox of loyalty that early 20th century African American soldiers faced when they returned home, victorious from World War I, yet were lynched in their uniforms. Having fought against foreign enemies, they would now face their own neighbors-as domestic enemies. This essay on the Tulsa, Oklahoma race riot, war and massacre of 1921, describes the paradox faced by those soldiers to provide a historically relevant lens for viewing the paradox of loyalty that black Americans face today.

> The hand of World War I was felt most keenly here. Our Uncle Sam summoned 250 black boys at one time. These boys did not hesitate, but bravely heeded the call, many never to return to their then-beloved Tulsa. These brave boys gave their lives to make the world safe for democracy. Is it safe? Let Tulsa, the city that suffered thousands of its innocent, law-abiding citizens to be made homeless, answer.[3]

It was a Monday morning, May 30, 1921. When a nineteen year-old, African American, Dick Rowland, headed to the top floor of the Drexel Building at 319 South Main Street in downtown, Tulsa, Oklahoma, it was also "Memorial Day." A shoeshine and delivery boy, Rowland was a high school dropout—a rarity for the Black Tulsa community—who made ends meet shining shoes and delivering packages for the businessmen thriving in what was then known as the "Magic City." But Tulsa was also a Jim Crow city. Thus, Rowland needed to travel to the top floor of the Drexel Building. Upon reaching the elevator, he stepped on the threshold and presumably stumbled upon the foot of the white elevator operator, 17 year old Sarah Page. This, at least, is the common story; but no one really knows what happened on that elevator. Sent to investigate, Walter White, then the National Association for the Advancement of Colored People's Assistant Secretary, provides interesting insight and greater depth than anyone has been able to muster thus far, even in 2002. According to White, Dick Rowland "rang the bell for the elevator" after he had delivered his package to an office in the Drexel building. Then:

The operator, a young white girl, on finding that she had been summoned by a Negro, opened the door of the car ungraciously. Two versions there are of what happened then. The boy declared that she started the car on its downward plunge when he was only halfway in, and that to save himself from being killed he had to throw himself into the car, stepping on the girl's foot in doing so. The girl, on the other hand, asserted that the boy attempted to rape her in the elevator.[4]

Both of these stories are fantastic news for historians because they reveal the extent to which various versions are shaped by social conditioning and biased perceptions. Much of the story is entirely plausible in Jim Crow Tulsa and in the same state that was so proud to be the first to declare its telephone booths segregated.

No matter what happened on that elevator, however, Sarah Page let out a loud enough scream for the white male clerk from Renberg's, the first floor clothing store, to hear her and come running. Jolted and scared, Dick Rowland fled back to Greenwood, the Black residential and business section of Tulsa now popularly referenced as "Black Wall Street." When the Renberg's clerk came upon the "hysterical" Sarah Page, he assumed that she had been sexually assaulted and called the police.[5] There is no record of Sarah Page's testimony to the Tulsa police department, but on the following day, Tuesday, May 31, 1921, Dick Rowland was arrested in Greenwood. After the proper exchange of information without the false interpretations of the clerk (and possibly Sarah Page), the incident could have been easily resolved as a misunderstanding and concluded to be an unfortunate happenstance—but it was not. The racial polarization of Tulsa, mixed with the recent disparaging of Black Tulsa's after hours "choc joints" where Blacks and whites had been found mixing to the sounds of jazz, the taste of spirits and the prohibited explorations of sexuality, made it impossible for the interaction of a Black boy and a white girl (within the confines of a small elevator) to carry anything but an inflammatory interpretation.

Damie Rowland Ford, Dick's grandmother and guardian, quickly hired a white attorney to defend him. As news of the "attempted rape" swept through the barrister's circle, it also swept into the newsrooms of the *Tulsa Tribune* and the *Tulsa World,* two popular newspapers that clearly reflected the racial mores of the times. For this story the *Tulsa Tribune* proved to be more insidious given the opportunity. Having missed the news for the morning edition, the editor ran a front-page story entitled, "Nab Negro for Attacking Girl in Elevator" in which there were descriptions of Dick Rowland's behavior with Sarah Page as, "scratching her hands and face and tearing her clothes."[6] In addition to this front-page article, eyewitnesses say that there was an editorial that ran a few pages into the paper entitled, "To Lynch Negro Tonight." In 1998, hired researchers from the State of Oklahoma Tulsa Race Riot Commission went searching for the microfilm of the *Tribune;* they found that someone had neatly sliced out both the front-page article and nearly all the obviously inflammatory editorial page of the microfilmed reel, thus leaving oral history with the final record.

The *Tribune* paper had run at 4:00 pm in the afternoon and by 7:43 pm, there were already hundreds of whites gathered outside of the Tulsa County Courthouse, where Dick Rowland was being held. According to one of Greenwood's Black political and business leaders, Andrew J. Smitherman, some of them were screaming, "Lynch him, kill him!. . . Let us have the nigger!"[7] Previously, no African American had ever been lynched in Tulsa, although the city did not bear a pristine image in terms of whippings, beatings and other forms of disenfranchisement.

Perhaps adding insult to injury, Dick Rowland's nickname was stated to be "Diamond Dick" and the Tulsa newspapers wasted no time in utilizing his adopted moniker for specious purposes. Such usage was particularly insidious because Dick was only nineteen years old, he was living in the "wild, wild West" and "Diamond Dick" was actually just the rival character to "Deadwood Dick," the hero and namesake of the popular dime novels of the era. Such villainous characterizations were useful to racist Whites already embittered by class envy of even the sight of Blacks thriving, in any manner, in the "Negro's Wall Street" or the "Negro's Broadway of Tulsa," and one of the best Negro business streets in the whole U.S.A.[8] An assault upon a white girl by a "Diamond Dick," played up by the newspapers, was especially incendiary to already envious whites.

As the "lynch-talk" circulated the White Tulsa community and greatly assisted in the formation of the crowd around the courthouse, such talk also reached the Black community in Greenwood. Conversations took place in the Williams Dreamland Theater, up and down commercial streets, in citizens' homes and, without question, in the *Tulsa Star* newspaper office of Andrew J. Smitherman, the editor and owner of Black Tulsa's printed voice.[9] Well-known for advocating armed resistance against lynching in order to uphold the law, Smitherman and others undoubtedly concluded that they must assist the sheriff in securing Dick Rowland's safety and to prevent his lynching. Smitherman, Black war veterans and concerned community men, totaling approximately twenty-five men, traveled down to the courthouse to offer their armed assistance to the Sheriff. As Ellsworth describes:

> Some of the men . . . decided that they could wait no longer. Hopping into cars, small groups of armed African American men began to make brief forays into downtown, their guns visible to passersby. In addition to reconnaissance, the primary intent of these trips appears to have been to send a clear message to white Tulsans that these men were determined to prevent, by force if necessary, the lynching of Dick Rowland. Whether the whites who witnessed these excursions understood this message is, however, an open question. Many, apparently, thought that they were instead witnessing a "Negro uprising," a conclusion that others would soon share.[10]

Most rumors of a Negro uprising would occur because the men chose to fight back following the eruption downtown. They had not gotten to that point yet and were actually seeking to secure peace and justice by demonstrating their willingness to assist the Tulsa police force. Upon their arrival they were told of Rowland's safety and were asked to return to Greenwood.

According to Ellsworth, "the visit of the African American veterans had an electrifying effect, however, on the white mob, now estimated to be more than one thousand strong . . . the visit of the black veterans had not at all been foreseen. [Thus,] shocked, and then outraged, some members of the mob began to go home to fetch their guns."[11] Perhaps some members of the mob were shocked because there had been no previous lynching of Black people in Tulsa. Or, perhaps individual personalities were shocked by some of the familiar faces that were in the crowd of armed veterans and community members.

Whatever the specificity of personal effrontery, this initial crowd of twenty-five armed, Black men would be the ones considered to be the "lawless Negro leaders," "bad niggers" and "black ruffians" responsible for causing the riot.[12]

Long before it had gotten to that point, however, there was hustle and bustle in the Greenwood community. Had it been a normal day in Tulsa, Dick Rowland might have finished shining shoes for the day and been found relaxing in Greenwood. Instead, he was hemmed up in the Tulsa county courthouse surrounded by hundreds of people longing to lynch him. Awareness of the incident occurred at varying levels in Greenwood. Some who had been in the Dreamland Theatre were well aware of the ensuing controversy. Students at Booker T. Washington High School had been preparing for their Spring prom while other youngsters were playing around the schoolhouse and outside their homes. Still others, such as Mary E. Jones-Parrish, an African American school owner and teacher, had been oblivious to the mounting tensions until her daughter called her to look out of the window and see the Black "men with guns." She described in her memoir that:

> Going down stairs to the street, I was told of the threatened lynching and that some of our group were going to give added protection to the boy. I am told that this little bunch of brave and loyal black men who were willing to give their lives, if necessary, for the sake of a fellow man, marched up to the jail where there were already over 500 white men gathered, and that this number was soon swelled to over a thousand.[13]

By 9:30 p.m. the crowd outside of the Tulsa courthouse that had been one thousand had doubled. Among the crowd were men, women, children, ruffians, community leaders, the curious, the enraged, the bloodthirsty and the befuddled. Ellsworth relates that in Greenwood, "possibly spurned on by a false report that whites were storming the courthouse, moments after 10:00 p.m., a second contingent of armed African American men, perhaps seventy-five in number this time, decided to make a second visit to the courthouse."[14] After being rebuffed once again by the Tulsa police and upon leaving a second time, one White man is presumed to have stated to a tall, African American war veteran, "Nigger . . . What are you doing with that pistol? . . . [Y]ou give it to me." When the veteran, who was carrying an army-issued revolver, refused, a tussle ensued and in the midst of the struggle, the gun went off and "a shot rang out." Choc Phillips, a Native American man who passed for White, recalled in his memoirs that some white men had come armed and/or had armed themselves following the Black men's initial visit, and they had been, "holding a rifle or shotgun in one hand, and grasping the neck of a liquor bottle with the other [and] some had pistols stuck into their belts."[15] This initial shot was like yelling "fire" in a theater. The Tulsa race riot began with immediate deaths on both sides. In reality no one is absolutely sure who fired the gun and for what reason, though the speculation discloses much about the city's underlying racial animosity and tension. But essentially every researcher, scholar, journalist and artistic writer who sought to pen the origins of the Tulsa race riot, all point to an initial gunfire shot that set off the first battle and one of the worst race wars in the country's history. Says Ellsworth:

> While the first shot fired at the Courthouse may have been uninten-
> tional, those that followed were not. Almost immediately, members of
> the white mob—and possibly some law enforcement officers—opened
> fire on the African American men, who returned volleys of their own.
> The initial gunplay lasted only a few seconds, but when it was over, an
> unknown number of people—perhaps as many as a dozen—both
> black and white, lay dead or wounded.[16]

Undoubtedly, Smitherman added his own heroic interpretation, praising the Black men without mentioning any of them dying in the initial gunfire. In fact, he lyrically celebrated the deaths of the white mobsters calling them "victims of their hellish lust" as he described the further descension of their humanity:

> Quick they fled in all directions,
> Panic stricken, filled with fear
> Leaving their intended victim
> As the news spread far and near,

> Scattered now in great confusion
> Filled with vengeance all anew
> Leaders of the lynching party
> Planned for something else to do. [17]

The Tulsa race riot was in high gear. Though Smitherman sought in his poem to relay a minor victory in the initial battle, they were still, as Ellsworth relates, "outnumbered more than twenty-to-one [and no matter what occurred initially] the black men began a retreating fight toward the African American district.[18] That retreating fight, of course, was partially a result of the spontaneous mayhem at the courthouse, but also, resistance to a firm resoluteness on the part of the White mobsters to put Black Tulsa back in its place after such "impudence" displayed by those armed Black men. The mob most certainly "left their intended victim" and subsequently "planned for something else to do." The Dick Rowland incident was seen as but a mere excuse to exorcise blackness from the Tulsa community.

After an initial group of White Tulsans had run to their homes or broken into hardware stores to secure ammunition, they attempted to encroach upon Greenwood, engaging in a fierce battle with many of the Black men who had gone down to the courthouse. Black men aligned themselves along the Frisco railroad tracks that separated Black Tulsa from White Tulsa. Their intent was not to commit an offensive against White Tulsans, but to defend the Black community from a racial onslaught.

Given the fact that some of the armed Black men had shot white men dead at the courthouse, all of these Black war veterans, leaders, laymen and even some ruffians and criminals knew that they were greatly outnumbered and that the battle against the white mobsters would be fierce. Despite the likelihood of their deaths, as Claude McKay had written of Black men resisting similar racial onslaughts throughout the Red Summer of 1919, these Black men now in Tulsa had decided to remain, "pressed to the wall, dying but fighting back".[19] Smitherman was particularly proud of their bravery because of the manner in which they had initially resolved to assist the sheriff and stand on the side of justice to protect Dick Rowland; and then later to organize themselves to protect the entire Greenwood community. He describes both individual and communal dialogue to indicate the level of what he considered to be the cowardice the mobsters engaged in versus the bravery the Black defensive team exhibited:

"Ready, Fire!" And then a volley
From the mob whose skins were white
"Give 'em hell, boys" cried the leader,
"Soon we'll put them all to flight."

But they got a warm reception
From black men who had no fear,
Who while fighting they were singing:
"Come on Boys, The Gang's all Here." [20]

The desire to "put them all to flight" was, not only a concoction of Smitherman's imagination, but also a testimony to the resistance against white racial violence across America. Thus, when the Black men gave such incivility and anarchy a "warm reception," they helped change the course of American history forever. Such a history bears witness to the righteous resistance of the Black men and a miraculous victory for law, order, democracy and freedom. Writes Smitherman:

Rapid firing guns were shooting,
Men were falling by the score,
'Till the white men quite defeated
Sent the word "We want no more."

Nine p.m. the trouble started,
Two a.m. the thing was done,
And the victory for the black men
Counted almost four to one.

This passage deals with one of the most controversial, contentious issues surrounding the Tulsa race riot, war and massacre. For some, even acknowledging this version of Tulsa history is completely unacceptable. How could there be a "victory for the black men" when they were so far outnumbered? Although there are both definite and approximate numbers of the death count, this was no video game and there was no way to perform an analysis of how many people had died, where they died and what were the colors of their skin. There are no historians, survivors nor documents that can accurately and fully detail what happened the night of May 31, 1921.

What is Terrorism?

Prior to the discovery of this "Descriptive Poem of the Tulsa Riot and Massacre," written by Smitherman, only circumstantial evidence and third-person narratives were offered to explain the thoughts, intentions, positioning and actions of the armed Black men who defended Greenwood. Smitherman was both an eyewitness account and a willing participant intent on setting the record straight regarding those whom had previously been regarded as "law-less negro leaders." For Smitherman there was simply no question that the Black men who fought and died on the night of May 31st and early morning into June 1st were heroes, not just for Black Americans, but for civilization itself. In his "Eulogy to the Tulsa Martyrs," Smitherman declared that because of their human sacrifice, "the hope of our race looms brighter/and the world has been made some better." Even Smitherman knew that in a white supremacist society, any image of an armed, Black man killing whites and speaking of liberty would never be welcomed with open arms. He also knew that it would be an uphill battle to help "fair-minded, justice-loving white people" to see that, not only was the battle against mob violence a battle for their own safety, but also Black men were intent on eradicating such violence by combating it with their own militancy in order to secure a better quality of life for all humanity.[21]

For the whites who witnessed what occurred at the courthouse at the Frisco railroad tracks, and the sporadic fighting that erupted throughout the city, those intent on "running the Negro out of Tulsa" would soon get their chance to seek revenge for their losses.[22] In the next section of his poem, Smitherman tells of what befell Black Tulsa, despite the valiant efforts of their men of war and their women of rescue:

> Then the whites went into council
> Helping to reprise their loss,
> Planned the massacre that followed,
> Dared to win at any cost.
>
> June the First at five a.m.,
> Three long whistle blasts were heard,
> Giving sign for concert action
> To that cold blood-thirsty herd.

At the signal from the whistle
Aeroplanes were seen to fly,
Dropping bombs and high explosives,
Hell was falling from the sky!

On all sides the mob had gathered
Talking in excited tones,
With machine guns, ready, mounted,
Trained upon a thousand homes

Hark! The sounds of roaring battle
As they charged without relent
Shooting women, men and children,
Plying torches as they went. [23]

The Tulsa race riot and war had turned into an all-out massacre, with people being killed and assaulted indiscriminately. Again, Smitherman promotes the idea that there has been a "loss" by the white men, thus leading them to go "into council" and plot out another manner in which they might "win at any cost." Such "council" matched with the subsequent description of damage may have been hyperbole on Smitherman's part. The details sound hellacious and extreme with the images of airplanes flying and machine guns "trained upon a thousand homes" that the early 20th century mind would have no choice but to dismiss Smitherman's story as exaggeration beyond belief. But scores of stories gathered from eyewitnesses of the massacre repeat much of what Smitherman formed into poetic verse; and provided their own description of the massacre as well:

> After watching the men unload on First Street, where we could see them from our windows, we heard such a buzzing noise that, on running to the door to get a better view of what was going on, the sights our eyes beheld made our poor hearts stand still for a moment. There was a great shadow in the sky and, upon a second look, we discerned that this cloud was

caused by fast approaching aeroplanes. It then dawned upon us that the enemy had organized in the night and was invading our district, the same as Germans invaded France and Belgium. The firing of guns was renewed in quick succession.[24]

It goes on to describe chaotic, horrifying scenes of people rushing from burning homes, running with babies in their arms and fleeing amidst rapid gunfire, some being shot down in the streets.   Carrie Kinlaw described attempting to take her mother to safety and seeing "an aeroplane [shoot] down a man right in [her] path".[25]   Attorney Richard J. Hill, stated that, "In the morning the shooting was more severe in front of our house. The whites were firing on colored who, seemingly unaware of the trouble, were on their way to work and in passing were met with volleys of shot."[26]   A woman who requested that her name be withheld described that, "in the early morning the whites were stationed on the hill with machine guns and high-powered rifles upon our people as they tried to run for safety."[27] A man listed by the name of "A.H." offered his description of the massacre, stating that:

> As daylight approached, they (the Whites) were given a signal by a whistle, and the dirty, cowardly outrage took place. All of this happened while innocent Negroes were slumbering, and did not have the least idea that they would fall victims of such brutality. At the signal of the whistle, more than a dozen aeroplanes went up and began to drop turpentine balls upon the Negro residences, while the 5,000 Whites, with machine guns and other deadly weapons, began firing in all directions. Negro men, women and children began making haste to flee safety, but to no avail, as they were met on all sides with volleys of shot. Negro men, women and children were killed in great numbers as they ran, trying to flee for safety.[28]

Not all "Negroes were slumbering" and at least 75 men in Tulsa had been well aware of the odds they were facing and chose to stay and fight. A.H.'s testimony seems most appalling in describing the massacre. Another community member testified anonymously that, "As one woman was running from her home, she suddenly fell with a bullet wound. Then I saw aeroplanes, they flew very low. To my surprise, as they passed over the business district they left the entire block a mass of flame . . . Tuesday night, May 31st , was the riot, and Wednesday morning, by daybreak, was the invasion".[29] Story after story and witness after witness attest to the destruction of Greenwood mostly from the ground but also in the air.

Law and Disorder: The Aftermath

It was with the assistance of the "special deputies" and, presumably, the Tulsa Home Guard units that so much of Greenwood was damaged and so many people killed. Interviewed by Mary Parrish shortly after the riot, the testimony of E.A. Loupe, a plumber and resident of Greenwood, corroborates accusations verified decades later:

> Most people, like myself, stayed in their homes, expecting momentarily to be given protection by the Home Guards or State Troops, but instead of protection by the Home Guards they (the Home Guards) joined in with the hoodlums in shooting at good citizens' homes. This was my experience, so after seeing no protection from them, I took my family and a few friends in my car and drove four miles into the country where we were gathered up by State Troops who were perfect gentlemen and treated us like citizens of real America.[30]

The National Guard units (described as State Troops by local Tulsans) had yet to arrive in Tulsa and hours still before they would be able to bring back law and order. The State Troops or National Guard must be differentiated from the local Home Guard units who were co-conspirators with Tulsa police officers, "special deputies" and White civilians in the destruction of Greenwood. What remains clear is that despite the tally of certifications and credentials amongst the Home Guards, war veterans and the Tulsa police, Black Tulsans received little to no protection from and were often victimized by them.

In the meantime, the civilian, "special deputies" began disarming and arresting Black men in droves, physically abusing or killing anyone who did not comply. Once in the hands of local police officers or "special deputies," the arrested men were marched through the streets of Tulsa with their hands held high in the air, in full surrender, prior to being searched and sent into McNulty Baseball Park or Convention Hall. Once thousands of Black men and women were arrested and held within the detention camps, the white rioters brought a whole new meaning to the idea of a "free market economy." Here, Smitherman tells of the looting that followed the mass arrest of Black men and women:

> In the meantime rabid hoodlums
> Now turned loose without restraint
> Helped themselves to things of value,
> More than useless to complain.
>
> Guns were taken by the hundreds,
> Ammunition all in sight,
> Reign of murder, theft and plunder
> Was the order of the night. [31]

Although this passage clearly describes the subsequent looting of the "Negro's Wall Street," it effectively indicts the mobsters as being far more than upset about an alleged assault upon a white woman or the fact that armed Black men showed up at the courthouse. The victims of "theft and plunder" provided testimony that offers substantial validity towards the notion that some white Tulsans envied and coveted the material possessions gained by Black Tulsans and, if nothing else, wanted to ensure that Black men and women would no longer maintain ownership over their property. When Dr. R.T. Bridgewater returned to his home on June 1st, what he found was horrifying. He describes the scene as follows:

> "I came by my home to see if it was destroyed and to get my medicine cases. On reaching the house I saw my piano and all of my elegant furniture piled in the street. My safe had been broken open, all of the money stolen, also my silverware, cut glass, all of the family clothing and everything of value had been removed, even my family Bible. My electric light fixtures

148

were broken, all the window lights and glass in the doors were broken, the dishes that were not stolen were broken, the floors were covered (literally speaking) with glass, even the phone was torn from the wall. In the basement we gathered two tubs of broken glass from off the floor. My car was stolen and most of my large rugs were taken. I lost seventeen houses that paid me an average of over $425 per month.[32]

An anonymous eyewitness implicated white women in the mayhem, describing that, "After they had the homes vacated, one bunch of whites would come in and loot. Even women with shopping bags would come in, open drawers, take every kind of finery from clothing to silverware and jewelry. Men were carrying out the furniture, cursing as they did so, saying, "These d__ Negroes have better things than lots of white people."[33] The listing of crimes echoes, in a much more detailed manner, the "theft and plunder" Smitherman describes in his poem and the results of such mayhem. Forty-one blocks of homes and businesses were completely destroyed, miles of charred soil marked the civility of Tulsa and thousands would remain homeless well into the winter. Millions of dollars of damage was the result and few people would recoup their losses, since all of the insurance companies pointed to the "riot clause" in their contracts. Thus, as Smitherman relates:

When at last the fight was over,
Might not right had won the day,
Blocks of homes and business places
Now in ruins and ashes lay. [34]

Martial law was declared in Tulsa on June 1, 1921 at 11:29 a.m., more than fourteen hours from the approximate time at which the first shot was fired and more than five hours from the time at which the full-fledged, white, riotous onslaught had begun. Unlike the behavior of the Tulsa Police Department and the local Home Guard, the National Guard units were considered to have ushered in law and order, disarming whites, closing businesses, issuing a seven o'clock curfew for everyone else to be indoors.[35] This order did not include most African Americans in any practical manner, however, because many had already been disarmed and/or arrested. This was the resulting paradox from the arrival of the National Guard, the declaration of martial law and the restoration of law and order.

Despite the fact that Black Tulsans and the Black men who had resisted the onslaught had been "greatly outnumbered" by thousands of whites, it was Black Tulsa who was put under mass arrest and could not leave the baseball park, fairgrounds and Convention Hall in which they were being held unless they were vouched for by a white employer. The irony, of course, is that many of them had no white employers from whom they might receive assistance, as they were self-employed. In yet another example of adding insult to injury, Black men were specifically asked to clean up the ruins of the Greenwood district for a paltry sum per hour. When not a single volunteer came forward over the course of a day or two following the offer, any Black men who did not have former employment were forced to clean up the district with *no pay*, thereby effectively reducing those already imprisoned to a condition of enslavement.[36]

In addition, there were many who could not leave even if they wanted. An exceedingly increasing number of Black Tulsans were sick, dying and/or in critical condition, unable to get the full kind of assistance they needed and grateful for the Red Cross "angels of mercy" who did as much as they could to treat their wounds.[37] Similarly, there was a humanely spirited element that existed throughout Tulsa among both individual and collective bodies of people who also assisted as "angels of mercy".[38] Without question, the Red Cross brought a tremendous amount of relief to the sick, horrified and/or wounded. Both Black and White doctors, nurses and others volunteered to assist in every manner they could, using the Booker T. Washington High School as another hospital ward. Echoing Smitherman's description was Parrish's eyewitness testimony upon entering the makeshift ward:

> I can never erase the sights of my first visit to the hospital. There were men wounded in every conceivable way, like soldiers after a big battle. Some with amputated limbs, burned faces, others minus an eye or with heads bandaged. There were women who were nervous wrecks, and some confinement cases. Was I in a hospital in France? No, in Tulsa.[39]

The American Red Cross assisted from June 1 through the winter, finally closing its disaster relief work center on December 31, 1921, leaving behind the Maurice Willows Hospital.[40] But the spirit that had initially encouraged lynching and mob violence did not die in the ruins of the Greenwood ashes.

One of the first incidents to exemplify the resilience of the lynching spirit after the riot, war and massacre, emerged where it had begun—in the Tulsa newspapers. The "Reconstruction Commission" organized, purportedly, to assist in dispersing money, clothing and other resources to assist Black Tulsans, had consistently refused outside aid, creating the illusion that they were effectively caring for the victims in Tulsa themselves. Further, the Tulsa city commission passed a fire ordinance on June 7, 1921 that created strenuous obstacles in the path of those who wished to rebuild on their land. Quickly following the passing of the ordinance were more newspaper articles celebrating the availability of open landscape from the charred area, inviting investors to consider the area for a potential industrial center.[41] Such occurrences provide circumstantial evidence to the land conspiracy claim that there was far more to the riot than the spark surrounding the Dick Rowland incident. Whether or not some White Tulsans plotted a conspiracy before the riot, it was most certain that following the riot, a mad rush for Greenwood land ensued. This tactic was foreshadowed when Mrs. Rosetta Moore confided to Mary Parrish that during the riot, "Old and young had to pile on trucks and when we were being driven through town, men were seen clapping their hands, rejoicing over our condition." Similarly, this idea was later reinforced by an inscription on a picture found by the State Commission describing the destruction of Greenwood as "running the negro out of Tulsa."[42] Many so-called Negroes *did* leave Tulsa, never to return, including the poet Andrew J. Smitherman. No matter how much of Greenwood was rebuilt following the riot, the city— and America—had been changed forever; and there would always be those without recompense for their suffering.

Whatever happened to the spark that caused such an explosion? Although mystery continues to surround what type of relationship Dick Rowland had with Sarah Page (if any) and what actually occurred on the elevator, Rowland was never charged with any crime and Sarah Page later testified that he had not accosted her in any manner.[43] The grand jury left no question that despite the evidence, the weight of the Tulsa travesty would have to lay upon the shoulders of the Black men who armed themselves, came down to the courthouse and sought to prevent Dick Rowland's lynching stating that:

> We find that the recent race riot was the direct result of an effort on the part of a certain group of colored men who appeared at the courthouse on the night of May 31, 1921 . . . [but] the crowd assembled about the courthouse being purely spectators and curiosity seekers resulting from rumors circulated about the city . . . . There was no mob spirit among the whites, no talk of lynching and no arms. The assembly was quiet until the arrival of armed Negroes, which precipitated and was the direct cause of the entire affair.[44]

In addition to blaming the victims, Black Tulsa's fearless heroes would be criminalized as the justification for white racial violence and the re-appropriation of land.

Nevertheless, Andrew J. Smitherman found it important to call upon "higher laws" that superceded the narratives scripted in the Tulsa newspapers and the conclusions stated by the legalese of the Grand Jury. For Smitherman America as a whole had to be weighed in the balance:

> You have heard the awful story,
> How it made the world see red,
> When the Huns invaded Belgium
> On the strength of might, 'tis said.
>
> But such crimes against the Negro
> In these proud United States,
> Meet the plaudits of the masses
> Even burnings at the stakes.
>
> Tulsa with her teeming millions
> Paid the toll for racial strife,
> But her black men won a victory
> With their blood they paid the price.

Nobly they had stopped a lynching,
Taught a lesson for all time,
Saved a man the Court had since found
Innocent of any crime

Though they fought the sacrificial
Fright, with banners flying high,
Yet the thing of more importance
Is the way they fought—and why![45]

He and others chose to leave a different narrative and a legacy of resistance for anyone interested in understanding the larger causes of the Tulsa race riot, war and massacre and, perhaps most importantly, the commitment to democracy and a just law, that could serve the people and help prevent such a disaster in the future.

Contemporary Implications

Neither Smitherman's words, nor the legacy he sought to leave are given high priority in the telling of the Tulsa story in 1921. In fact, the mysteries surrounding the role of the armed, Black men who went down to the courthouse and engaged in the subsequent rioting and warfare, in addition to the resulting conspiracy and culture of silence created after the riot, begged for this closer examination of the related Africana narratives. Numerous scholarly works have attempted to retell the story of the Tulsa tragedy.[46] It was not until the 1995 bombing of the Oklahoma City federal building, with a push from Oklahoma legislators Don Ross and Maxine Horner, that the Commission to Study the Tulsa Race Riot of 1921 was created. As a result of the contributions of those on the Commission, a voluminous amount of evidence has been uncovered. There are still, however, a number of voids in this story; and the various misinterpretations by those who contributed to the final report are cause for serious alarm, particularly since such a report is seen as "official" and the case closed. The case is not closed at all. This author's dissertation, on which this essay is based, serves to fill that void and render a new understanding of the psychology, actions and resulting narrative of those

Africana men who chose to be men of war, physically, legally, lyrically, scholastically and spiritually engaging the system of white supremacy, as a threat to American democracy and to civilization itself.

What occurred in Tulsa was no aberration. The racial violence and destruction of Africana communities across the country swept across the nation throughout the entire late nineteenth and early twentieth centuries. Having survived such white American, riotous assaults throughout history, the Africana experience in America holds special meaning in the quest for freedom.

When Americans of all hues were stunned into prioritizing the value of human life over fast food, football, the stock market and crossover hip hop on September 11th, the psychological need to call upon Black America was instantaneous because the strength, resilience, courage and spiritually renewing capacity of those who have suffered the ills of terrorist attacks remains a part of the American historical landscape no matter how often such experiences go unrecognized. Black America has always known that one must affirm one's humanity even in the midst of inhumanity and embrace the fullness of life, even whilst others seek to take it away. On September 11th, all eyes were on New York and Washington. Shortly after, the movement for reparations for such tragedy was essentially immediate. Within weeks, plans had been drawn up to compensate for the loss of life, the loss of corporate stability and the loss of "innocence."

White Americans cannot imagine that anyone could tell them to "just get over" September 11th eighty years from now. Yet this is precisely what happened when African Americans sought to engage with and heal from the Tulsa tragedy that was swept from the front pages of the newspapers when all eyes were on the city in 1921—and remained hidden from history for over 80 years. To date proper reconciliation and compensation for such losses have remained unpaid and the framework for memorials and the redevelopment of the business district has received little more than lip service. Such benign neglect would never occur in New York in this same manner.

As Vernon Jordan related in the commencement address to Howard students, terrorism is not and was not "new to us." The fact that American citizens committed such atrocities against their own neighbors is also not something new. When Barbara Lee and other conscientious citizens were threatened, terrorized and called "unpatriotic" for exercising their rights to freedom of speech and in seeking a balance to Presidential powers, that was not new either.

What would be new for America, however, would be the opportunity to learn from the history of its Africana people here and use such lessons to ensure that all of humanity benefit from the quest for freedom and the drive for self-determination.

From a song that Sweet Honey in the Rock sings, "It will only be until the killing of Africana peoples all over the world is as important as the killing of white peoples all over the world" (realizing that the terror inflicted upon one group is easily the terror afflicted in return), that we might find some peace. It stands as both a testament and a challenge that, "we who believe in freedom cannot rest." The sincere struggle for these ideals can make America new again, and can make us truly neighbors, both foreign and domestic.

Notes

1. Washington NNPA
2. James Carville on "Crossfire", CNN, May 30, 2002
3. Mary E. Jones-Parrish, *Race Riot 1921:Events of the Tulsa Disaster* (Tulsa: Out on a Limb Publishing, 1998), 11.
4. Walter White, "I Investigate Lynchings" in *American Mercury* 16 no. 61, January 1929, 83
5. Scott Ellsworth, "The Tulsa Race Riot" in The Tulsa Race Riot of 1921 Final Report Submitted to the State of Oklahoma (Oklahoma City: State of Oklahoma Commission to Study the Tulsa Race Riot, February 28, 2001), 77; Walter White, "The Eruption of Tulsa" in *The Nation*, June 29, 1921, 1.
6. Ellsworth, "The Tulsa Race Riot," 80.
7. Andrew J. Smitherman, "The Tulsa Race Riot and Massacre," (NAACP Papers, 1922), 1; Tulsa World, June 1, 1921, "Final Edition" 1, 8; Ellsworth, "The Tulsa Race Riot" 84; Walter White, "The Eruption of Tulsa," 1.
8. David Hamilton Murdoch, *The American West: The Invention of a Myth* (Reno: University of Nevada Press, 2001), 52; Parrish, *Race Riot 1921*, 17; "Statement of A.H.", Parrish, *Race Riot 1921*, 63.
9. Parrish, 99-101; Letter from Walter White to Morefield Storey January 16, 1922 (Schomburg Center for Research in Black Culture, New York Public Library, New York).
10. Ellsworth, "The Tulsa Race Riot," Final Report, 62.
11. Ellsworth, "Scholar's Report," 87.
12. *Tulsa Daily World*, June 2, 1921; "Tulsa's Job," *The Tulsa Tribune*, June 2, 1921.
13. Parrish, *Race Riot 1921*, 18.
14. Ellsworth, "Scholar's Report," 63.
15. Choc Phillips, Unpublished Memoir, Tulsa Race Riot Collection, Tulsa Historical Society, Tulsa, Oklahoma.
16. Ellsworth, "Scholar's Report," 63; Walter White, "The Eruption of Tulsa," 1; Tulsa World, June 1, 1921, "Final Edition," 1.
17. Smitherman, "The Tulsa Riot and Massacre," 2.

18. Ellsworth, "Scholar's Report," 63.
19. Claude McKay, "If We Must Die," *Claude McKay: Rebel Sojourner in the Harlem Renaissance* by Wayne F. Cooper(Baton Rouge: Louisiana State University Press, 1987), 99-101.
20. Smitherman, "The Tulsa Riot and Massacre," 2.
21. Andrew J. Smitherman, "How Tulsa Has Treated the Negroes Since The Riot," *The Boston Herald* January 15, 1922, 60.
22. Anonymously inscribed picture of Tulsa ruins, Greenwood Cultural Center; Tulsa Race Riot Collection, McFarlin Library, Tulsa, Oklahoma, June 1, 1921.
23. Smitherman, "The Tulsa Riot and Massacre," 2.
24. Parrish, *Race Riot 1921*, 20.
25. Carrie Kinlaw in Parrish, *Race Riot 1921*, 51.
26. Robert T. Hill in Parrish, *Race Riot 1921*, 41.
27. Name withheld by request, Parrish, *Race Riot 1921*, 55.
28. A.H. in Parrish, *Race Riot 1921*, 62.
29. Name withheld by request, Parrish, *Race Riot 1921*, 65.
30. E.A. Loupe, "Fourteen Years in Tulsa," in Parrish, *Race Riot 1921*, 49.
31. Smitherman, "The Tulsa Riot and Massacre," 2.
32. Dr. R.T. Bridgewater, in Parrish, *Race Riot 1921*, 45.
33. Name withheld by Request in Parrish *Race Riot 1921*, 53.
34. Smitherman, "The Tulsa Riot and Massacre," p2.
35. Parrish, *Race Riot 1921* 24-25
36. *The Tulsa Daily World, The Tulsa Tribune*, June 2-5 1921.
37. "My Experience in Tulsa", Parrish, *Race Riot 1921*, 23.
38. A number of different stories in Mary Parrish's *Race Riot 1921* and in Scott Ellsworth's "The Tulsa Race Riot of 1921," discuss White Tulsans taking Black Tulsans into their homes for protection and vouching for them as employers even if they were not actually their employers. One Mexican woman is said to have saved a Black boy from being shot in the street. A number of Black Tulsans describe saving other Black Tulsans via warnings, shelter, rides or other various forms of assistance. And following the disaster, countless White Tulsans contributed food, clothing, shelter and money to offset the extensive damage suffered by Black Tulsans.
39. "The Emergency Hospital" in Parrish, *Race Riot 1921*, 29.

40. The role of the Red Cross is discussed extensively in Bob Hower, "Angels of Mercy": The American Red Cross and the 1921 Tulsa Race Riot; "American Red Cross," in Parrish, *Race Riot 1921*; Ellsworth, *Death in a Promised Land*; Ellsworth, "Scholar's Report" and in Ellsworth, "The Tulsa Race Riot of 1921."
41. *The Tulsa Tribune*, June 7, 1921; Parrish, *Race Riot 1921*, 58.
42. Mrs. Rosetta Moore in Parrish, *Race Riot 1921*, 42.
43. Smitherman, "The Tulsa Riot and Massacre," 3; White, "The Eruption of Tulsa," 2.
44. *The Tulsa Daily World*, June 26, 1921, 1, 8.
45. Smitherman, "The Tulsa Riot and Massacre," 3.
46. See Kaye M. Teall, *Black Oklahoma History* (Oklahoma City, Oklahoma Public Schools, 1972), Richard Halliburton, The Tulsa Race War, Ellsworth, Death in a Promised Land and the State of Oklahoma Commission, The Tulsa Race Riot of 1921, Final Report.

WHERE WERE YOU WHEN THE REVOLUTION WAS TELEVISED?

Reginna A. Green

Having the "Where Were You _____?" conversation is an activity that has value precisely because of its universal applicability. That universality simultaneously makes it easy to pose the question; yet somehow makes asking it in bars or at parties seem inappropriate. We are not really interested in where our cubicle mate was when Reagan was shot, or Kennedy or King. We care about the actual moment. The conversations we have about those moments in our nation's history that hold captive our hearts and heads we have because despite the horror of a President's assassination or an aerial attack on Hawaii, now our 50th state, the unity that always followed-however brief-was awesome. At those moments, everyone in America had something in common. We did not all have the same reaction, but everyone's reactions were sharp. When baseball fans pretend we care about our neighbor's whereabouts the day Nolan Ryan pitched a record seventh career no-hitter, we, like those who ask, "where were you on September 11th?", are actually seeking common ground, a connectedness, a unity derived from that moment.

"Where were you on September 11, 2001?"

African American Unity and Cohesion

The common ground, connectedness and unity Americans of all races, sexes, colors and creeds sought immediately following the terrorist attacks of September 11th was especially needed, to hear political scientists tell it. Robert Putnam, in his landmark work, *Bowling Alone: America's Declining Social Capital,* identified and addressed a marked decreased in Americans' social and civic interaction in recent years. For example, folks in Buffalo might tell you that over the past few years membership in bowling leagues has dropped. In the south, Junior League chapters may report that membership has plummeted. All over the country, for sure, fewer and fewer parents regularly attend PTA meetings and hold potluck dinners.

159

What is Terrorism?

I remember watching the evening news on the days immediately following the attacks. Almost daily it seemed, a news reporter was in a grocery store or at the post office, asking folks how they were handling the tragedy. Often, people reported that they were going to take a short family vacation-or have that potluck dinner, family game night or neighborhood barbecue. On Halloween, parents reported that they would be spending the night in with their kids. On Thanksgiving, families suggested that the dinner at Grandma's house this year would be huge. I remember thinking it peculiar that it would take a tragedy like 9/11 for families and communities to renew the familial and community bonds that had been weakened by time binds created by long school hours, long work hours and multiple jobs with multiple responsibilities.

I found it peculiar because the African-American community had always been a closely-knit one, historically because of a lack of opportunities outside of it. When mainstream banks refused to lend to African American borrowers, they instead went to the more affluent among them to borrow money (these days, those of us who are unable to get loans at prime rates from mainstream lenders are forced into nefarious loan schemes that, were it possible, could probably draw blood from a stone). My parents actually remember segregation and they frequently speak of the fact that back then, every black teacher entered the classroom knowing that every black child could learn. The books may have been old and the ceiling crumbling, but even the schools were home to a strong sense of community and purpose. The institutional racism blacks in America have suffered for hundreds of years has forced us to create an alternative world, indeed, a bifurcation of our selves: the white world that discriminates, punishes, marginalizes and ignores and the black world that comforts, soothes, protects and cares. This is why old, black communities are almost always home to a multitude of churches. Georgetown, one of Washington, D.C.'s tonier sections that now are mostly white, was once a vibrant black neighborhood. This explains why it's difficult to walk two blocks without passing a place of worship. The reason for all of this is clear; no one knows spiritual renewal like the descendants of slaves. This is why black gospel music is popular among more than just black folks. Though I rarely attend church, I know I am always welcome at my father's church and the church of my childhood, Bethesda Missionary Baptist in Georgetown,

South Carolina. I would probably be welcome at any other black church in America, for that matter. To be sure, there are times when I feel like I must go, to hear the gospel that sits in compact disc players across the nation, to hear the kind of preaching that has made Bishop T.D. Jakes a household name and, perhaps, just to be around people who believe.

I do have a slight problem with black America's position as America's spiritual savior during this crisis. While we may be the nation's immediate reference on spiritual matters, and rightly so, what about our contributions to the discussion unrelated to faith and spiritual renewal? To be sure, African American voices need to be heard on public health concerns, public safety, racial profiling, defense and homeland security spending and all the other myriad issues that have come to the fore since 9/11. It is simultaneously flattering and frustrating to see African Americans enclosed in this spirituality box. However, this stereotyping is not unexpected. The racism fueling our paradox of loyalty is the same racism that encloses us in the role of America's spiritual leader. We can and should be voices of vision, clarity and inclusion on issues beyond faith and strength. Can the obvious lack of black voices post 9/11 fuel a stronger commitment to newsroom and newscast diversity? Perhaps. The truth remains, however: no one knows unity and spiritual renewal like the descendants of slaves. Indeed, Kwanzaa, the celebration of the culture and history of African Americans and other Africans of the Diaspora, is traditionally also a time of bonding with families and communities. It is particularly telling that on the first night of seven, we celebrate the principle of *umoja*, or unity. On the last night, we celebrate *imani*, or faith.

"Where were you on September 11, 2001?"

The unity and cohesion that has been a trademark of the African American community has now, however ephemerally, enraptured America to a degree. While there are those among us who disagree with our country's "war on terrorism," who among us can say that we are not affected by it and the attacks of which it was borne? It took a terrorist attack for us to realize that the next day is never promised. It took the perpetrators mere minutes to wreak havoc on a nation. It took seconds before we sought solace in each other. It took hours for us to turn to black America for guidance during this tragedy- and with good reason.

Plenty of black intellectuals have noted that terrorism is not new to African Americans. How else could one describe the arrival of slave ships in

West Africa and the start of a practice that qualified as nothing short of the hunting of humans? How else could one describe Rosewood in 1923? The Tulsa race riots in 1921? Watts in 1965? Los Angeles in 1992? Cincinnati in 2002?

"Where were you when the "Black Wall Street" burned to the ground?"
"Where were you when hundreds fled Rosewood, Florida?"
"Where were you when Emmett Till hung like strange fruit from a tree in Mississippi?"
"Where were you when Cheney, Schwerner and Goodwin were murdered?"
"Where were you the first time L.A. burned? Where were you the second?"

The fires this time were in New York. In Pennsylvania. In Virginia. African Americans had already seen the fires in Los Angeles, in Florida and in Oklahoma. This does not mean we were prepared for September 11, 2001. It does not mean we were not shocked, mortified and disgusted. It instead means that we knew how to react. It's always easier to get somewhere when you've been there before. No doubt this is part of the reason African Americans possess a cohesion that is the envy of the world: a search for comfort always follows tragedy. Since we have seen tragedy like no other group on these shores at the hands of those with power, it makes sense that we seek solace within ourselves, our families and our communities. Comfort follows tragedy, remember? "Where were you on September 11, 2001?"

Was the Revolution Televised?

At my Columbia, South Carolina high school, seniors were required to give "senior speeches" on a topic of their choosing at our Friday assemblies. I was alphabetically scheduled to give my speech on Friday, November 24, 1995. Because I had had my first "Where Were You _____?" moment two weeks earlier, on the occasion of Israeli Prime Minister Yitzhak Rabin's assassination, I felt that I needed to speak about that man, this world and the peace he tried to bring to it. The following Monday, I politely requested to switch speech dates with Harriett Gettys because she was to speak on November 10th, the Friday immediately following Rabin's death. On the 10th, I stood before my classmates, certain that most of them probably did not find in the assassination a source of unity, cohesion, and connectedness. That morning, Friday, November 10, 1995, I crackled with the energy of a speech worth giving. My voice cracked with the weight of a dispute far older than me as I spoke of the Middle East peace process through frowning lips and salty tears. I eventually crumbled. I had never heard the gymnasium so quiet. I had never experienced 250 people watching my eyes and my mouth, waiting in silence for words to come out. Who did I think I was, talking about the Middle East peace process and the death of an Israeli statesman to 250 over-privileged Christians in South Carolina? Suddenly the moment and, indeed, my presence seemed a bit absurd. I was confused and embarrassed, and still emotional as I spoke about the words my mother scrawled in a journal the year I was born: "September 17, 1978: peace in the Middle East possible?" This was the date the Camp David Peace Accord was signed. The tears came and went. So did the speech. My guidance counselor told me to expand it into an essay. Then she said I "would have to work on controlling the tears."

After my first "Where Were You —?" moment, I wrote a speech. I write this essay with September 11, 2001—my last, but certainly not final life changing moment in mind. What are the similarities? What are the differences? Many believed that peace in the Middle East would cease to be possible following Rabin's assassination. They were the cynics among us and it appears that they were right. What do we believe about our nation post-9/11?

Could we believe that 9/11 was the beginning of our own revolution?

Will the feelings of unity and patriotism in the wake of 9/11 fuel a commitment to racial harmony or an end to the proliferation of the prison industrial complex? Will we make sure that the workers displaced by the terrorist attacks can still feed their families six months from now?

Can leftist voices of dissent to the "war on terrorism" triumph in the court of public opinion? Can we build on the realization that official U.S. foreign policy, as well as our unofficial Goliath complex, did indeed have a hand in last year's attacks? Biblically speaking, we did "deserve" what happened if you believe the "eye for an eye, tooth for a tooth" maxim. That does not mean I think it should have. Post-9/11, scores of black progressives immediately invoked the words of Malcolm X, suggesting that America's "chickens had come home to roost," a phrase mentioned in other essays in this volume. Instantly, I could see their point. A free society encourages, perhaps requires even, a degree of responsibility for one's actions. What are we if not a free society? Then why can we not acknowledge the pain and destruction our actions have caused across the globe for decades? Moreover, what will be the long-term effects of the 9/11 attacks on the American psyche? After all, *it still affects the survivors' psyche everyday.* Can the entire nation take a page out of black America's manual for life, namely the pages about unity, connectedness and support?

"Where Were You on September 11, 2001?"

On the morning of September 11, 2001 I walked into work with the proverbial spring in my step. It was a gorgeous morning. I had on comfortable shoes. Au Bon Pain had not yet run out of the crème de fleurs of which they appear to only make fifteen on any given day. It was my fourth day at my new job located a block away from the White House. The day seemed — even then, but certainly in retrospect—almost suspiciously placid, peaceful and just.

Later that morning I walked out, but this time the aura of placidity and calm had been replaced by clouds of smoke and terror.

On the morning of September 11, 2001 at 8:30 a.m. I was sitting on a Metro train, the Green line to Gallery Place/Chinatown. At 8:36 I was standing on the Red line train to Metro Center. At 8:41 I was in line at Au Bon Pain, getting impatient with the woman before me who chose to pay, very slowly and very carefully, for her banana and bagel with what appeared to be pennies. I sighed repeatedly, shifted my weight from one leg to the other and made conspiratorial eye contact with the people unfortunate enough to be behind us both. By 8:52 I was at my desk. At 8:53 I received a message from a friend in midtown Manhattan. "The weirdest thing just happened. A fucking plane hit the World Trade Center."

I blinked.

"What? That is weird" was all that initially fled across my mind. I did not immediately think about the hundreds who could—indeed, would—die. I did not immediately think "sneak attack" as some who were alive on December 7, 1941 may have. I certainly did not immediately think "terrorists!" My immediate thought was "The World Trade Center? Jesus. Those poor people! They were just bombed in 1993." Shortly thereafter, the second plane hit the second tower. Then the gestalt of half-baked thoughts and prejudices in my brain held hostage any true cognition of events.

"We're under attack."

After United Airlines flight 175 and American Airlines flight 11 crashed on the morning of September 11, 2001 and I was still sitting at my desk, I tried in vain to find any source of news as to what was transpiring in Manhattan, which would by midmorning clearly be the most devastated of the terrorists' targets; I only knew what I could learn from quick and dirty e-mails from friends in the city as phone circuits were busy and internet servers down. Were people hobbling uptown? Were there people trapped in the Holland tunnel? Were people trekking across the Brooklyn Bridge to get home? Soon the phone at my desk was ringing and my e-mail box was flooding. The third plane had struck the Pentagon, less than a mile from my desk. I ran down the hall through our conference room and to our balcony.

I saw the smoke. There were no mirrors. This was for real.

Then I was clueless about New York and Arlington both. I had no idea what was happening in Manhattan, but also I had no idea what was transpiring one mile south of me either. Where was the Pentagon hit? Were people trekking across the Key Bridge to get home? When am I going to get to go home? The last place I wanted to be was with my coworkers. At that moment—with the knowledge of the World Trade Center and the view of the Pentagon—I cried. I cried because the United States had walked all over this earth and expected no retribution. I cried because whoever was responsible for the day's grievous attack on humanity had played dirty and found it acceptable as this nation has done repeatedly throughout history. I cried because the United States has stood at the intersections of greed and welfare, the environment and globalization, starvation and over-consumption for years, and so many times has perpetrated egregiously unjust acts against others just to guarantee that the road most traveled is the road we paved. At that moment — for one moment — I was ashamed to be human.

However, the shame need not be permanent. The United States and its citizens can learn from this tragedy. We can renew our commitments to each other, to our communities and to our children. We can practice true diplomacy. We can respect the people of foreign lands and welcome the contributions they make to our society. If there is a silver lining to the cloud of terrorism this country has witnessed, suffered and survived, it is that perhaps our community and civic engagement has strengthened. It could possibly be that we believe; believe that we can be renewed, believe that we must be strong and believe that we should not be the big bullies on the playground of the world just because we are strong. We might believe that we can indeed depend on, care for and learn from each other. We might even believe in lofty notions like universal health care, gay marriage and universal family and medical leave, the necessities of which became obvious post-9/11.

Gil Scott-Heron is a mighty fine musician, but he was not a soothsayer. I believe the revolution was televised on September 11, 2001. It just wasn't ours. Still, we can decide what we will do with someone else's revolution. We can choose to ignore the realities terrorists brought to light. Or we can embrace the knowledge and use it to reinvent our relationships with each other and the world.

We will continue to ask each other "Where were you on September 11, 2001?" And while we now have "Where Were You _____?" conversations with dates and times filling in the blanks, our children may fill in the blanks with concepts.

"Where were you when America was reborn?"

CHAPTER SIX

This Land Was Made for You and Me

THIS LAND WAS MADE FOR YOU AND ME

This land is your land
This land is our land
From the redwood forest
To the golden highland,
This land was made for you and me.

Back in my girlhood, I sang this folk song around camp fires without really thinking about what the words meant. Who is this land made for, exactly? Who did our nation's founders actually steal it from? Does domestic public policy serve all of us, that inclusive "we" known as "the people"? Or have we developed selective policy that serves some to the detriment of others? Writers in this section look, in many ways, at the concept of shared status and the ways that domestic public policy hits us unevenly.

The actor and activist Danny Glover speaks of the death penalty in "this great nation of ours" and rejects it as a solution to crime and violence. Like Congresswoman Barbara Lee, he paid for his views with some measure of public censure, but Glover's activist roots were stronger than the water of right-wing disapproval. Laura Murphy dissects the notion that racial profiling will make us all safer, focusing on the many ways that racial profiling increases oppression in a post 9/11 world.

As a member of a group of African American leaders who meet twice a year to contemplate the ways we engage in the world, I have participated in the development of a series of concepts called "The Ethics of Sharing". One of our key principles is that of shared status, the notion that hierarchies are divisive and disruptive and that there is a moral component to the ways that we value others in comparison to the ways we value ourselves.

Who is this land made for? The concept of shared status demands that we claim it for every single human being everywhere on the planet, not just rich, privileged, media-enhanced Americans.

— J.M.

Danny Glover, a former Black Panther, an anti-death penalty activist and Chairman of TransAfrica Forum, makes the connection between the illegitimacy of the death penalty in America and the U.S. government's seemingly unlawful incarceration of individuals of Middle Eastern, South Asian and Arab descent that followed in the wake of last year's terrorist attacks in this speech originally given at Princeton University in November of 2001. The speech is brief, but the message clear. In a way much similar to our use of the death penalty, we have embarked on an unclear path with our launch of the war on terrorism. Just as we know the death penalty is not a deterrent to crime and just as we know innocents have died at its hands, we do not know of the numbers of potential casualties in this war on terrorism, and yet we continue to fight. We dismiss civil liberties momentarily because they are bothersome and an impediment to this vague war. Aside from knowing we are definitely hunting for Osama bin Laden, the rest of the WANTED list of the war on terrorism reads like a dragnet's suspect sheet: people who are terrorists, harbor terrorists and help terrorists. We have no idea what we are getting ourselves into, but we resolutely vow to fight.

Those among us who disagree with the U.S. declaring a "war on terrorism" especially appreciate the freedom of living in the United States because this nation affords our citizens the right to disagree, publicly and often, if necessary. After Mr. Glover delivered the following speech in New Jersey, and during a panel assembled to discuss the death penalty, a student asked if Mr. Glover advocated the death penalty as a punishment for Osama bin Laden. His response was that he was opposed to all instances of using the death penalty. Individuals like conservative talk show host and Iran Contra poster boy Oliver North make a mockery of the freedom of thought and expression the dissenters among us hold dear when they call for someone's head because they support an opinion contrary to the status quo. North, et. al, attempted to paint Mr. Glover as unpatriotic and called for a boycott of his latest film, "The Royal Tenenbaums". The Modesto City Council withdrew Glover's invitation to speak at their Martin Luther King Jr. Day celebration. The Council eventually reissued their invitation and Mr. Glover did indeed speak, but North's inflammatory, reactionary and un-American response to the words Mr. Glover spoke last November had already caused enough damage, not necessarily to Mr. Glover, whose film, "The Royal Tenenbaums", appears to have done well despite any boycott, but to the whole of what our society believes in. Progressives believe in the freedom of thought and expression and the justice that often follows and precedes such thought: "When I believe in something," Mr. Glover told Teresa Wiltz of the Washington Post earlier this year, "I have a sense of justice in my beliefs. I try to make decisions which are morally right."

It is also interesting to note that the title of Mr. Glover's speech is "The Death Penalty in This Great Nation of Ours." This country is indeed a great nation. A great nation blemished by our employment of the death penalty. A great nation blemished by our wholesale war on terrorism. A great nation blemished by our response to systemic injustice on other shores and a blindness to the injustices on our own.

—R.G.

THE DEATH PENALTY
IN THIS GREAT NATION OF OURS
Danny Glover

Good evening. Tonight I would like to discuss with you a practice that separates the United States from every other country in the Western Hemisphere. This, of course, is the use of homicide as an official tool of the state, otherwise known as the death penalty.

But first I would like to talk to you for a moment about consumer protection. You see, in this great nation of ours, we have laws on the books that protect consumers from faulty products. We protect consumers from drugs that are dangerous. From foodstuffs that are poisonous. From toys and appliances that are defective. The list goes on and on. We have many regulatory agencies that hire thousands of inspectors and adopt reams and reams of regulations to protect us. The Food and Drug Administration. The Environmental Protection Agency. The people who inspect our eggs and beef and poultry and milk.

Imagine, if you will, that you visited your doctor, and she or he prescribed a drug that works miracles for six out of every seven people who take it. But due to a defect with the drug, one out of every seven people who take the drug end up dying.

You can imagine the many lawsuits that would ensue. You can imagine how quickly this drug would be yanked off the market. You can imagine the congressional hearings, the charges and countercharges, the acrimony and finger-pointing that would follow as we rushed to keep our people safe in this great nation of ours.

Now. Let's talk about the death penalty.

Since the Supreme Court allowed executions to resume in the 1970s, 741 people have been executed in the United States. Unfortunately, as I give this speech, that number is climbing to 743, courtesy of the states of Georgia and Texas.

And yet 98 people, or about one out of every seven executed, have walked off death row after new evidence emerged that proved their absolute innocence.

Let me be very clear here. I am not talking about people whose sentences

171

or convictions were overturned on what some might call a technicality. I am talking about actual innocence.

Think about it. If one of every seven car tires sold in this country was subject to a blowout, if one of every seven chickens taken to market infected someone with salmonella, if one of every seven cars manufactured had a faulty engine that exploded every now and again, these things would be taken off the market.

But for every seven people executed since 1976, one actually innocent person has been sent to death row. Yet the death penalty remains "on the market."

There are, of course, many reasons why I oppose the death penalty, in addition to the fact that I believe innocent people can be executed and in fact have been executed.

I'd like to share with you some of these reasons.

Many of you know I worked on the case of Gary Graham. Gary came from the fifth ward in Houston, Texas. He was convicted and sentenced to death for the robbery-murder of a shopping clerk. There are many things about Gary's case that are illustrative of the kind of problems caused by the death penalty.

Number one: Gary was a juvenile when it was alleged he committed the crime for which he was convicted. Only five other countries are known to have executed children in the past decade, Nigeria, Pakistan, Saudi Arabia, Iran, and Yemen. But in the U.S., 13 states, including Texas, allow for the execution of people who commit crimes as juveniles.

Number two: Gary was Black. Black people make up 12.1 percent of our nation's population, but comprise 43 percent of death rows across the United States. Racial disparities continue to define who lives and who dies under this punishment.

Number three: Gary was convicted on the very shaky eyewitness testimony of one person. The Bible in the Book of Numbers says we shouldn't convict on the testimony of one eyewitness. But our courts say otherwise.

Number four: When Gary's supporters discovered new evidence of innocence, the courts wouldn't hear it. You see, the Congress and the State Legislatures have put time limits for the introduction of new evidence. New evidence can show a person's innocence, but if it is not introduced in time, it may not be heard. The Supreme Court has even ruled that as long as a person has received fair trial, it is not unconstitutional to execute an innocent person. Now does that make any sense?

Number five: Gary was from Texas. Texas has executed 253 people since reinstatement or more than one third of the people executed in the United States. Many of those executions were from Houston, Gary's home town. Harris County, which encompasses Houston, has sent 63 people to the death chamber since 1976. If it were a state, Harris County would rank third in the number of people executed, behind Texas and Virginia.

Gary Graham was executed in the summer of 2000. His case pointed out the many problems the death penalty brings to our system of justice. Incompetent legal counsel, racial bias. The possibility, in this case the probability, of innocence, the very issue of disproportionality, Gary probably would not have been executed if he was from a different state or if he had drawn a different prosecutor or a different jury.

But the tide is turning. The very same tide that swept up Gary Graham and so many like him is now turning. Consider these developments:

The U.S. Supreme Court this term is set to take up the question of whether mentally retarded people can be executed. Eighteen states have banned this barbaric practice, including five states this year alone. Across the globe, a strong international consensus against execution of the retarded has emerged. Of those countries that still employ capital punishment, only two, the United States and Kyrgyzstan, regularly put the retarded to death.

Fifteen states have banned the execution of people who commit crimes as juveniles. Next year, Arizona, Kentucky, Ohio and Missouri will consider similar legislation.

Across the nation, a healthy moratorium movement is battling the notion of state-sponsored homicide. The Republican governor of Illinois declared a moratorium in his state after many innocent people were discovered on death row, some with rapidly approaching execution dates. States like California, Texas, Tennessee, Maryland and Pennsylvania are giving birth to healthy moratorium campaigns. In the state of North Carolina alone, elected officials in fourteen towns and cities have passed resolutions supporting a moratorium on executions.

Nationwide, fifty-eight towns, cities, and counties have done likewise and polls consistently show that more than 60 percent of the American public supports a moratorium on the death penalty. Since September 11, 2001, the poll numbers have only risen slightly.

Around the globe, 110 nations have abolished the death penalty, either in law or in practice. This growing list includes Chile and Yugoslavia, both of whom outlawed the practice earlier this year.

So yes, the tide is turning, but now we face a new and profound challenge. I refer of course to the events of September 11th.

It has been said that war is never the friend of social justice movements. When we fear, we clamp down on those who do not think like we think or do not look like we look.

Since September 11th we have seen our federal government incarcerate without trial or access to bail more than 1,000 people, mostly of Middle Eastern or Southern Asian descent. Now it is revealed that Attorney General John Ashcroft wants to allow Federal Authorities to listen in on privileged conversations between these detainees and their lawyers. Furthermore, the government will no longer reveal how many people are being illegally incarcerated or where they are being held—this despite the fact that the FBI has admitted that 99 percent of those detained have nothing to do with the events of September 11th.

It gets worse. Just this week, President Bush unveiled a proposal to create special military courts to operate outside the nation's boundaries and, possibly, even outside the boundaries of the Bill of Rights of the United States Constitution. These courts will make it easier for the prosecutors to seek-and get-the death penalty.

It is clearly a slippery slope we are on. We cannot be silent while such tactics are employed by a president who makes his political career off the backs of those condemned. We must stand vigilant against Bush in these times and work onward and together toward abolition.

WHITE MAN'S PASS
The Heightened Danger of Racial Profiling in the Post 9/11 World
Laura W. Murphy

More than a decade ago, the New Jersey Turnpike came to be known in the African-American and Latino communities as the "White Man's Pass," a term that signified the growing realization that skin color, not the suspicion of criminal activity, had become the primary catalyst for law enforcement encounters along that stretch of highway. [1]

The Garden State experience became one of the notorious poster children for an emerging national outcry against racial profiling. In 1998, reforms were finally initiated in New Jersey and laws passed against race-based policing. During the two years directly before the tragic attacks of September 11th, ten states passed laws to discourage racial profiling and thirteen brought legislation under consideration.

As late as July 2001, President Bush himself told the National Organization of Black Law Enforcement Executives, "we owe you something in return ... for your service, and that is justice. And that's why I've asked the Attorney General and the Deputy Attorney General to examine racial profiling. It's wrong in America, and we've got to get rid of it."[2] The President's remarks followed similar attestations by Attorney General Ashcroft and other members of the Bush Administration.

On September 11th, things changed intensely for the worse. The emerging, ideologically crosscutting consensus against racial profiling began to dissolve in the panic and uncertainty of a country suddenly attacked. The Administration's strong promises to investigate and end racial profiling fizzled into ambiguous generalizations. Affirmative support for racial profiling experienced a renaissance among pundits and opinion leaders around the country and, more frighteningly, among average, generally liberal-minded Americans.

An African-American ACLU member from New York expressed this newfound, and profoundly troubling, acceptance of racial profiling during a series of focus groups held there in November of 2001. As I sat behind the one-way

175

mirror watching these discussions, I almost felt a chill wind blow past me as I heard her declare her antipathy toward racial profiling, but then concede that the practice might be necessary to fight terrorism.

Fear does funny things in this country. In this case, the result of September 11th vis-à-vis racial profiling was a sudden and wrenching sea-change in how large segments of the literati and the general populace viewed the practice. Gone was the popular rejection of the premise that certain minority groups are more likely to be engaged in criminal activity. In its place, unfortunately, was the idea; (a) that racial profiling might be a necessary evil, or (b) that while targeting motorists for driving while black is of course unacceptable, singling out people guilty only of flying while Arab or Muslim or Middle-Eastern is probably a good idea because they are the ones most likely to be terrorists.

It is exactly this paradox (driving while black is not cause for a traffic stop but flying while Arab is an acceptable rationale for the unceremonious expulsion of a law-abiding Middle Easterner from an airplane) that showcases exactly how flawed the two ideas above really are.

Racial profiling is; (a) never a necessary evil, and (b) poses just as much moral and practical danger when applied on the New Jersey turnpike against African Americans as it does when applied in LaGuardia Airport against Muslims.

It is the practical danger that is the most significant and disturbing outgrowth of the new support for racial profiling after September 11th. In reality, law enforcement or intelligence gathering apparatuses that engage in racial/ethnic/religious/national origin profiling risk putting the country in more danger.

Consider how the harrowing implications of a "White Man's Pass" cut two ways. First, the idea of law enforcement informed by the erroneous folk wisdom that blacks or Latinos are more likely to be drug couriers is, in itself, morally reprehensible. America is nothing if its denizens are not treated equally under the law. But, second, and more important in a post 9-11 world, is the realistic danger of a "White Man's Pass."

When law enforcement focuses its resources based on the idea that certain skin colors or other unchangeable characteristics are more likely to carry with them criminal activity, actual criminal activity among groups who do not share these characteristics goes unchallenged.

Therefore, if we begin to profile based on race, ethnicity or nation of origin in terrorism interdiction efforts in America's airports, seaports, train stations, bus depots and along our borders, the chance of our stopping a terrorist who does not fit the racial/ethnic/national origin profile diminishes accordingly. It is an ugly and scary concept.

As in domestic law enforcement, the only way to stop international terrorism within our borders before it happens is to convince prospective terrorists that security has, in fact, been stepped up for everyone, regardless of race, ethnicity, religion or home country. However, if we convince al Qaeda that only individuals of Middle Eastern or Muslim extraction will receive high scrutiny when entering the country, the terrorist leaders will logically seek out potential terrorists who do not fit the mold.

Couple this heightened, practical danger with the deep social injuries caused by racial profiling and the need to combat its use becomes clear. Not only is racial profiling perilously ineffective, it is also corrosive to relations between target communities and the authorities. Just as the African-American community has been forced by decades of police bias to distrust law enforcement, so will the Arab-American community draw in upon itself and become less willing to cooperate with the authorities if it is treated unfairly on the nation's planes, trains and highways.

Since September 11th, the fight against racial profiling has shifted from what was an increasingly successful campaign to a series of defensive skirmishes on the local, state and federal level.

The rest of this essay will deal specifically with these skirmishes: the emerging crisis of ethnic and religious profiling against Arabs, Muslims and Middle Easterners, and the ever-increasing similarities between the experiences of the Arab and Muslim communities and the African-American community. Finally, it will offer several recommendations on how to alleviate the situation and force the shameful practice of racial profiling back into the legislature and the courts for its eradication.

Racial Profiling Today

September 11th brought another visible minority group into the exclusive and tragic club of communities targeted by racial profiling. While America has yet to make significant strides in combating the more famous kind of racial profiling, euphemistically known as Driving While Black or Brown (with the catchy acronym DWB), the terrorist attacks have also dredged up the same kind of discriminatory treatment for the Arab and Muslim communities in the United States.

As mentioned before, there has been much furor from the right for an established and systematic racial profiling scheme in the nation's transportation facilities. Columnists and opinion leaders from all over the political spectrum began to argue after September 11th that the "Constitution is not a suicide pact" and civil rights, liberties and the American tradition of individual freedom are expendable in the interests of national security. Within this argument is the rationale in their minds for racial profiling.

At the ACLU, we have been on the frontline of this fight and we realize just how extensive the erosion of liberty is, especially as regards the profiling and discriminatory treatment of the Arab and Muslim communities in America. Arab-Americans have not merely experienced—as some might suggest—slight inconveniences at airports or around national monuments. They, as a community, have been singled out as the target of round-ups, dragnet interrogations, invasive and undeserved searches in airports, summary expulsions from airplanes, run-of-the-mill mob violence and secret detentions.

In November, the Department of Justice announced that it would begin conducting 5,000 "voluntary" interviews of Middle Eastern and Muslim men living in America, selected because of their ethnic background. To allay fears of profiling, the Attorney General publicly stressed that these interrogations would be wholly voluntary; the government was simply asking for help. Significantly, however, the Attorney General's beneficent public statements were misleading at best and wholly inaccurate at worst. The INS memo outlining the interrogation program explicitly stated that even minor visa violators who cooperated with the sting would be arrested, jailed and probably deported.

At no time did the Attorney General or the INS Commissioner ever give any public indication that they were aware of the acute potential for such a program to alienate the Arab and Muslim-American communities. Frankly they should have been. When the government treats individuals who belong to a social group unfairly simply because they belong to that social group (a phenomenon the African-American community knows all too well), the entire group is likely to lose faith in the government.

In addition to the dragnet questioning, the Department of Justice then had an internal memo leaked to the news media that detailed a plan to target a very small minority of so-called visa absconders (i.e. those who have over-stayed their visas), based on ethnicity and nation of origin. While no one objects to the enforcement of the law, the problem grows worse as it does in turnpike racial profiling when the law is used as a tool of prejudice and enforced selectively based on unchangeable characteristics.

This kind of official profiling breeds prejudice. In early June, the ACLU sued four major airlines—American, Continental, United and Northwest—for blatant discrimination against five men who were ejected from flights based on the prejudices of airline employees and passengers and for reasons wholly unrelated to security.

There is ample historical precedent for this kind of activity. While not yet as extreme, the recent mistreatment of Arab-Americans and Muslims in this country harkens back to the Japanese-American internment of World War II.

Arguments similar to those of the new defenders of racial and ethnic pro-filing were as widespread in the early 1940s as they are now. The urgency of the situation— today's World Trade Center is yesterday's Pearl Harbor — dic-tated drastic action, or so the argument went. Yet today, there are few who defend that shameful period in history, let alone recognize any success what-soever in the internment. President Ronald Reagan himself called the intern-ment a "grave wrong," a "mistake" and an action completely outside the pale of the American commitment to "equal justice under the law."[3]

What is of real significance as well is that, over the course of the war, only ten Americans were ever convicted of spying for Japan and all ten were white.[4] This is just another example of why racial profiling cannot work. Racial pro-filing targets and, then, alienates the good guys and lets the bad guys go free. And it is this alienation that is particularly destructive. Had those interned, and vastly loyal, Japanese-Americans been accorded their constitutional rights and permitted to remain in their homes on the west coast, might they not have been more able and more willing to help in the war effort?

The same hypothetical can be turned on its head and applied now equally to both Arab-Americans and African-Americans: if we do our utmost to treat minority communities in America equally under the law, will we not reap added benefits in social harmony and cooperation with authority? As Attorney General John Ashcroft himself has said, notably before September 11th, "And freedom is respected when the law is enforced uniformly, impartially, and without regard to race or color or creed."[5]

Just as tragic as the recent treatment of Arab and Muslims in America is evidence that suggests that the fight against African-American or Latino racial profiling has also suffered significant setbacks. Notwithstanding legal and procedural reforms in New Jersey, recent statistics show that the Turnpike is still beset by race-based traffic stops.[6] Other racial profiling lawsuits in Rhode Island, Montana and California also highlight the ongoing national problems with bias in law enforcement.

The above measures, however, pale in comparison to the two most immediate threats to equality under the law that have emerged in the past ten months. Both the USA PATRIOT Act, passed into law last year, and the recent popularity of national identification system proposals almost guarantee an increase in the level and severity of racial/ethnic/religious/national origin profiling in the United States.

The USA PATRIOT Act

It is one of the most American ideals — individualized suspicion before a law enforcement encounter — that is illustrated by racial profiling. As most of us know, both the Constitution and a wide and vibrant body of law guarantee each American that he or she will be treated equally under our laws. The very core of our political ideal immunizes Americans from law enforcement attention based solely or primarily on an unchangeable characteristic such as race or ethnicity. Therefore, law enforcement encounters cannot be initiated when there is no collection of indicators independent of race that suggest criminal activity is ongoing or about to occur. Racial profiling flies in the face of this longstanding American protection.

Unfortunately, so do many provisions in the ponderously named "Uniting and Strengthening America by Providing Appropriate Tools Required to Intercept and Obstruct Terrorism Act of 2001" or USA PATRIOT Act, which was signed into law by President Bush in late October 2001.

Passed by a Congress under enormous pressure and signed by a President seemingly eager to provide any and all new powers to his law enforcement and intelligence gathering apparatuses regardless of the cost to civil liberties and individual rights. Much of the USA PATRIOT Act runs counter to the concept of individualized suspicion.

For example, the law creates a new definition of "domestic terrorism" that allows the government to target individuals for investigation based on constitutionally protected associational activity. What this means in reality is that the government may on a whim decide that a group like Greenpeace or Operation Rescue is engaging in activity that warrants a label of domestic terrorism. Law enforcement can then investigate and even prosecute as domestic terrorists individuals involved with these groups.

From an African-American and civil libertarian perspective, one major problem with this smudging of the boundaries between what is protected speech and what can elicit government investigation is when the target group correlates with a particular ethnicity, nationality, political ideology or race within America. The new law could theoretically be applied to the Nation of Islam or the New Black Panthers, groups with memberships that are racially defined and that engage in political speech often at odds with the perspective of the powers that be. Not only would this be racial or ethnic profiling, it would cause a chilling of necessary and democratic dissent.

One can only imagine the damage a law like USA PATRIOT could have wrought during the decades of civil rights and anti-war ferment. Could the Rev. Dr. Martin Luther King Jr. have been investigated as a domestic terrorist? If used to its full and troubling potential, the USA PATRIOT Act entices the government to abandon individualized suspicion in its investigation and prosecution of Americans, leading to police and intelligence gathering practices akin to, if not identical to, racial profiling.

National ID Proposals

Another unfortunate outgrowth of the tragedy of September 11th is an increasing enthusiasm for the creation of a national identification system. These proposals have taken a number of forms. Some are fairly straightforward, some less so. One of the most troubling proposals is being lobbied for by the American Association of Motor Vehicle Administrators and would standardize driver's licenses across the country. The proposal has created controversy in Washington and around the country and is being fought by a shocking bedfellows coalition, including the ACLU and the conservative Eagle Forum.

Proponents of the system have long argued that a national ID system would actually be quite successful in preventing racial profiling. Nothing could be further from the truth. The reality of racial profiling today is that police use an enormously complex traffic law, which contains what seems like an infinite number of minor violations, to provide pretexts for search and detention. These pretexts allow police officers to essentially cast out their hooks on the nation's highways in constant fishing expeditions for criminal activity, a practice utterly at odds with the American criminal justice system.

Now imagine that every human being within the borders of the United States is required by law to carry a national ID card at all times. Visible minorities will be swept up in ever-greater numbers. Instead of using a broken taillight or the failure to signal a lane change, police out on the turnpike or in the airports can now simply demand our new internal passport—our 'Papers, please!' And if we do not have our identification in hand, law enforcement has been given the ultimate pretext to detain, search, question and even jail us even though we have done nothing wrong.

Couple the national ID with biased law enforcement and America runs the risk of an almost unimaginably powerful regime of racial profiling.

Conclusion

The panic and fear created by September 11th and nurtured by the continuing threat of future terrorism have also tragically compounded the losses of that day in early fall by eating away at our ability as a nation to consider the long-term consequences of our response. We want to be able to answer terrorism effectively and shield our country from its reach. Yet, at the same time we still have divisive forces in our country that have been overarched and made worse by the fear of terrorism.

Racial profiling is one of these problems. Not only has our attention been brought away from the reality of the "White Man's Pass" in New Jersey and across America, but many in our government have actively sought to enlarge that figurative Pass in both contemporary law enforcement and in the fight against terrorism.

It is a dangerous juncture. African-Americans, Arab and Muslim Americans and any other Americans of conscience need to get in sync, protest loudly and act promptly to make sure racial profiling does not come all the way back into vogue on the tailfeathers of September 11th.

Congress also needs to act. Our lawmakers need to engage in more thorough deliberation when passing future legislation that could encourage racial profiling and they need to turn back many facets of the USA PATRIOT Act and other anti-terrorism bills that go too far.

The legislature should also address the problems of DWB by passing the End Racial Profiling Act of 2001 (S 989; HR 2074), sponsored by Sen. Russell Feingold (D-WI), Rep. John Conyers (D-MI) and many other members from both chambers of Congress. The ERPA is easily the most comprehensive and promising fix to come down the pike in years. It defines racial profiling and provides added funds for data collection on traffic stops, early-warning systems, the use of monitoring technology such as dashboard video cameras in patrol cars and other proactive anti-profiling measures. The bill also grants the federal government and private parties the ability to bring legal action against police departments that racially profile.

The danger of the "White Man's Pass" and how we, as a nation, enforce our laws and ensure our security is by far the most immediate and important problem for the civil rights community today. Racial or ethnic or religious or national origin profiling threaten both our principles by their rejection of the constitutional demand for individualized suspicion and our physical safety by their ineffectiveness. Racial profiling in the post 9-11 world is a newly invigorated, fanged beast chomping at a tenuous leash, which is close to breaking. Once it gets free we will all suffer less liberty, less safety and, equally bad if not worse, less unity.

Notes

1. Roane, Kit R., "A Risky Trip Through 'White Man's Pass' In New Jersey, A Losing War on Racial Profiling," *US News and World Report*, 130:5, April 16, 2001.
2. "Remarks to the National Organization of Black Law Enforcement Executives, July 30, 2001," Weekly Compilation of Presidential Documents, 37:31, p.1116, August 6, 2001.
3. "Remarks on Signing the Bill Providing Restitution for Wartime Relocation and Internment of Civilians, August 10, 1988," Weekly Compilation of Presidential Documents, 24:32, p.1034, August 15, 1988.
4. Carter, Tom. "Profiling is a 'flawed' tool to beat terror," *The Washington Times*, January 14, 2002.
5. Remarks to the Fraternal Order of Police, August 14, 2001, reprinted on the Department of Justice website at http://www.usdoj.gov/ag/speeches/2001/081401fop.htm
6. Schwaneberg, Robert. "Blacks Still Pulled Over At Higher Rate on Turnpike," *The Star-Ledger*. Newark, NJ, June 27, 2002.

SHARED STATUS: A GLOBAL IMPERATIVE
Julianne Malveaux

September 11, 2001 was not the first time in world history that 3,000 people died in one day in one incident. That bears noting, especially because as teeth gnashed and tears flowed, we were all prepared to describe September 11, 2001 as an "unprecedented" occurrence. Horrible. Unthinkable. Unfathomable. It had happened before, though. Globalization began when Christopher Columbus intruded himself in the Americas, supposedly discovering people who already lived here. He marked his discovery by leaving corpses in his wake. Don't tell me there was not another day when 3000 people died. Maybe a slave ship sunk, and all the people on it perished. Maybe a reservation was invaded and those who resisted Custer lost their lives. Maybe Pilgrims invaded a rock and eliminated the people who were their gracious hosts. It is not unthinkable that the carnage that accompanied the deaths of 3,000 people had happened before. It was unfathomable to people in this country that it should happen here, on our turf, especially when we had presented ourselves as the invincible masters of the globe, the impenetrable fortress of market dominance and capitalism.

Even the modern era, the time we measure from 100 years ago, has a legacy of broken lives. There had to be one day, during the Holocaust, that 3,000 people died. If half a million lives were lost in Rwanda, it is likely that 3,000 died on one particular day. Perhaps in Bosnia, on one particular day, 3,000 people lost their lives. Arguably, in Tulsa, Oklahoma, in 1921, 3,000 lives were lost, with some descriptions of the event revealing that bombs were dropped from planes that flew over the community described as "Black Wall Street".[1] So shameful is that carnage that people would not speak of it openly until a few years ago. Yet, white Tulsans whose ancestors participated in the carnage have never recoiled from it in strong terms. For them it is simply history, but it is not abhorrent, unthinkable, and unfathomable. It just happened.

The events of September 11th are events that need a global and historical context. Yes, they were horrible events that have changed the way the United

States engages with the rest of the world. Yet, they do not change global engagement for the South, for those developing countries who have seen lives lost on massive scales time and again, and have endured the world's indifference to those lives lost. While it is important to respect and mourn the lives lost on September 11th, if we believe in the concept of shared status, which means that a life is a life is a life, then we must also mourn, both in history and in context, the loss of other lives.

The attempt to give the lives lost on September 11th some special status was apparent from the outset. Former President Bill Clinton and former Senate Majority Leader Robert Dole joined forces in an attempt to raise money for college scholarships for children of the survivors. More than a billion dollars was raised within a month of the carnage of September 11th.[2] The federal government offered compensation for those who agreed not to sue the airlines. But there seemed to be a class bias in the way that compensation was being offered with the question being raised, albeit briefly, about whether families of undocumented workers could collect compensation. There was no notion of shared status; instead privilege, knowledge, and access seemed to shape the way the families of September 11th victims were treated with the white, middle class (or upper middle class), and educated having a much easier time negotiating red tape than others. One widow estimated that her husband's lost earnings were over $8 million; her lawyer filed a claim for that amount! But there are millions of widow-women who will collect only a fraction of that sum.

On August 7, 1998, a truck bomb ran into the U.S. Embassy in Kenya, killing 213 people and injuring 4500. On the same day a truck bomb was parked outside the U.S. Embassy in Tanzania. Its explosion killed 11 people. Although these explosions happened on U.S. property, initially those killed or injured were not offered the same kind of government-sponsored compensation as the victims of September 11th. Indeed, it was only after lobbying that the families of the American citizens who were killed were allowed to participate in the victims' fund (which may reach billions of dollars) established for the victims of September 11th. The concept of shared status, the notion that a life is a life, was absolutely ignored in the treatment of the victims of the embassy bombings. Why? Because those tragedies did not happen on this soil?

The terrorists who used four airplanes as weapons of destruction, who pointed them at buildings occupied by people, who deliberately, willfully, and hatefully murdered thousands were callous individuals worthy of all contempt; their cohorts worthy of all punishment. They had no respect for the value of life, and they are not to be excused. Still, we live in a time where disrespect for life is common. Three thousand people probably die of hunger every day. More than 19 million people have died of AIDS on the African continent. There are at least 28.5 million Africans living with HIV/AIDS, with 3.8 million new cases diagnosed in the last year. A 15 year old teenager in Lesotho has a 74 percent chance of contracting AIDS on or before her 50th birthday. A third of Zimbabweans live with the disease.[3] Yet foreign aid to the African continent is miniscule, representing less than one percent of GDP in the United States. There has been a deliberate and willful indifference for human life outside the industrialized west. We have been quick to write off those who are starving or dying, because we have not humanized them.

We humanized the victims from September 11th. They were, of course, our own. So, we learned that a Jamaican immigrant who lived in Queens was engaged to be married. We learned that a stockbroker and his wife had just had a second child. *The New York Times* brought us short sketches accompanied by postage-stamp sized pictures, and they served to remind us of our common humanity, of the things that Langston Hughes calls the sweet flypaper of life, the details that transform someone from a casualty to a person. What if we had postage-stamp sized pictures of AIDS or hunger victims, if we learned that Ariane Tadeska who died of hunger at age 8, did sums in the dirt with twigs and cared for her younger sister? Would our brittle hearts bend if we read that South African Linda, at 30, had succumbed to AIDS, but loved her children passionately and held them close to her until she died, and that her son, 15, is at the top of his class? In mourning our losses of September 11th, we illustrated our capacity for domestic compassion. We did not illustrate the belief in the concept of shared status, in the notion that a life is a life, and that all lost lives deserve to be mourned. Our own losses have not made us more sensitive or compassionate toward global losses of life, not only of terrorism, but also of global economic injustice.

Globalization means linked future, and generally, modern globalization has linked the economic futures of the west with those of the rest of the world.

This has been the case since Columbus came, ostensibly on a mission to Christianize the Indians. Just as mercenaries went to Africa in the fifteenth century to theoretically "Christianize" the Africans; a whole lot of nonsense has happened in the name of Christianity. At the bottom line, though, Columbus came seeking rare goods and services to trade in Italian markets, just as European merchants invaded Africa in search of labor, gold, and other commodities. In modern times, globalization has meant the search for markets, for consumers to purchase our goods and services. It can be argued that the U.S. economic expansion of the late 20th century was largely a function of our ability to manipulate trading conditions to our advantage.

The United States has come into world space with a swaggering posture that has been reinforced by global financial organizations, the World Bank and the International Monetary Fund — supported largely by our money. The IMF has arrogantly insisted that developing economies comply with our narrow views of the world, focusing on interest rates instead of education and development. The World Bank has been only slightly better, as it has placed some focus on issues like poverty and gender in the last decade. Still, the bank has insisted on implementing structural adjustment programs that are environmentally and socio-economically damaging to developing countries. In some cases, deforestation is accelerated by the pressure to sell raw materials to earn foreign exchange. In other cases, educational and medical expenditures are postponed to accommodate debt repayment schedules. The West has failed to understand the tremendous disparities that emerge from a world where 1.2 billion people survive on less than a dollar a day, and 2.8 billion, or 45 percent of the world's population, live on less than $2 a day.[4]

The United States had GDP per capita of $31,500 in 2000; in Nicaragua the GDP per capita was $2,500. GDP per capita was $1800 in Ghana, $1,300 in Benin, and $730 in Tanzania.[5] How do we contextualize the "linked futures" of security issues? In the United States, we speak of "homeland security" and assert that we can create it by some new bureaucratic arrangement, more money, more guns, more vigilance, yet few people enjoy any kind of security inside or outside our borders. Security. That word comes up a lot since September 11th. We have a new near-cabinet Department of Homeland Security, headed by former Pennsylvania governor Tom Ridge. We have a series of colored alerts to remind us how insecure we are -- red, yellow, orange all signal different levels of danger. Yet we cannot be sure of the scope of the danger we face because the announcements are so vague. We are on red alert one day, yellow alert on another, and red, white and blue alert on the Fourth of July.

Security means safety, refuge, sanctuary, shelter, well-being, happiness and comfort. The majority of the people who live in this world never know security. Many have never been given shelter, many do not know or expect safety. Some do not know what it is to have sanctuary or refuge, happiness or comfort. They scramble through life on less than $2 a day, hoping for food, not for security. Thus the term security needs to be placed into some context, and we need to look at security in a global, not national, sense. We in the United States think we can create security by forming a new bureaucracy or by putting a new set of dollars around a problem. The security we seek is the same security that people seek around the world. The extent to which we are able to attain our own security is the extent to which we are able to understand that others, too, have security needs.

Globalization is about linkages, and when we link the concept of security, both inside and outside the United States, we have to understand that most people never experience security. Never mind the security of going into a building or getting on a plane and having the presumption that everything will be okay. What about the simple security of getting up in the morning and breathing air and thinking that everything will be okay? More than 3 million Americans live on the streets.[6] Some of them are children. Where is their security? Half of all women who work full time full year earn about $25,000 a year. Those who are married do okay financially when their partners are working. Those who aren't married, those single moms, hustle to make ends meet. Where is their security? Where is the security for the women who have been pushed into the workplace by welfare reform? What security do their children have when they are left home alone because their mothers cannot find childcare for them? What security do their families have when women are charged with child neglect and their children sent to foster homes because they have committed the crime of failing to find childcare? For too many Americans, the notion of "homeland security" was elusive and amusing, even before September 11th.

Does anybody experience security in our globalized space? Jobs race to the bottom, from New Jersey, to Mississippi, to the maliquadore zone in Mexico.

Security? For whom? Those with an add water and stir version of security that says if you throw enough money at a problem security will follow. If you throw enough money, enough troops, and enough young men with guns at the problem, you can ensure somebody something. If all it takes is dollars, why aren't we throwing them at the AIDS crisis, making prescription drugs available to people all over the world? If all it takes is dollars, why can't we throw money at the hunger problem, buying food? Instead, while conservatives tout the need for "market-based" solutions to domestic and world hunger, our Congress is actively into market distortions, developing a special welfare program, Temporary Aid for Needy Farmers that further disadvantages the agricultural sectors in developing countries by subsidizing U.S. agriculture. "We can't throw money at a set of problems that have deeper roots than dollars," has been a refrain for those who don't want to spend more money, even when it is clear that dollars make a difference. I would argue that dollars wouldn't necessarily make a difference in "homeland security" and point to the millions spent on "airline security" to questionable end.

Words like terrorism and security must be placed in a global and historical context, especially in the wake of September 11th. In the days after September 11th, we heard a lot about a "state of emergency" and the ways we needed to respond in the middle of an emergency. We were supposed to mobilize because we had been attacked. Congress was supposed to appropriate funds, emergency funds, because we were in the middle of a state of emergency. People were supposed to change their behavior because, again; it is an emergency, a state of emergency.

African Americans have always lived their lives in this country in a state of emergency. We have always felt assailed, at risk, under siege. We have had twice as much of the bad things, half as much of the good things, twice as much infant mortality, half as much of the educational access, twice as much of the stress, diabetes, and heart attacks, half as much, and sometimes not even that, of the wealth, the valuable positions, and the political influence. When statistics blare our disparities, disparities that speak to a state of emergency, there has been indifference. It is galling to watch the rapid response to our national state of emergency, understanding that we live in a state of emergency within a state of emergency.

What we learn from this state of emergency is that mobilization is possible. It is possible to suspend ideology, scrap the rules, dig deep and come up with the resources to combat "terrorism" or whatever blight plagues our country. Why haven't we been able to work as hard to close the racial economic gap? To attack the disparities that exist in education? Our emergencies have always been emergences for which the solution could be postponed. Now that we are confronted with a "real" emergency, it has become clear that emergencies can be handled expeditiously.

One aspect of the current emergency has been the leadership factor, the "jawboning" factor, and the ability to wrap unifying rhetoric around a problem. Our President stands up to them and says, Let's roll. Imagine that we could "roll" our nation around a set of social problems that, if solved, could transform the tone and tenor of our civic lives. Imagine that we could roll around education, health, and economic disparity to eliminate some of the nihilism that plague inner cities. When Mr. Bush says, in the parlance of the streets, it's on, some of us wonder what took so long and why the targets are so distant. Had someone called it "on" in regards to disparity, we might have been able to switch it "off" so that African Americans could fully participate in the social, economic, and political life of our nation.

Instead, what's "on" now is the economic burden of terrorism, a burden that will be unevenly borne by our nation's taxpayers. George W. Bush gave high-income taxpayers a break when he cut taxes in April 2001. Now, we are facing a deficit that is partly a function of his tax cut, and partly a function of the increased expenditures that will come from this war on terrorism. The airlines have lined up for bailout money, but the national rail system is slated for collapse because, as energy-efficient as it is, it has been deemed unworthy of subsidies. The airlines will get a break, but those ancillary travel and tourism related industries have also been hit, and there is no relief for their workers. Class matters. Pilots and flight attendants, mostly white, get a bailout, while maids, porters, janitors and food handlers, mostly black and brown, get the shaft.

Conversations about budget priorities have been suspended, and the military industrial complex will again be rewarded for our war against terrorism. Military contractors can expect a windfall, but the money that shifts from the social and civic sector to the military brings a shift of jobs with it. The Republican Party, hard on government spending, is soft when spending turns into profits. They are prepared to cut budgets for social spending to beef up spending on "defense" (or offense, depending on how it is defined). We are not only prepared to track down terrorists, but also to predetermine which countries we will define as terrorist, anticipating trouble before it comes. We are prepared to do this with out paying attention to the financial implications of instigating conflict. And while our global allies stand behind us in any fight against the perpetrators of September 11th, they are less willing to support us in a door-to-door search for a new enemy.

The fiscal implications of the war on terrorism are especially important for people at the bottom. The Bush administration, while asserting that we are all in the same boat, has been eager to provide financial rewards (in the form of tax cuts) to corporate allies, even as the matter of corporate chicanery has generated headlines. If fewer dollars come in through tax revenue, and more go out through wartime expenditures, this means that there are fewer dollars left to support social programs. Thus, the Bush Administration has often talked the talk of economic justice, asserting initiatives, for example, to close the homeownership gap, while failing to walk the economic justice walk with money to support rhetoric. More importantly, when deficits occur, social programs are the first to be cut in both Democratic and Republican administrations. The war on terrorism abroad is also a war on poor people at home.

The impact of this war is compounded when we understand that poor people didn't get a break in the past decade. While the economy expanded, the minimum wage has remained at a stagnant $5.15 per hour since 1996. While stock portfolios expanded from 1997 through 2000 by about 20 percent a year (although the stock market has faltered in the last year), incomes at the bottom grew by less than 3 percent a year.[7] There has been macroeconomic ecstasy and microeconomic angst, most characterized by increasing levels of hunger and homelessness in the midst of prosperity. The Bush "free market" approach to these problems was not designed to elevate the least and the left out, but the added stress on our national budget from the "war on terrorism" pushes those at the bottom even further from the mainstream.

There is an irony in the way that the old "free market, deregulation" line coexists with the new regulation that is a necessary outgrowth of the war on terrorism. In Washington, D.C., for example, the only public hospital was closed in a privatization move that occurred in the slave (as in non-voting) city in the name of fiscal efficiency. But when the anthrax plague threatened postal workers, the closed DC General Hospital was re-opened, making the case for public health. Further, it is both interesting and amusing that foes of big government would create a Department of Homeland Security that will employ more than 170,000 workers. The anti-big government message has now been compromised by reality. Will the reality hold long enough for us to explore the potential positive role government may have in managing resources both in time of war and in the face of other national emergencies? The Bush Administration, instead, has cleaved to free market solutions around issues like education, favoring a voucher system that erodes confidence and resources in public education. Imagine, though, that we "farmed out" aspects of the war on terrorism, providing market outcomes to those with innovative solutions. I don't think we are prepared for a free-market war, and the legislative climate after September 11th suggests we aren't even prepared for a free speech environment. Still, the Administration supports unfettered markets in education, a tribute to both their pragmatism and to their hypocrisy.

How can we expect all Americans to embrace the "war on terrorism" as some national rallying cry? Too many have not participated in the good times, but are now being asked to shoulder a burden in the bad times. As unemployment rates have risen since September 11th, they've not risen uniformly with African Americans bearing twice the unemployment burden of whites.[8] Layoffs, too, have not had an even impact, with those in the service sector more likely to experience cuts than those in the professional sector. If we are all in the same boat, some folks are riding and some folks are rowing, and the sense of extra burden erodes the sense of shared status. Just like a life is a life, a tragedy is a tragedy and a burden is a burden. Yet the early 2002 corporate debacles have clearly illustrated the ways that the "just us" system can be manipulated with Enron and Arthur Andersen crooks invoking the Fifth Amendment to evade investigation. It is similarly ironic that the Inglewood, California police officer that beat a young black man on videotape was free a week after the beating while the man who shot the tape was incarcerated.

In another time, under other circumstances, a beating that may be racially motivated would provoke outrage. At another time, under other circumstances, corporate chicanery would have outraged Democrats and enraged lefties notching up the rhetoric about the evils of capitalism. In this context, with the war on terrorism looming in the background, the protests are muted, the criticism contained, the tone and tenor dictated by the fact that we are in the middle of a war.

The Bush administration has gotten a pass on its domestic policy because of the focus on the war. Even as opinion sifts, people are uncertain about the amount of dissent that our nation can stand, and so they edit themselves. The Democratic Party was silent for nearly a year, and then only gained voice when the Republican National Committee wantonly ignored the bipartisan terms of engagement by selling photographs of the President making post-September 11th calls. Even then, Democrats were too often cowed when they were described as "obstructionist" and "unpatriotic" as if patriotism is the same thing as silence. Indeed, it seems that the most patriotic thing that Democrats (and others) can do in this climate is to offer respectful voices of dissent and analysis. There has been too much talk of people "coming together" under siege, without acknowledgement that we should not come together without discussion and negotiation.

The Administration's complicity in issues of corporate chicanery, with the President's own involvement in stock options from the Harken Group, on whose board he served, and Vice President Cheney's checkered leadership at the Halliburton Group, has also given Democrats leverage. This leverage has not been used, though, to redirect the budget toward the people who have been economic victims, and are in greatest need of economic assistance. Domestically, that group would include the 25 percent of the black population, and 12 percent of the overall population that lives in poverty. Internationally, Democrats have not challenged the Administration's paltry genuflection to African poverty with its scant contributions ($200 million in 2001) to fighting AIDS in Africa.[9]

The Administration's indifference to poverty, domestic and international, is at odds with its compassion to the loss of life that our nation experienced on September 11th. If we believe that a life is a life is a life, then we must also believe that we can save lives with our fiscal intervention. Had we the resources—the money, the intelligence, the will, the wherewithal — to turn al Qaeda away on September 11th, we would have used them. We would have done everything in our power to make the terrorists unsuccessful. We know that we have the resources—the money, the intelligence, the will, and the wherewithal—to eradicate poverty and hunger both here and abroad. When our resources can make a difference, somehow we chose not to use them, avoiding the universal principle of shared status; the notion that a life is a life is a life.

What Are Our Priorities

While the war on terrorism may have changed the terms of engagement between the United States and the rest of the world, it does not change the internal challenges that our nation faces. Instead, it forces us to focus on the rhetoric that we offered in the hours that followed the debacle of September 11th. "It will never be the same," people said to each other. They hugged and reconnected and claimed to reach a set of "core values" after the foundation of their value was shaken.

"Now I know what is important", a banker sobbingly proclaimed to eager cameras. He had lost much of his immediate family and was devastated by that loss. Whether we suffered individual losses or group challenges, many of us felt as the banker did, devastated and challenged, wondering whether we would do things differently if we had the opportunity.

We have the opportunity. The challenge of September 11th is to reconfigure the ways we think about the United States in context with the rest of the world. The challenge is, also, to consider the many ways that our arrogance and superiority has eroded the concept of shared status, the many ways that we can universally mourn life. From an economic perspective, the challenge is to bring sensitivity to the way that we allocate resources. When do we offer relief from suffering? To whom? How? The relief we offered to victims after September 11th did not adhere to the concept of shared status, but instead to a concept of privilege. September 11th victims, based on the legislation, are the most favored victims of terrorism. Those who died from the truck bombings at African embassies, from hunger in Somalia, from AIDS in South Africa are lesser victims, worthy of less concern.

We have the opportunity. Our challenge is to look at our domestic budget and to figure out how we make that budget conform to our rhetoric. We say that education is important. How much money do we spend on education? We say that it is of ultimate importance. Does the budget reflect that?

We say that we car about world hunger. How much money do we spend on that? If the money doesn't match the rhetoric, we don't walk the walk, we just talk the talk. We say we believe that children are the future, but our budgets don't suggest that. Children go missing in Florida, in California, but we ignore them and expend resources looking for grown women gone missing, mainly because they have been connected to political figures. What does this suggest? If we have been chastened by September 11th, we should have been chastened to consider the principal of shared status, the notion that you can't look for Chandra Levy without explaining to the hundreds of mothers of black girls missing that their daughters are important, too.

The optimist in me feels that it is not our intention to elevate some victims over others, while the pessimist in me looks at the expanse of our nation's history to conclude that the United States has never been able to embrace the concept of shared status. And yet, if status is not shared, unity is not fostered, and resonance never takes place. Our challenge is a moral one, a political one, and an economic one. Our challenge is to take our national pain and turn it into an inclusive passion to eliminate terrorism not through counter-terrorism, but through an effort to embrace and eliminate all actions that diminish human life and self-determination.

Notes

1. Scott Ellsworth, *Death in a Promised Land: The Tulsa Race Riot of 1921,* Louisiana State University Press, 1992.
2. See http://nonprofit.about.com/cs/september11 for information about September 11-related giving.
3. See Cinua Akukwe and Melvin Foot, "The Death March Continues," www.allAfrica.com, July 12, 2002.
4. Joseph E. Stiegletz, *Globalization and its Discontents.* New York: W.W. Norton, p. 25.
5. World Bank Data, 2001.
6. See Food First and Children's Defense Fund data on economic disparity.
7. Lawrence Mishel, Jared Bernstein, John Schmitt, *The State of Working America 2000-2001.* New York: ILR Cornell Paperbacks.
8. www.bls.gov
9. Alexis Simendinger, "Cutting a Deal on Death." *National Journal,* June 29, 2002.

CHAPTER SEVEN

An Island of Tranquility in a Sea of Discontent

An Island of Tranquility in a Sea of Discontent
U.S. Foreign Policy and the War on Terrorism

While African people around the globe live in extreme poverty and with political turmoil, African American people, despite our often-challenged circumstances are an island of tranquility in a sea of discontent. Similar, the United States of America has also often been seen as a refuge and haven, a magnet for immigrants from all over the world. Yet September 11th has reminded us of the status of others in the world, and of the high price we pay, that we extract, for the relative tranquility we experience.

Dr. Orville Taylor incorporates an Afro-Caribbean perspective into this conversation about the war on terrorism, looking at the ways that Americans have shaped global culture, and the ways that African people around the world are affected by the war on terrorism in the United States. His contribution reminds us of the many ways that we, African people, are connected. His work also cautions us about the complications of globalization.

Dr. Ron Walters is one of or nation's most gifted political analysts. His concept of foreign policy justice expands the notion of shared status into a global space. How can we take one country and elevate it over another, demanding immediate democracy in some places but tolerating a time line for compliance in others? We do it, of course, in the name of our strategic interests by ignoring the concept of foreign policy justice that Ron Walters explores in his thought-provoking and expansive essay.

—J.M.

GLOBALIZATION, RACISM AND THE TERRORIST THREAT

Incorporating an Afro-Caribbean Response
Orville W. Taylor

To begin any discussion of the terrorist attack and the African American response while excluding any reference to Afro-Caribbean Blacks is to unwittingly go precisely to the heart of the dilemma. The fact is, any serious notion of African American concerns as they relate to international matters should, ideally, incorporate at least some recognition of the affinity with those which emanate just south of the South. Part of the explanation for the crisis presented by the attacks on the World Trade Center (WTC) lies in a perception of the process of globalization, global domination, ethnocentrism, and social, cultural and economic exclusion. While Anglo-America has been historically accused of not demonstrating a sensitivity about others, including their own fellow citizens of color, such a luxury is not to be afforded to a people whose very history has been one of marginalization.

A Common History

The history of the peoples of the Afro-Caribbean has long been intertwined with that of the African Americans, even before slavery was abolished in the United States. The Caribbean, and in particular Jamaica, and Barbados, had been a transshipment port for slaves to other territories including the American colonies, between the seventeenth and nineteenth centuries. According to Winston James *"Up to 1700, it is safe to assume that all of the slaves in South Carolina came from the Caribbean. It has been estimated that between 15 and 20 percent of slaves to South Carolina in the eighteenth century, came from the Caribbean,"* (James 1998:11) When the slave trade ended in 1806 and the impending abolition of slavery itself was to follow in the British empire in 1838, many plantation owners moved with their slaves to the Carolinas. Contact between the Carolinas and the Caribbean continued such that, *"the significant influence of the Caribbean on South Carolina endures to this day."* (James 1998:11)

An Island of Tranquility in a Sea of Discontent

It is no secret also that the emancipation of slaves in the Anglo-Caribbean had bred a set of African descendants who, by the civil war in the 1860s, had long been accustomed to a life of freedom, in societies where they were the racial majorities. These cousins of the African Americans were spared the post slavery lynchings by dint of the fact that the white minority had reason to fear being engulfed in a national tide of angry Negroes. Similarly, the Haitian Revolution, which ended in 1803, had not only presented an example to the American slaves, but more importantly was a 'wake up call' to the American planter class. Thus, despite the orthodox fallacy of a benevolent North led by Abraham Lincoln, a point also well challenged by Lerone Bennett (2000), slavery really ended in the United States because of the North's recognition that it was sitting on a time bomb as exemplified in the Caribbean.

By the late nineteenth century, the Caribbean had begun to export some of its free sons and daughters to the United States. Among the 'importees' of significance is, of course, Alfred Dubois whose son, William Edward Burghardt, emerged as one of the prime leaders of the race in the late nineteenth and early twentieth centuries. Marcus Garvey, Otto Huiswoud, and Stokely Carmichael (Kwame Toure) have also made indelible marks on African-American history.

Today, many African Americans of Caribbean descent people the 'Who's Who' list in America. Sidney Poitier, Harry Belafonte, Louis Gossett, Jr. and the late Madge Sinclair are but a few. More recently, Delroy Lindo, Carl Lumbly, Sheryl Lee Ralph, Garcelle Beauvais, Wyclef Jean, Shaggy and a pantheon of rappers and hip-hop performers , Doug E. Fresh, Young MC, Pepa, the late Notorious BIG, Heavy D, Busta Rhymes and doubtless many others yet unnamed, have colored the American entertainment landscape.

It has also been suggested that there is more than a 'casual' link between the origins of rap and dance hall DJ music (Jamaican rap). Arguments have been advanced to the effect that given the emergence of Jamaican rap in the 1960s and the historical connections between both peoples, the relationship is, in fact a 'causal' one. Even if there is room for debate about the birthing influences of either, there is little arguing that there is much commonality of social location of the music as an expression of urban lower-class Black culture in Western society. As such, rappers from both countries share most of their characteristics, including the negative ones, and are involved in an incredible cross-fertilization. Thus, the Black *Jamerican* bond is a tight one.

Interestingly, at two ends of the spectrum we find two very prominent African Americans of Caribbean descent, Colin Powell and Louis Farrakhan. The former, viewed with some suspicion by the African-American community, is often seen as a rigid conservative, who is unmindful of the issues surrounding his 'brothers' and 'sisters' and the latter is regarded with some ambivalence, as a race leader and a racist advocate of anti-American sentiments. Whether the image of either is correct is not significant. The point is these are men with stature beyond American soil who have deep Caribbean roots.

What is also significant is that despite being different populations, the Caribbean and American Blacks do not only share a common history, but they to some extent have similar experience in a world that is dominated by a white Western elite.

Looking at America from the Caribbean

In the modern era Black Caribbeans have been constantly aware of the achievements and struggles of their American counterparts. Among sports aficionados the breakthrough of Jesse Owens in 1938 and the Black power salute in 1968 are Black events, not simply African American history. News of the death of Martin Luther King was received with great horror. My own recollection as a first grader was of Jamaicans crying. *Cleopatra Jones, Coffey, Black Belt Jones* and all of the 1970s 'Blacksploitation' films were well accepted on the islands. The Afro hairstyle and soul and R & B music were as much part of the staples of Caribbean culture as were the dashiki and jazz. Alex Haley's *Roots* was made into a film that evoked tears and deep anger among West Indians to the extent that some governments did not wish to allow it to be continuously shown because of fear of anti-white sentiments in a region where the whites are a minority, but well-located in the upper echelons of the society.

Simply put, Caribbean Blacks have for a long time had a fairly strong affinity with African Americans. There is also some degree of admiration for and aspiration towards things American. Thus, if one speaks with an American accent, the response is usually that he/she is 'talking nice.' They have known for a long time that the experiences are, not only similar, but also connected. However, the extent to which the reverse is true is not so obvious.

There is far more knowledge of the lives of Black American and American culture on the whole that Afro-Caribbeans have, than Americans have about them. The truth is, there is little in American culture or ideology that advocates a serious 'anthropological' approach to the cultures of other peoples. A very ethnocentric people, Americans, perhaps unconsciously, downplay the significance of anything that is not Anglo-American. Therefore, one who does not speak like an American (even outside of America) 'speaks funny' or 'has an accent'

The Caribbean response to this hegemony is in itself ambivalent. On one hand one finds a positive perception of American culture, even the dysfunctional aspects, and a desire to ape it. Yet there is an equally resentful approach to the lack of significance given to their local identities and culture. A dualism pervades the Caribbean psyche.

Notwithstanding this dualism, which even Black Americans share towards their own country, Caribbean Blacks on the whole are pro-American and see themselves connected to America. Still there is some degree of discontent with respect to the extent to which they feel disregarded and insignificant, in a world dominated by Anglo-American culture and agendas.

EconAmerica

Apart from the historical relationship that Caribbean Blacks have had with the United States, in more recent times it has represented an economic Mecca of sorts. According to renowned anthropologist Nancy Foner, *"Today, after several decades of large-scale migration, there are nearly a million West Indian immigrants living in New York City alone, where they represent well over a third of the city's black population".* (Foner 2002) It has been estimated that more than 250,000 Jamaicans live in South Florida, and this figure is considered to be significantly underestimated (*Miami Herald* 1996:22). At a rough appraisal, at least four million people from the Anglophone Caribbean as a whole can be found on American soil. This basically means that an almost corresponding number of West Indians who live in the region inhabit the States.

A combination of factors and programs has contributed to this. All the relevant theories on migration recognize the economic pull of the northern neighbor. The temporary work program in the agricultural and semi-skilled sector has absorbed a significant number of Caribbean workers under the H2 program. At the height of its operations in the 1980s it employed more than 20,000 Jamaican workers each year. These workers contributed in excess of $16 million in remittances to Jamaica in 1990 alone. Not surprisingly, there is always a noticeable number of workers who disappear instead of returning to their countries of origin. On the average close to ten percent of these workers is reported as 'absent without leave' (AWOL) (Ministry of Labour Jamaica 1998). This group, adding to the mass of undocumented aliens in America, makes America home and provider for scores of Caribbean nationals.

At the macroeconomic level America is undoubtedly the largest regional trade partner. More than 55 percent of imports and just under 50 percent of exports in the English-speaking Caribbean are accounted for by the United States. This compares with 15.8 and 13.7 percent between the region and the European Union (EU). Of all the tourist arrivals to the West Indies, Americans comprised about 67 percent. For the 1990s Jamaica received on the average of a million tourists per year. In simple terms, this means that more than 750,000 Americans visited Jamaica in each year of the last decade. (PIOJ 1990-2000).

In terms of direct foreign investment in the English and Dutch speaking Caribbean, America is unrivaled. The United States invested some $5.3 billion in the region in 1994. For the years 1996 and 1998, the figure was $5.4 and $6.8 billion respectively. In 2000 the total was $9.8 billion. (BEA 2002) The EU total is less than a fourth of this.

Yet, this very economic dependence on the United States has in itself been a source of national dissent and ambivalence since the post war period began. American foreign policy has historically been hegemonic, to the extent that it seeks to instruct local ones. Thus, when the Michael Manley government of the 1970s pursued a pro-socialist policy, there was a tremendous backlash, resulting in a decline in investment and aid. Manley's socialism, though seen as anti-American, was simply nationalist. Ironically, it is the reaction of America which might have been seen as hostile.

The Drug Connection

Another area in which the interests of Americans and Caribbean are connected is in regard to drugs. Despite the extensive expenditures and programs to curb their usage, illegal drugs have a ready and constant market in the United States. Inasmuch as drugs are consumed in the Caribbean as well, the sheer numbers of users in the United States make it a very lucrative market. In fact it is the single largest drug-consuming country in the world. Estimates put American consumption of cocaine at 300 of the 575 metric tons produced internationally in the mid-1990s. (Griffith 1997:55)

Writers such as Ivelaw Griffith have scrupulously examined the subject. Consistent with the historical patterns of inter-cultural exchange, he argues that *"legal and illegal migration between the United States and the Caribbean facilitates drug-use emulation by West Indians, both at home and in North America."* (Griffith 1997:51) He furthers argues that the geographical proximity of both regions, added to the mass media, results in the transmission of American values and attitudes.

However, for the purposes of this paper, the greater problem posed by the drug trade is the impact that it has on the economic profile of the Caribbean societies. First of all, given the desire for conspicuous consumption, and the *'American Dream'*, the drug trade presents a real alternative for many Caribbean residents. With the displacement of workers in the agricultural, manufacturing and tourism sectors, the available pool of drug dealers, smugglers and collaborators is swelling.

In larger territories such as Jamaica and Trinidad there are sizeable populations of inner-city residents, who are economically, socially and politically marginalized. According to Taylor (2002), they comprise a separate social order. Even without the involvement of the international drug trade, there is the constant need in such communities for the defense of turf. In these communities there is a greater propensity towards violence. Thus, with the advent of large scale drug distribution comes the influx of firearms. Consequently, there is an increasing concern with the impact that these firearms are having on governance. In July 2001, the police and members of a downtown Kingston community were engaged in a day-long battle that left 24 civilians and three police personnel dead. Between January and July 2002, ten police officers were murdered with firearms.

206

But firearms are not produced in the Caribbean. Therefore, for them to be available they have to be imported. The popular weapons found in the Jamaican underground are both American and Russian made, suggesting that they may indeed be connected to other international axes. The link between drugs and organized crime in the Caribbean is a large enough issue to raise questions about the capacity of a government to manage the country. With the apparent targeting of police personnel in Jamaica, reminiscent of the pattern in Colombia, it may be successfully argued that there is a link between the international drug trade and terrorism within the Caribbean states. There is some evidence to support the link between Colombian drugs and terrorism (POINT 2002). The connection between the trade in the Caribbean and Colombian drugs has been documented (Griffith,1997). The drug trade is more of a threat to authority and stability in the small Caribbean states than it is to the United States.

Less convincing, however, is the alleged connection between the trade and international terrorism a la bin Laden. Despite the statements to the contrary points to the use of income derived from the international drug and weapons trade to finance the operations that led to the events of 9/11, little evidence has come in to support it.

Thus, what is clear is that the drug trade is related to all aspects of the subject under discussion. Yet, perhaps myopically, the foreign policy of the United States may be leading to a deepening of the links between Caribbean nationals and the drug trade.

McDonaldization:
The Negative Aspects of the American Way in the Caribbean

Apart from the obvious drug connection between the United States and the Caribbean, American influence has penetrated the Caribbean with some negative consequences via a process described by George Ritzer as *'McDonaldization'*. According to Ritzer, late twentieth century American society has a greater drive to efficiency than that which existed from the late nineteenth century to the early part of this century. Characterized by a new model of organization, typified by the fast food restaurant, McDonaldization has four key elements; efficiency, predictability, calculability and control. They epitomize the new American culture. Thus, "Almost all social institutions (for example, education, sports, politics and religion) were adapting McDonald's principles to their operations. And McDonald's was spreading around the world...." (Ritzer 1996: xviii)

Nevertheless, in as much as the concept refers to a process that is manifested in all sectors of society the fast food industry is being singled out because of its high visibility.

The current process of McDonaldization operates on a pre-established pattern of the 'industrialization by invitation' strategies of the 1950s and 1960s. Like the earlier transnational of the 1960s and 1970s they do not utilize many local inputs. As franchises they pay fees and, having only few linkages with the rest of the economy, they contribute to the expatriation of capital, pressure on the balance of trade, inflation and in some cases, influence the decline in the value of the local currency. Recently Burger King broke the cycle by agreeing to buy a small percentage of Jamaican local beef production. Kentucky Fried Chicken is committed to buying local Jamaican chicken. However, given the forces of globalization, it from time to time sources and purchases cheaper imports, leaving local producers with unsold surpluses

Yet apart from the obvious economic impact there is also a cultural aspect. Writers such as Rex Nettleford, V.S. Naipaul, C. L .R. James, the aforementioned Frantz Fanon, and others consistently struggled to raise the issue of racial and cultural identity and integrity as essential components of nation-building and development strategies. These writers, recognizing that 'cultural imperialism' mitigated against true development, critiqued the 'Afro-Saxon' phenomenon. Yet paradoxically, there are elements in the society that see aspects of Euro-American culture as the ideal. Consequently, the Creole languages, based mostly on West African syntax, spoken by the Black majority (50 to 90 percent across the region) are stigmatized as 'talking bad.' Conversely, as indicated, the individual who speaks with an American or British lilt is likely to be seen as 'talking nice.' The North American brothers and sisters in their own dilemma with Ebonics share the same issue of language validity and inferiority.

Still, the issue of cultural hegemony and acculturation is not limited to self-identity and stigmatization. As mentioned before it has to do with all aspects of lifestyle. Therefore, corn flakes in the Caribbean are seen as more prestigious than the local, more nutritious, cornmeal porridge. A meal of the unhealthy American fare of pancakes, topped with synthesized maple syrup is regarded with prestige. American fast foods typically have this status. This cultural intrusion is resented by some ethnically, and health conscious locals, such as the Rastafarians. Thus, there is a constant ambivalence of aspiration and resistance to American culture.

However, for a large number of persons, Burger King and Kentucky Fried Chicken are 'holy grails'. Based on information from the Burger King subsidiary in Jamaica, the branch in Half Way Tree in Kingston sold in absolute volume five times more than its counterparts on the north coast, which caters to tourists. According to the management of the branch, it had the proportionally highest volume of sales of all stores internationally in 1998. KFC is the most common fast food with more than seventeen stores across the island. On a personal note, it is a bit saddening that a product trademarked by a Southern Confederate Colonel has such popularity in a population which was free and seeking to improve its position while its brothers and sisters to the North were both subject and object of a civil war in which his ancestor was an antagonist.

The demand for McFood, not only has implications for identity, but it also has health consequences. The fact is life expectancy of 'African-Islanders' is well above 70 years for the entire Anglophone Caribbean region. This compares favorably with that of African Americans, and is even not far from that of white Americans, who have far better access to a wider range of, and better health services. Given that a significant number of the ailments that are diet related affect African Americans, such as hypertension, and diabetes, McFood is a deadly lure.

Compared to prices in the U.S.A., it is expensive. A typical combo meal sells for between $1.99 for the Whopper to around $3.50 for the BK Broiler. This represents around 1/100 of a U.S. $250 a week minimum wage. In comparison the Jamaican national minimum wage, which is below the poverty line, is JA$1800 per week. Therefore, a Whopper combo of around JA$200 is actually 1/10 of a week's salary. Thus, to consume a burger is not only unhealthy nutritionally, but it also takes up a sizable portion of an already meager income.

The economic hegemony is also obvious. Because of the exclusive nature of the enterprises, McDonaldized type food stores do not tolerate similarities. Where there are pre-existing enterprises in the local economies with names that resemble or suggest their names or products, they obtain legal instruments to prevent them from continuing. Beyond that they compete with local providers of ethnic food and attempt to undersell and eliminate them, canceling out any positive employment effect.

Finally, but not least importantly, workers in these industries have lower labor standards than their counterparts. Fast food restaurants have one of the lowest rates of trade union membership/representation and are thus largely unprotected from arbitrary dismissals. In Jamaica less than 10 percent of workers in the industry are unionized. This compares with 20 percent nationally.

In summary, McDonaldization is the process of Americanization. It is a form of cultural diffusion that transmits much of the negatives in the United States without the concomitant benefits. The issues of race, though important, are ignored in the discussion of globalization. McDonaldization is globalization and vise versa. Still, if it is a process that is so inimical to the development of the Caribbean, which has historical connections and loyalty to the United States, one can only imagine how and why the non-friendly countries may develop deeper feelings of hostility.

Globalization, Jihad and the Terrorist Attack

There is somewhat of a causal link between terrorism and racism and globalization. It perhaps does not have the kind of connectivity that is suggested in the American media, but it exists. Globalization has led to the marginalization of a wide range of persons of non-European origin, including Blacks, and has brought a concomitant antipathy for America, which ultimately is connected to terrorism. Though bantered about for the better part of a decade, the term 'globalization' is not clearly defined. Nonetheless, a working definition is, *"the process in which nationality and geographic location become increasingly irrelevant.* (Antweiler 2002:4) The process occurs on three fronts; economic, cultural and political. Normally presented as seamless, globalization is far from equitable. Rather, it involves the domination of a particular set of cultural patterns, political agendas and economic regimes.

As regards culture, most of the elements have been discussed in the preceding treatise on the process of McDonaldization. It is, in essence, the spreading of American culture irrespective of the resistance of the local. With all of the positives that it may be said to carry, there are negative consequences and much resentment and resistance. Political dominance is not a recent phenomenon; it has characterized American foreign policy since the turn of the century. This is particularly true for the Caribbean basin, where the '*Monroe Doctrine*' and notion of '*Manifest Destiny*' were axiomatic in American orthodoxy. Simply put, the ideology underlying these is that the region was the footstool of America, being in its backyard. Consequently it was the prerogative of the United States to oversee the activities of the emergent nation-states.

That globalization is a historically established and ongoing process is not up for debate. What is true though is that it has taken on a different dimension since the middle of the 1990s. In 1994, the World Trade Organization (WTO) was formed and fully inaugurated in January 1995. Its agenda was specific with the intention of establishing common standards relating to international trade. In summary it introduced a regime which prevents a country from enjoying preferential treatment and from implementing protection for its own industries. Further, with a commitment to free movement of trade and capital, it virtually enjoins member states from restricting imports. In a nutshell, it attempts to create a status quo resembling what economists call perfect competition, eliminating unfair advantages to any member state.

On the surface this may appear to be just. The principles of equality that underline American ideology are consistent with this. This is not surprising, since, despite the declaration to the contrary, it is a body, like the International Monetary Fund and the World Bank, dominated by American interests. On deeper examination it reveals a bias that should cause much concern in the Afro-Caribbean community. It does not place labor issues on its agenda. This is more than an incidental omission. In 1996 it defined its own role, "*identifying the International Labour Organization (ILO) as the competent body to deal with labour standards*". (WTO: 51) However, the ILO does not have the powers to sanction a country that has breached its core labor standards. This thus translates into an advantage for the countries with poor labor practices, given that labor standards are cost-related. With this imbalance between enforceable standards related to trade and none for labor, investment will and does move in the direction of countries where workers operate under sub-standard terms and conditions of employment.

Such an inconsistency poses a serious dilemma for the Anglophone Caribbean in particular. This region has entrenched labor democracy and has had a symbiotic relationship between its trade unions and political parties. Workers in this area have legislated rights that are missing most of the other countries in the Third World. With higher labor standards, it is difficult to compete with other countries in Latin America which do not have the same democratic traditions.

Yet, on the other hand, pressure has been put on the Caribbean industries to compete 'fairly' under the rules of the WTO. The recent example of the banana industry is a poster case. In 1997, a motion was brought before the WTO to remove the preferential treatment that Caribbean bananas was receiving from the European Union (EU). These Caribbean countries have been receiving specialized access via a quota to the European and in particular the British market since the post World War II period. In terms of global trade in the commodity, the Caribbean's share is miniscule. It comprises less than three percent of world supply. Even with the privileged treatment West Indian bananas only constitute approximately nine percent of the European market. (Smikle: 2).

The West Indian producers are vulnerable and have difficulty competing with the American companies based in Latin America. Apart from having higher transportation and production expenditure, their labor standards are better, thus, the labor costs, as would be expected, are higher than in the Latin American countries. It is also of note that they utilize more organic productive and pest control methods and are therefore more environmentally friendly. (FOE 2002)

The case was brought by the United States government even though not one single American worker was affected. Investigations revealed that the government was taking the action due to the interest of Chiquita Banana, which was owned by an American, but located in Central America. Interestingly, this 'entrepreneur' is a large contributor to both the Democratic and Republican parties, but more to the latter. (Smikle:1) According to a fact-finding mission of European parliamentarians in 1997, the loss of the banana trade with the EU would have *"devastating consequences for the livelihood of hundreds of people across the Caribbean."* (Panda 2002) In Dominica the industry is listed as one of its essential services. It contributes between 60 and 80 percent of foreign exchange earnings (Morris:1) while employing one half of the labour force. More than 50 percent of the employed labor force in St. Vincent and 30 percent in St. Lucia, are engaged in the industry. Significantly, close to 20,000 banana growers have already been forced out of production. (Bryan 2002:2)

The banana issue goes to the heart of what is wrong about globalization. Chiquita, Del Monte and Dole combined control more than 60 percent of world banana production. (Morris 2002:1) Thus, the total share of the Caribbean is not a significant threat to their market share, as the little islands are not de facto competitors. It is a combination of greed and untrammeled capitalism.

In a paper presented by Montrope and Taylor (2000), it was argued that the impasse between the EU and WTO over the Chiquita controversy, was *'internationalizing racism'*. It is not inconsequential that the Congressional Black Caucus had taken up the matter, because more than 90 percent of the affected producers are persons of distinct African descent. Of particular note has been Rep. Maxine Waters, who in arguing that *"This multinational corporation was determined to put small Caribbean farmers out of business,"* also recognized that the industry was essential to the stability of the countries' democracies (Waters 1999 & 2000).

Given what appears to be the insensitivity of Washington to the needs of its Black neighbors in the Caribbean and an apparent willingness to sacrifice the livelihood and well being of thousands of people of color for the interest of one white American it can only lead to anti-American feelings. It says, like the cultural elements of globalization, that black people in the Caribbean do not count.

The ruling of the WTO against the EU and the Caribbean is likely to have ironic effect. The paradox is that the demise of the Caribbean banana industry will, in all probability, result in the farmers and workers resorting to the production and shipment of illegal drugs, to the US, which has an infinitely elastic demand for it. Similarly the flow of illegal immigrants will probably increase as well, since there will be a decrease in economic opportunities for them in their domiciles. Thus, two of the critical areas of pre- and post-911 American foreign policy are being worsened by the action.

Apart from the impact of the WTO-led globalization on the banana industry, all sectors in the Caribbean economy have felt the effect. To cope with the inequity caused by the enforcement of trade standards, but none for labor, employers with some collaboration with the regional governments have begun a trend towards employing *contract labor*. Workers employed under these contracts are traditionally not covered by most of the statutes which give basic rights such as paid vacation, sick leave, and protection from arbitrary employment. They also have no severance package. This is particularly so in the private security and tourism sectors. (Taylor 2001:14) The result is a pressure on real wages and an increasing inability of the labor force to subsist from wages. Ultimately this may make paid employment less desirable and push marginal members of the workforce towards 'other activities'. Doubtless, migration, legal or otherwise, will also be a real alternative.

Globalization is in itself a paradox for Afro-Caribbeans. In many ways it has been a betrayal of a set of people who have been Americanized (though with some resistance) and then marginalized. It is leading to attitudes and behaviors that America can ill-afford.

What the World Trade Center Represented

Although much older than the World Trade Organization, there is much that the Center shared with it. It housed 430 corporations from some 28 countries, and international agencies. Though in existence more than two decades prior to the formation of the WTO, it easily epitomized the heights and importance of a national monument. As an icon that represented the essence of a Western capitalist system headed by America, it was the natural target for anti-American action. Similarly, it represented to America, the symbol of its economic way of life.

According to Benjamin Barber: *"global economic forces weaken the nation-state in developed areas where it is most democratic and strengthen it in the third World where it is least democratic, imperiling liberty in both cases."* (Barber 1995:56) In his view, anti-American sentiments brought on by the process of McDonaldization, have led to *'Jihad'*. He uses the term to describe the range of local responses and resistance to the processes.

214

It is difficult for Anglo-Americans to understand why and how a set of individuals could have been so cruel. Yet, as abominable as it was it must be recognized that the perpetrators did not value their lives enough to preserve it either. These suicide bombers themselves represent an extreme counter-ideological response to what they consider to be the demise of their ways of life due to the spread of American culture. Though extreme and repugnant, it differs in degree to the attempts of America's historical 'friends' to wrest its culture from the grasps of Americanization in more peaceful ways.

From an Afro-Caribbean perspective, the entire range of anti-American ideology and action is not difficult to understand. The fact is, America has long disregarded things that are not Anglo-American. It is the center of the world. Thus, it has its private games that it considers the World Series. It invented a game and appropriated the name of another sport, which is used in over 200 countries. It refers to its Super Bowl champions as World Champions in 'football'. Irrespective of the fact that it is an entirely North American affair.

Even the name of the ill-fated WTC is a display of what could be termed as American arrogance. What made it the 'World' trade center? Was it truly representative of a global constituency? Twenty-eight countries are hardly the world. Though not directly related to the WTO, the names may very well bring about a correlation of sorts and thus associated resentment.

The difference between the Afro-Caribbean reaction to the suicide attacks on September 11, 2001 and those of other nations in the third world is the close historical and cultural bonds, though ambivalent, that have existed between the Caribbean and the United States. American political, economic and cultural hegemony and insensitivity has been tempered by a paradoxical pro-American identity. The geographical proximity is both a source of affinity and resistance. People with a different history and geography do not have the buffer of historical cultural links and identity to soften the American antipathy. Thus, as repugnant and reprehensible as the 'attacks' were, many Afro-Caribbean citizens can understand it.

Ironically, the response of the United States by targeting and bombing Afghanistan utilized the same paradigm as the terrorists. First of all a tangible target was made, even though the country of Afghanistan did not itself lead the attack on the Center, and the Taliban were not all Afghani, and bin Laden is not a citizen of that country. In fact, the jihad is an ideological network unembodied and unlocated physically. The members of bin Laden's 'army' are as spatially located as the Internet, cable television and other elements of American culture.

The attack on Afghanistan itself may lead to further Anti-American feelings. While it may have 'liberated' the country, many individuals have suffered as the United States swept with a wide broom. Non-participants in the 'war' have been killed or maimed and the physical infrastructure has been further damaged. Only time will tell how deep the scars will go and whether the seeds for further repercussions have been sown.

Ironies and Paradoxes in Addressing the Terrorist Threat

When the World Trade Center was impacted by the two aircraft on September 11, 2001 and the events described as the *attack of 9/11*, consistent with the process of globalization, the event was broadcast via satellite and cable television. Therefore, it was simultaneously relayed to several parts of the world. In the Caribbean the news was received with shock as several persons of Antillean origin perished in the explosions. More than a hundred persons from the Caribbean died in the blast. When one looks at the total percentage of Caribbean fatalities as a fraction of the population, it is not a small figure. Proportionally it may even be greater than the United States' loss.

With some degree of irony America sought an immediate response to a tangible enemy. Thus, the enemy was constructed and personified in Osama bin Laden and his Taliban cronies in Afghanistan. At best, the support from the third world was divided, as once again America was seen as a forceful bully by some. A non-scientific survey of the newspaper opinion polls across the English-Caribbean suggests that less than half of the populace supported any armed incursion into Afghanistan.

With much justification, security was increased at all ports of entry and officials demanded a more scrupulous examination of travel documents. Of course whenever the issue of increased security arises there are invariably questions of human rights violations. Travel has become more onerous as passengers now have to wait on the average 45 minutes to an hour more at international airports. Coupled with that, visitors to the United States, who are required to be processed in separate immigration lines, are subject to sniffer-dogs invading their intimate parts.

As with internal policing in the United States, security personnel at the airports have profiles that supposedly identify the 'typical suspect'. In doing so many innocent Caribbean travelers are viewed with the same suspicion as terrorists. The general consensus that many Caribbean visitors to the United States now share is that more than before, the encounter with American immigration and security officers at the major international airports leaves them feeling like suspects and criminals. Consequently, they develop deeper resentment to their 'antagonists' and by extension the American authorities.

Directly related to the heightened security in the American airports is the concomitant increase in security checks at the Caribbean airports. In the Point Salines Airport in Grenada, passengers are required to clear a civilian security guard. Next, a uniformed police officer checks the luggage. Finally, a fully-armed soldier in military fatigue conducts both body and baggage searches. Added to all of that, there is the likelihood that a plainclothes police officer will select any individual 'at random', to check his/her travel documents. The truth is, the selection of suspects is not random in the scientific sense of the word. Far from being the result of probability sampling, the methodology utilized by the Caribbean security personnel is also based on stereotypes. Again with some measure of irony, a region with the overwhelming majority of its population being of African descent, uses a typecast based on race and class. Citizens who fit the profile of the lower-class Blacks from the inner cities and rural areas are more prone to be targeted. In simple language, there is an element of a racial bias, perpetuated by people of color, against their peers. It is a sort of 'Black-on-Black' racism.

In the zeal to comply with the security standards dictated by the United States, other Caribbean airports have followed suit. Invasive body searches are not unusual. There are increasing reports of security officers and police personnel carrying out excesses in maintaining vigilance. Recently, a Jamaican citizen sued the government for breaches of his rights in unlawfully detaining and searching him prior to boarding (*Week End Star* 05/10/2002).

Given that at least part of the explanation for the events of 9/11 lies in the anti-American sentiments that emanate from the encounters between America and other nations, the ironic consequence of the enhanced security measures is that they run the risk of further marginalizing some of the erstwhile pro-American neighbors in the Caribbean.

Interestingly, the Caribbean governments do not have the same vigilance in searching visitors and cargo entering their countries. Therefore, there is still the possibility that the aforementioned contraband trade, suspected to indirectly help in the financing of the very international terrorism that is being targeted, is not being curtailed.

Even more, there is also what appears to be some degree of inconsistency in the adjustment that the airlines have made. As mentioned, the Caribbean airlines have implemented a more restrictive regimen. For example it is impossible to take a nail clipper or nail file on board a BWIA or Air Jamaica flight. Yet Air Canada still issues metal forks and spoons without any furor by United States security. Needless to say the latter is the airline of a country that is manifestly white.

Added to the increased security measures, the United States foreign policy was modified to throw out the proverbial baby with the bath water. Several changes in immigration policy were made, as America sought to close its borders. More recently, holders of visitor's visas of the 'B' type were advised that they would no longer have the privilege of staying in the States for more than thirty days unless it could be established that they had reason to remain. Previously, visitors could remain for up to six months. Typically, Caribbean holders of these visas would spend lengthy periods of their three to four months summer vacations. Of course, there are also a number of them who engage in activities leading to economic gain, however unlawful it may be. As has been the case with nationals from many other pro-American countries, visitors to the United States, who earn incomes during these short stints, remit money to their families in the Caribbean or at a minimum, spend it on themselves. Due to the obvious undocumented nature of this phenomenon, the actual economic contribution of this type of endeavor is unknown. However, its contribution to the economies of the Caribbean could compare favorably with that of the H2 program. Notwithstanding this last observation, the great majority of Caribbean nationals who hold these visas comply with American law and return to their places of origin.

What American policy makers are overlooking is that Caribbean visitors to the United States do not only return with or send economic benefits. Beyond that they also transmit or transport positive images of America to their fellows. This good public relations impression that is carried home does far more than the mass media could possibly do for America's image. The reverse is also true.

The new regimen is unfavorable to legitimate Caribbean nationals who desire to maintain their historical relationships with the United States. One cannot help but conclude that there may be elements of racism in the way in which the problem of terrorism is perceived and addressed. As is the case with the banana industry, the post-9/11 reaction of the United States government is likely to create a paradox. September 11th has perhaps affected the Caribbean tourist industry most. Tourism in the English-speaking Caribbean contributes between 30 and 60 percent of GDP. (PIOJ 2000) It is the single largest earner of foreign exchange and employs one out of every four Caribbean nationals. In the two weeks after the event, the impact on flight and tourist arrivals was devastating. The multiplier effect is yet to be felt. However, estimates are in the region of close to $300 million. The loss of jobs in this industry could exceed 50,000. (Observer 2001). With diminished opportunities for earning a living, again pressure is exerted on Caribbean nationals to seek other means. These very means are themselves a threat.

Conclusions

For Caribbeans of African descent, the attack on the World Trade Center and the subsequent response of the American government represents the paradox of paradoxes. As quasi-Americans they have historical ties to the land of opportunity. America is a source of economic and cultural diffusions. As people of color they share much of the suffering and issues of their northern counterparts. They live in a region dominated by white American interests. Though by and large protected from the micro, face to face manifestations of racism, they are affected by the racist nature of the globalization process. This coupled with the historical contacts between both sets of Blacks must lead to a sensitivity to some of the injustices being perpetrated against them.

Globalization has integrated the Caribbean in a network of American culture and economic relations. The new direction that globalization has taken has had an overall negative impact on the lives of the Caribbean peoples of African descent. On the one hand it is further integrating them in an increasing 'McWorld' while at the same time sacrificing their economic well being on the altar of a narrow set of interests.

Yet, they both absorb and aspire towards American culture and reject its hegemony at the same time. In the mix, however, they are pro-American. It is ironic also that many Caribbean people have been directly affected by the loss of lives of their family members and friends. Nonetheless, in being targeted as undesirable immigrants, and visitors, they are made to suffer twice. With the loss of earnings they are even more imperiled.

Still, as America seeks to close its borders to its 'friends' in the Caribbean it perhaps unwittingly increases the threat. Not only will it marginalize its allies-ordinary pro-American citizens-in the Caribbean, but also it narrows their choices, making the alliances with the drug traders more enticing. These, who have been portrayed to have a link with the international 'enemies' of the United States, may very well find easy access to American soil. Still ironically, it may very well be the small Caribbean states that are more threatened by the drug trade.

The situation is an irony twice over.

References

1. Antweiler, Werner (May 21,2002) "Economic Globalization and its Consequences." http://pacific.commerce.ubc.ca/antweiler/apsc450/
2. Barber, Benjamin (1995) *Jihad vs. McWorld*, New York, Ballantine Books
3. Beckford, George(1972) *Persistent Poverty*. London, Oxford University Press.
4. Bennett, Lerone (2000) *Forced into Glory: Abraham Lincoln's White Dream*, Chicago, Johnson Publishing Company.
5. Bryan, Anthony (June 24, 2002) 'US Caribbean Relations Strained over US- European Banana Dispute.' www.miami.edu/nsc/pages/newsup dates/Update.htm.
6. Bureau of Economic Analysis [BEA](2002) International Investment Data, US Direct Investment Abroad: Income. www.bea.doc.gov/bea/d./usdiainc.htm
7. Girvan, Norman (1972) *Foreign Capital and Economic Underdevelopment in Jamaica*, Kingston, Jamaica, Institute of Social and Economic Research, University of the West Indies, Mona.
8. The Gleaner Company, editorial (03/10/02) *Week-End Star*, Kingston, Jamaica, The Gleaner Company.
9. Griffith, Ivelaw L (1997) *Drugs an Security in the Caribbean*, Pennsylvania State University Press.
10. Fanon, Frantz (1967) *Black Skins, White Masks*, New York, Grove Press.
11. Friends of the Earth [FOE] (June 28,2002) 'WTO Scorecard: WTO and Free Trade vs. Environment and Public Health,' www.foe.org/inter national/wto/scorecard.pdf
12. Foner, Nancy (11/5/2002) Hearing Testimony to 'Subcommittee on National Parks, Historic Preservation, and Recreation' http://energy.sen ate.gov/hearings/national_parks/5_11Cats&Dogs/Foner.htm
13. Hall, Kenneth and Benn, Dennis (eds.) (2000) *Contending with Destiny: The Caribbean in the 21st Century*, Kingston, Jamaica, Ian Randle Publishers.
14. Henry, Zin (1971) *Labour Relations and Industrial Conflict in Commonwealth Caribbean Countries*, Port of Spain, Trinidad, Columbus Publishers
15. Jamaica Observer the (September 13, 2002) The Jamaica Observer
16. James, Winston (1998) *Holding Aloft the Banner of Ethiopia: Caribbean Radicalism in Early Twentieth Century America*, New York/London, Verso.
17. Miami Herald (August 12, 1996) 'The Jamaican Miracle', 20-23.

18. Ministry of Labour (1991-2000) Statistical Bulletin, Kingston, Jamaica, Ministry of Labour
19. Mittleman, James H. (ed) (1997) *Globalization: Critical Reflections,* Boulder/London, Lynne Reinner Publishers.
20. Montrope, Darrel and Taylor, Orville (2000), 'The WTO and Caribbean Bananas: Globalizing Racism.' Unpublished paper presented at Association of Black Sociologist Conference, Washington DC.

THE U.S. WAR ON TERRORISM AND FOREIGN POLICY JUSTICE

Ron Walters

The manner in which the United States pursues its security interests both at home and in the Middle East will have a profound impact on the promise of the administration of George Bush to guarantee the security of the average American. Thus, the issue of the "War on Terrorism" in the United States; the military engagement of al Qaeda in Afghanistan, Pakistan and other venues in the Middle East; and the threatened invasion of Iraq, at this writing, are all linked in their origin to the American posture with respect to the Arab-Israeli question. In fact these issues are linked to the minds of Middle Easterners as indicated by a poll of 3,800 Arabs in countries, such as, Egypt, Jordan, Lebanon, Kuwait, Morocco, United Arab Emirates, Saudi Arabia and Israel. This was revealed in a poll conducted by John Zogby in 2002, "What Arabs Think: Values, Beliefs and Concerns." Therefore, this issue should be linked by Americans in an examination of what factors will contribute to peace in both areas.

The policy of the United States government in the Middle East, and in particular the Arab-Israeli question, is characterized by significant confusion over its role, rather than the clarity which contributes to a resolution of the conflict because the U.S. poses as both an ally of Israel and as an "honest broker" to the dispute. This contradiction—as mediator between Palestinian and Israeli leadership and sponsor of the state of Israel in the region as an outpost of American interests—has limited the legitimacy necessary for the U.S. to exercise the maximum leverage in resolving the problem fairly, most especially, in the eyes of the Arab public. While in the 1980s President George Herbert Walker Bush attempted to court Arab states, somewhat to the detriment of Israel in order to secure American oil interest in the region, the Clinton administration returned to the basic Israel-U.S. accord framework as enunciated in a speech by Martin Indyk, senior National Security Council aide on May 18, 1993 to the pro-Israel Washington Institute for Near East

Policy. He said, "Our approach to the negotiations will involve working with Israel, not against it. We are committed to deepening our strategic partnership with Israel in the pursuit of peace and security." Indyk goes on to say, that "No similar pledge was made to work with the Arabs."[1]

This Israeli first and only approach is problematic because the precondition for successful negotiations in the Middle East conflict and its modern manifestations has resided in the ability to create an environment in which the proposals could attain the necessary confidence, especially by the Arab world, that they are in their interests as well. This complication that resulted in failure by the Clinton administration is now most vividly revealed in the failure of American policy in the Middle East at this time, led by George W. Bush.

This essay will spell out several critical dimensions of that policy failure that are rooted in the contradictions of the American position, which further complicates its ability to create the proper environment for policy success. This failure, regarded here as foreign policy injustice, has in turn contributed to the more intensive alienation of the "Arab Street" creating the environment which challenges American internal security. I will discuss the basis of this injustice and suggest that a just policy, one that balances interests of both Israel and Palestinians in ways proportionate to Palestinian suffering, is the path to justice in the Middle East and to security for American citizens.

Dimensions of Foreign Policy Injustice

First, in the full flush of this quagmire, supporters of the Bush administration have failed to understand the problem and allowed the Israelis to cast the problem in the region in a law enforcement, crime and punishment context for "terrorism," rather than a serious attention to the political demands of the Palestinian/Arab revolution, that are central to understanding both the motivations and the lack of flexibility on both sides. The Bush administration is complicit in that failure because it has approached the attack on the World Trade Center and Pentagon in the same vein, pursuing a war based on the false proposition of "defeating terrorism."

The pretense of the West, including the U.S., is that the Arab revolution is unconnected to the just struggle for self-determination among Third World people that they encountered as the price of undoing legal colonialism. Thus, the roots of the Palestinian struggle is related to the wider Third World Revolution and its grievances against the West, begun with the 1936 Palestinian revolt against British colonialism, which included not only the occupation of their land, but the inferiorization of their culture. To suggest that citizens of the West are naive about this history and therefore, the reasons for the use of terrorism (traditionally the poor man's nuclear weapon) is to lose credibility in the eyes of those whose demands are at issue. The loss of American credibility is related to the loss of Arab trust which makes it impossible that any settlement agreed to will be honored by either side.

This lack of credibility expands in the pretense that Yasser Arafat—or any one person—"controls" or could control the full set of revolutionaries such as Hamas, by making him personally responsible for the tactics of militants or Palestinian rejection of proposals put forth by the U.S. In fact, at the time of President Clinton's Camp David meeting in the summer of 1999, Hamas officials threatened Arafat with going too far in the direction of negotiation suggesting that they would not honor any such agreement struck that took away the basic elements of their nationalist struggle. Then, as late as mid-May 2002, Sheik Yassin, founder and leader of Hamas said that, although he respected Yasser Arafat's recent call to end the violence against Israelis, his organization would not do so—for to do so would be to end the resistance and to betray the cause for which they were engaged in the struggle in the first place.

In his words, "when he asks me to stop the self defense, he asks me to surrender and die."[2] In this sense, then, the error has created an impasse of viewing Arafat as a totally autonomous actor when he is as much a hostage to the revolution as he is its leader because his lack of control sets substantial limits on his flexibility with Israel and, thus, with the United States.

This has led to a third problem which is the substitution of Western arrogance in the so-called "peace process" for the legitimacy of Palestinian leadership. The current crisis is replete with comments by American officials demanding what Yasser Arafat must do and how he has not been receptive to offers that would lead to a peace settlement, even to the point of casting inferences that he should be replaced with someone more malleable. This has led to the attempt to manage or even de-legitimize Arafat with an arrogance typical of the Western management of this crisis.

For instance, in a widely anticipated speech on the Middle East of June 25, 2002, Bush chided the Palestinians for mismanagement of funds and failing to develop an adequate governmental infrastructure. While holding out the promise of supporting a Palestinian state, he argued that reform and indeed a change in leadership was necessary and that the existing leadership was not legitimate as a partner in fighting terrorism unless it stopped "the flow of money, equipment and recruits to terrorist groups seeking the destruction of Israel, including Hamas, Islamic Jihad and Hezbollah."[3] Thus, Bush began to separate his government from the support of the Palestinian Liberation Organization and some suggested from the peace process itself because of a lack of an ability to be flexible on the issue of Palestinian leadership.

It would appear that the most rudimentary understanding of the ingredients of a legitimate process involved in achieving a peace agreement is missing, which is that you must deal with the obvious legitimate leadership that may be one not of our own choosing. This mistake is compounded by the domestic rationale which views Osama bin Laden as the problem, but realizes there is another cause for his attack upon the United States. So, rearranging the leadership of the Palestinian people in order to achieve an agreement on the terms of the West is ultimately a self-defeating exercise that would only enhance the volatility of the region and fan the flames of the deep-seated feelings against the West. This effort would appear to completely misunderstand the personal and institutional basis of moral capital.[4] The Palestinians derive considerable moral capital inasmuch as they have been the historic displaced victims of the imposition of the Israeli state in that region and have further been the disproportionate victims of Israeli military operations. Thus, the leadership status of Arafat is derivative of the moral capital of the Palestinian people, which they cede to him as a personal resource that he has attempted to husband in addressing the requirements of the negotiating process.

Impact on the War on Terrorism

The problem derived from the U.S. role as mediator/player contradiction is that by waging war against the Palestinians in the name of "rooting out terror cells" Ariel Sharon has caught the United States in a vulnerable place because of its own "war against terrorism" as a result of the 9/11 attacks on the

New York Twin Towers and the Pentagon. By pursuing a war against something called "terrorism" rather than acknowledging that there are people with grievances who perpetrated it and addressing those grievances, the United States is able to suppress the point that the attack constitutes evidence that all along it has not been perceived as a neutral agent, but as a partisan one.

In this context, Sharon's agreement that peace cannot be made with Arafat is counterproductive because, although he exercises superior military force, he cannot choose the leadership of the Palestinian people except by force; with the consequence that the process will make temporary whatever "peace" may be achieved by such an act. This was the effect of the attack on all of the Palestinian settlements, including Ramallah where tanks leveled houses to rubble, killing scores of people and the surrounding of Arafat's compound, eventually blowing up a large part of the Palestinian Authority buildings. It was a display of bravado that was ultimately stunted by the reality that, although Sharon might have wished for Arafat to be sent into exile, if it actually occurred, Sharon would be even more exposed to the violence of Hamas and other groups than ever before.

The speech by George Bush which sought to de-legitimize Yasser Arafat and which paralleled Sharon's statements, was roundly criticized when he attended the June 2002 meeting of G-7 countries plus Russia in Calgary, Canada, and he was unsuccessful in persuading any leader to support his call for Arafat's ouster. Rather, Bush himself was isolated in their sentiment that the selection of the head of the Palestinian people was a matter of their own self determination, not a function of any outside power.

Moreover, the so-called "Arab Street" is generally opposed to replacing Yasser Arafat because of their own understanding that he is the legitimate leader of the Palestinian people and that a successful replacement of Arafat could be a lesson which any of them might face, comparable to the Shah of Iran. In any case, at the Arab Summit in April of 2002, Crown Prince Abdullah of Saudi Arabia offered his own eight point peace plan, the elements of which are as follows:

1. Complete Israeli withdrawal from the West Bank areas recently occupied;
2. An end to the Israeli military siege of Ramallah where Palestinian

leader Yasser Arafat was trapped in his headquarters for four
weeks;

3. The insertion of a multinational force;
4. The reconstruction of destroyed Palestinian areas;
5. A renunciation of violence;
6. The immediate initiation of political talks;
7. An end to Israeli settlements;
8. Implementation of UN Resolution 242, which calls for Israeli withdrawal from territories occupied during the 1967 Israeli-Arab War,
   including the West Bank and Golan Heights.

At a meeting with Crown Prince Abdullah at his ranch in Texas on April
27, 2002, George Bush agreed to continue to talk to Abdullah about the peace
plan, but made no hard-fast commitments to all of its elements.[5]

It was clear that the thrust of this statement was to effect the withdrawal
of the Israeli military forces from the areas attacked, including Ramallah and
Jenin, to secure their re-development and to begin talks leading toward a
peace settlement. In his subsequent speech on the Middle East, however, Bush
made no mention of the Arab/Saudi peace proposals, in an astounding show
of either neglect or political devaluation of the role of Arabs in the peace
process. This important slight was another bow to Israel, but its effect was to
harden the chasm between Arabs and the West and the strategies that they
have pursued.

Foreign Policy Justice

To understand the plight of the Palestinians who have been victims of the
Western policy of displacement and disproportionate destruction and that of
other Arab sympathizers is to understand their perspective that opposition to
occupation is a "just war" as it was for Americans who fought against the
British; or South Africans who fought apartheid; or Algerians who fought
against the French; or any such similar situation. While one does not support
or justify suicide bombing, one understands that it is the weapon of a frustrated people who believe that they have no other means of resistance and,
thus, its use is beyond the Western standards of what is humane in war. All
such groups have used such tactics, including the Irgun, the Irish Republican

228

Army, the African National Congress and the Pan African Congress, and other groups.

Guerilla warfare has always been a way of seeking for the relatively powerless to equalize the power equation and this example is no different. What has always been known about guerilla movements is the demand that the poor and outgunned use the same tactics as the powerful amounts, in effect, to a demand for a default of their struggle. What one observes is that despite the wealth of American intellectual resources on global conflict, our understanding about the revolutionary process and its methods has no currency in this conflict and our intellectuals have abrogated their responsibility to transmit their understanding of the process to the general public. Instead, opposing terror is the base and shallow level of analysis that only supports an unjust, one-sided approach to both peace in the Middle East and the resolution of the internal security dilemma in this country.

American policy in the Middle East should be pursued from the values of the American people about justice and human rights. To this extent, inasmuch as public opinion polls of the black community have traditionally indicated a preference for the peace process over war and feel that American policy is too heavily weighted on the side of Israel, a large segment of the American people do not feel that the policy toward the Palestinians is just. In fact, many whites who feel as blacks do that Israel has a right to live within secure borders find no moral equivalence between two parties when it has been illustrated that Israel exercises superior military power in the region and is supported by the most superior military power on the face of the globe.

Like other aspects of American domestic and foreign policy, understanding the diplomatic gestures and the resulting formulae resides in the domestic elements that drive policy. In this case, an obvious key is the admirably high level of activity of the Jewish community as a whole with respect to its support of Israel and the effect of that support on the American political system. Here, economic resources are especially key, since the absence of such resources would make the Jewish community resemble the historical efforts of blacks to influence American policy toward the African continent, where only episodic gains have been made. One periodical reports, for example, that in the 2001-2002 election cycle pro-Israeli PAC contributions to Congressional candidates amounted to $828,097.00, while for the period 1978-2002, the total amount contributed was $35,435,279.00[6]. The level of these contributions have made possible actions such as, a letter signed by 235 House Members [including Black Caucus Members Alcee Hastings (D-FL), Carrie Meeks (D-FL), John Lewis (D-GA), Gregory Meeks (D-NY), and Diane Watson (D-CA)] urging that Arab groups such as, Al Aqsa, Martyrs Brigade, the Tanzim and Force 17 be added to the terrorist list.[7] This formidable influence on the Congress is led by lawmakers across the political spectrum, but, especially, by conservative leaders such as Tom Delay (R-TX). It is expected to increase with the passage of the new version of campaign finance reform which enhances the role of private donors.[8]

Then, another result of such influence is that in the debate over H. R. 240 a resolution that called for the support of Israel, most African American members of Congress either opposed it, abstained or did not vote. However, Congressman Earl Hilliard of the 7th Congressional District of Alabama subsequently lost his seat due to a primary challenge in the June 2002 primary election by a challenger Artur Davis who was heavily subsidized by out-of-state funding related to Israeli interests and who was able to raise over $800,000 for his bid.

Similarly, Representative Cynthia McKinney of the 4th District of Georgia was challenged by Denise Majette, a black female former state judge. McKinney became vulnerable over her comment that President Bush may have had information on the September 11th attack before it occurred, but he did not release it, so that his associates could profit from a war. These remarks drew significant opposition to McKinney from the local media and key white political figures, such as conservative Democrat, U.S. Senator Zell Miller. More importantly, her decision, like Hilliard's, not to vote in favor of a resolution of absolute suppport for Israel evoked an outrage from Jewish organizations outside of the State of Georgia. The combination of these factors saw the Majette campaign become the recipient of approximately 1.3 million dollars from those organizations. The result was that McKinnney was defeated in the primary election by 58% to 42% of the vote.

The combination of the losses of Earl Hilliard and Cynthia McKinney over the Middle East issue has angered many black political leaders, for example, Rep. Albert Wynn of Maryland who said, "The black community perceived Jewish opposition to them as racial. It appears some elements of the Jewish community have become more aggressive and it is unprecedented. I think it risks rupturing the traditional black-Jewish alliance." (Julie Hirschfield Davis, "Rift between Blacks, Jews Worries Democrats of Fall," *Baltimore Sun*, August 26, 2002, online edition)

The Movement Against Iraq

Foreign policy justice must be consistent in the treatment of nations, but what we find in the case of Iraq is a selective policy of persecution because that country and its leaders are attempting to manufacture weapons of mass destruction. Other countries in that region such as, Israel, Pakistan and India have succeeded in manufacturing these weapons, but the United States has done little as long as these countries were perceived to be within the Western orbit of influence and there was the likelihood that the use of these weapons could be controlled, or at least not used against the United States.

Americans, however, do not know that the development of nuclear capability by so many Third World countries was abetted by the official policy of the United States which shared technology and was lax in the enforcement of the nuclear non-proliferation policy of the International Atomic Energy Agency. In my study of the nuclear capability of South Africa I asserted that the racist regime had the capability to manufacture nuclear weapons in a scenario where the U.S. had given it a small nuclear reactor in the early 1960s under the "Atoms for Peace" program initiated by President Dwight Eisenhower. This enabled them, with one of the largest natural stocks of uranium in the world, to perfect a uranium enrichment technology and reprocess uranium into weapons grade material, probably with the assistance of Israel. The administration of Jimmy Carter covered up the 1977 South African nuclear test in the Kalahari Desert because to acknowledge that a test had occurred would have involved nuclear sanctions against South Africa, a friend of American corporate interests. Although nuclear experts derided the notion that South Africa had nuclear weapons, they finally had to admit it did possess them. (Ronald Walters, *South Africa and the Bomb*, Lexington/Praeger-1986).

War against Iraq is justified by its pursuit of nuclear weapons, not its known possession of the same. The United Nations has been enlisted in the search for such capability as well as for chemical or biological agents that may be used militarily. Meanwhile, the Bush administration has sought and received permission from the U.S. Congress to pursue war against Iraq unilaterally and independently whether or not the United Nations inspectors confirm that Iraq has such weapons. The ferocity and singlemindedness of Bush's war intention have been related to the oil reserves of Iraq which would come under the direct influence of the United States should Iraq be defeated. In this scenario the oil associates of Bush would undoubtedly benefit. Moreover, because of the Soviet interest in Iraq oil, suggestions from some quarters are that the U.S., France and Russia have already divided up the Iraqi oil reserves. (David Ignatius, "War and Oil", October 18, 2002, The Washington Post, page A37)

Foreign policy justice means that a policy must take into consideration that cost borne by American citizens and it must be configured that the costs are shared rather than a disporportionate burden being borne by one group. Thus, black Americans should oppose war against Iraq and all such wars whose motives cannot be considered to be just because they are positioned to bear a disporportionate share of the costs. For example, blacks comprise over one-fifth of the infantry units that are sent into a ground war. The presumption made during the Gulf War, which was based on the experience in the Vietnam War, was that blacks would suffer nearly one-quarter of the casualties. It did not occur in the Gulf War because the resistance from Iraq was not significant. Secondly, the economic costs of war cancel out the expenditures for human needs. The cost of the Gulf War was said to have been nearly one trillion dollars; the estimated cost of the planned Iraq War is two hundred billion dollars with the settlement(occupation) of the country costing another five hundred billion dollars over the next several years. Add to this amount the ten year tax cut that was achieved by the Bush administration which will go into effect in 2004. Thirdly, there must be an accounting for the moral cost of the war. Black tradition is not only to resist war because it is costly in economic terms, but also, because it is costly in terms of human suffering. Dr. Martin Luther King, Jr. was allowed to live through some of the worst phases of the Civil rights struggle; however, he probably gave his life for the fact that he began to actively oppose the American pursuit of the war in Vietnam. For these and other reasons the massive mobilization against Iraq, the bombing of Afghanistan, the adoption of a policy of "hot pursuit" into Pakistan and other belligerent actions should be opposed.

Conclusion

What I have argued in this work is that state posture structures the state policy orientation and that the American posture toward Israel has prevented its many negotiations from achieving the fruits of peace sought by all sides to this conflict. I used the term "foreign policy justice" in order to point out that analysts have not considered sufficiently the moral content or the racial interests of a policy in their determination of which party to a dispute should be advantaged. With the result that the handling of foreign policy by those in power often shielded moral content by striking a neutralist or defensive interpretation of policy, the existence of unequal power and unequal loss posed a substantial question of the justice in the resolution of the problem.

In the context of the Palestinian/Israeli conflict, the U. S. approached the policy problem as a fair moderator while at the same time attempting to maintain its own set of regional interests.

In doing so, it had to pretend that the political situation on each side was equal, even that the disproportionate victim had to exercise more responsibility than the victor in various military encounters. As such, their task was to persuade the parties that peace was in their mutual interests and to devise proposals and plans for achieving an agreement between them that was accountable to the losses suffered by each side. But once perceived as also representing one of the parties to the dispute by subtly absolving them of accountability and placing heavier burdens on the weaker party to accept the framework elements of negotiation, they were frustrated by the weaker party's rejection of their entreaties, demands and proposals. The weaker party did not consider the proposals just, essentially because they called for actions that were not reciprocated on the other side in similar dimension and were not rooted in the greater loss of life and property and greater risk of ceasing the attempt to regain their former political integrity. In other words, the proposals did not adequately take into consideration either the perspective or the realistic condition of the weaker party.

This contradiction at the heart of American foreign policy toward the Middle East can only be resolved by a serious shift in emphasis to legitimize Palestinian perspective and conditions which could improve the chances for peace resolution of the dispute by such actions as a restraint on Israel. Moreover, the war against Iraq will only intensify the problem of American security by adding to the Arab-Israel problem yet another source of alienation for those persons who are already opposed to American policy and presence in that region.

Otherwise, neither the American government as a moderator of the conflict, nor the subsequent protection of American regional interests may be secure. This situation becomes even more urgent as the seeds of the policy failure have now taken on domestic consequences, meaning that the roots of the security of American citizens is now dependent upon shoring up the integrity of American posture in the Middle East by pursuing fundamental changes that evoke credibility and trust in its position and proposals by those who are most oppressed in the region.

Notes

1. Avi Shlaim, *War and Peace in the Middle East*, Penguin Books, 1995, p.123.
2. Oral Interview, CNN Television, May 14, 2002.
3. "Mideast Turmoil: The President's Words of Warning: 'Things Must Change in the Middle East,'" *The New York Times*, June 25, 2002, transcript.
4. John Kane, *The Politics of Moral Capital*, Cambridge University Press, 2001, p. 35.)
5. "Crown Prince Gives Bush Eight-Point Middle East Peace Plan," April 27, 2002, Saudi Arabian Information Resource.
6. *Washington Report on Middle East Affairs*, May 2002, Vol. XXI, No. 4, p. 37.
7. Sheri McArthur, "Letters Show Depth of Anti-Palestinian Sentiment in Congress," Ibid, p. 33
8. Ibid, p. 35.

About the Contributors

Cheryl Poinsette Brown is a graduate of Howard University and Harvard Law School. She practiced law and later worked in a Fortune 500 corporation in San Francisco, California before moving to the South where she is now a writer, mother and wife. She is currently working on her first book.

Melanie Campbell is the executive director and chief executive officer of the National Coalition on Black Civic Participation, Inc. She has over twenty years of experience as a civic leader, political strategist and youth advocate. She has been featured in numerous national and local media outlets as an expert on Black civic participation, African American voting trends, and Census and election reform.

Paul Collins is a self-taught Michigan-based artist. His achievements have won him many national and international honors and awards for his skills as an artist and as an humanitarian. He was named in the Watson-Guptill Publication as one of the top twenty painters in America. He has won the Mead Book Award, Tadlow Fine Art Award, People's Choice Award in Paris, The Golden Centuar, Italy, and the Ceba Award for Excellence. Mr. Collins has served on many boards including the John F. Kennedy Center For Performing Arts, The Martin Luther King Board and the Arts Council.

Dr. Kimberly C. Ellis is Assistant Professor of English and Black Studies at DePauw University. She gives multimedia presentations on the Tulsa story and is currently completing a play based upon her research. Her dissertation on the Tulsa tragedy is entitled "We Look Like Men of War: Africana Male Narratives and the Tulsa Race Riot, War and Massacre of 1921."

Marcia Ann Gillespie is a pioneering feminist, trailblazing publishing industry executive, writer, editor and activist. She has been the Editor-in-Chief of both *Ms.* and *Essence* magazines. A popular lecturer, Ms. Gillespie's inspired remarks raise important questions about the intersections of race, class and gender. A member of the board of directors of Planned Parenthood, Ms. Gillespie lives in New York City.

Brian Gilmore is a D.C. area writer, poet, and attorney. His work has appeared in numerous magazines and newspapers, including the *Washington City Paper*, *The Progressive* and the *Washington Post*. He is the author of *Elvis Presley is Alive and Living in Harlem* and *Jungle Nights and Soda Fountain Rags*.

Danny Glover is a critically acclaimed actor of both stage and screen. He has been nominated for an Emmy Award for his performances in the miniseries *Freedom Song*, the miniseries *Lonesome Dove*, and the drama series *Fallen Angels*. Mr. Glover is also Chairman of TransAfrica Forum.

Congresswoman Barbara Lee has been representing California's Ninth District, which includes parts of Oakland and Berkeley, in Congress since 1998. Formerly, she represented her district in the California Assembly as legislator and senator. Active in global and domestic policy issues, especially around AIDS, poverty and economic development, Lee has been Vice Chair of the Progressive Caucus, Chair of the Congressional Black Caucus Task Force on Global HIV/AIDS and a member of the CBC's Minority Business Task Force.

Haki R. Madhubuti is a poet, educator and editor. He is the founder and publisher of Third World Press (1967), co-founder of the Institute for Positive Education (1969), the New Concept School and the Betty Shabazz International Charter School(1998). He is a Distinguished Professor and Director of the Master of Fine Arts Creative Writing Program at Chicago State University. He is the founders and Director Emeritus of the Gwendolyn Brooks Center at Chicago State. He has published twenty-five books, including *Don't Cry, Scream!* (1969), *Black Men: Obsolete, Single, Dangerous* (1990) and *Tough Notes: A Healing Call for Creating Exceptional Black Men* (2002).

Roland S. Martin is editor of BlackAmericaWeb.com and news editor of *Savoy Magazine*. He is the author of "Speak, Brother! A Black Man's View of America." Mr. Martin is also a nationally syndicated columnist and a national correspondent for the American Urban Radio Network.

Aaron McGruder is the creator of the syndicated comic strip *Boondocks* which has been "inciting angry black children since 1998." Mr. McGruder is currently working on two television pilots, in addition to his daily work that appears in hundreds of newspapers nationwide.

Gail E. Mitchell is a graduate of Boston University and New York University. She is a licensed real estate broker in New York State and on September 11, 2001 worked in the Real Estate Department of the New York Port Authority as Senior Lease Account Manager at the World Trade Center. An active member of Delta Sigma Theta, Inc., Ms. Mitchell also serves as Secretary on the Board of Directors of Steinway Child and Family Services, Inc.

Askia Muhammad is a photojournalist, poet, radio and television commentator and author. He is a panelist on Howard University Television WHUT-TV32's "Evening Exchange." He writes a column for *The Washington Informer*, is the White House Correspondent for *The Final Call* newspaper and is a contributor to the Opinion Page of MSNBC.com Interactive.

Laura W. Murphy is the Director of the Washington Office of the American Civil Liberties Union. She is the first woman and first African American to hold the position, and as a lobbyist was instrumental in the passage of the Voting Rights Act Extension of 1982. She is the recipient of numerous awards and is the Acting Chair of the D.C. Committee to Promote Washington.

Dr. Andrea Benton Rushing is a Professor of English and Black Studies at Amherst College in Amherst, Massachusetts. Professor Rushing is the Co-Editor of *"Women in Africa and the African Diaspora"* and the author of a collection of interlocking essays, "Rape: the Invisible Wound", as well as numerous articles and reviews published in academic journalsand collections. Her current work-in-progress is "Speaking in Tongues: the Language of Yoruba Women's Attire".

Dr. Karin L. Stanford is a former Assistant Professor of Political Science and African American Studies at the University of Georgia. She also served as Bureau Chief of the Washington, D.C. Office of the Rainbow/PUSH Coalition between 1997-1999. She has received numerous awards, including the National Conference of Black Political Scientists Outstanding Book Award in 1998, Congressional Black Caucus Fellowship and a Post-Doctoral Fellowship from the University of North Carolina, Chapel Hill. She is currently a writer and consultant.

Dr. Orville W. Taylor is a Lecturer in Sociology at the University of the West Indies, Mona in Jamaica. He is also an Associated Faculty at the Center for Labor Research and Studies at Florida International University. A member of the Association of Black Sociologists, he has done extensive research on international labor standards and globalization including collaboration with the International Labour Organization (ILO).

Dr. Ron Walters is Distinguished Leadership Scholar, Director of the African American Leadership Institute, and Professor of Government and Politics at the University of Maryland at College Park. He is a lecturer, media commentator, syndicated columnist, and author of several books on international affairs and Black American politics.

John Edgar Wideman is a Distinguished Professor of English at the University of Massachusetts at Amherst. He has written nearly twenty works of fiction and non-fiction and is the recipient of many awards, including the O' Henry Award for short fiction and the PEN/Faulkner Award.

Tamara A. Masters Wilds is a doctoral student in American Studies at the University of Maryland at College Park. She has worked as the Director of African American Outreach at the Democratic National Committee and as a Deputy Field Director for the Gore 2000 campaign. She is the recipient of the Women's Information Network Young Women of Achievement "Campaigner of the Year" Award and devotes much of her spare time to mentoring Washington, D.C. youth.

Rev. Willie F. Wilson is the pastor of the Union Temple Baptist Church in Washington, D.C. The church has been recognized by the National Conference of Black Churchmen, an organization representing over 68,000 churches as one of the 100 Model Black Churches in America. In 1997, President William Clinton awarded Union Temple Baptist Church the President's Service Award, the prestigious presidential recognition given for community service.

About the Editors

Dr. Julianne Malveaux is an economist, columnist, author and radio and television commentator whose work focuses on politics, economics, gender and race. She provides regular commentary to BET, CNN, Fox News and MSNBC. Her columns have appeared in the *Detroit Free Press*, the *Los Angeles Times*, *Black Issues in Higher Education* and *USA Today*, among other papers They have been collected in two volumes, *Sex, Lies and Stereotypes: Perspectives of a Mad Economist* (Pines One Publications, 1994) and *Wall Street, Main Street and the Side Street: A Mad Economist Takes a Stroll* (Pines One Publications, 1999). Her essays have been collected in several volumes including, most recently, *When Race Becomes Real* edited by Bernestine Singley (Lawrence Hill Books, 2002) and *Race and Resistance* edited by Herb Boyd (South End Press, 2002). She is also author (with Deborah Perry) of *Unfinished Business: A Democrat and A Republican Take on the 10 Most Important Issues Women Face* (Perigee Books, 2002).

Julianne Malveaux owns Last Word Productions, Inc., a multi-media research and production company. She is a board member of the Center for Policy Alternatives, the TransAfrica Forum, the Economic Policy Institute and the Recreation Wish List Committee of Washington, D.C. Malveaux is a former college professor who earned her Ph.D. in economics from the Massachusetts Institute of Technology, and her B.A. from Boston College. She is a San Francisco native who now lives in Washington, D.C.

Reginna A. Green is Research Associate at Last Word Productions, Inc. and a freelance writer. She has worked at the Appleseed Foundation in Washington, D.C., the Health Care for Homeless Veterans Program at the Columbia, South Carolina V.A. Medical Center and at the South Carolina Appleseed Legal Justice Center, also in Columbia. Ms. Green also worked at the Hawaii Foodbank in Honolulu and the Center for Women Policy Studies in Washington, D.C. as part of a year-long fellowship with the Congressional Hunger Center Mickey Leland-Bill Emerson Hunger Fellows National Program. A South Carolina native, Ms. Green studied political theory and journalism at the University of South Carolina. She lives in the Columbia Heights section of Washington, D.C.

Acknowledgements

We both wish to thank all of our contributors, talented and busy writers with schedules that required them to carve out time for us. Each of them did so, with a collegial goodwill that has been delightful and flexible. We are grateful to them for making this volume possible. We are also grateful to the individuals who pitched in and helped shape this manuscript, especially Dr. Andrea Benton Rushing, who edited two of the longer and more challenging pieces at short notice. Elaine Bonner-Thompkins, Michon Lartigue and Regina Martin also helped with editing. A. Robert Phillips and Dianne Robinson took time to read the completed manuscript and made useful suggestions on its development.

—Julianne Malveaux and Reginna Green

First of all giving honor to God from whom all blessings flow, and to the ancestors, the African American scholars who paved the way for this work, especially Dr. W.E.B DuBois whose statements on dual consciousness, "African and American, two warring souls in one black body" partly motivates this work. Thanks also to the community of supportive friends who nourish, support, and inspire me. I am especially grateful to Haki Madhubuti for being receptive to this idea, and to Third World Press for publishing this book. My siblings Antoinette, Marianne, Mariette and James, and my posse of friends, especially Cora Barry, A. Robert Phillips, Delores Sennette and Eddie Arnold, have been sounding boards for my ideas and my work. Finally, I am grateful to my co-editor, Reginna Green, an extraordinarily talented young writer. This project could not have been completed without her focused, motivated, and dedicated work.

—Julianne Malveaux

I first wish to thank my parents, Jesse Green and Linda Annette Grice, for supporting me in (nearly) every endeavor I have ever chosen to pursue. I thank my mother for having a keen eye and for being a careful editor. I thank Daddy for trying to keep me on the straight and narrow, however much in vain it was. I hope they are as proud to have me as a daughter as I am to be their daughter. I extend a very special thanks to Sanna Pennix, Tonyalle Ross and Joel Ross for always believing. Thank you to my circle of friends, especially, Elan Nissenboim, Dan Lee, Alisha Pennix, Megan Mell, Chris Hess, Gene Willis, Angela Ledford, Grady Harper, Veena Srinivasan and M. Eileen O'Connor. These people keep me as sane as can be expected. Thanks to Edward Deutsch for being the catalyst for my own contribution to this book and to Ed Wingenbach for his assistance at the eleventh hour. Lastly, my co-editor Julianne Malveaux has been an important individual in my life for the past six years. Her guidance and motivation has been a driving force during this time and I am eternally grateful. Her patience and support has always been unwavering and appreciated.

—Reginna A. Green